The Oklahoma Land Rush of 1889

The Oklahoma Land Rush of 1889

by
Stan Hoig

Oklahoma Historical Society
Oklahoma City, Oklahoma
1989

Library of Congress Catalog No.: 84-080258

Hoig, Stan
  The Oklahoma Land Rush of 1889
  1. Oklahoma—History. 2. United States—History. I. Title
ISBN 0-941498-41-7

Third printing, 1995.

Contents

	List of Illustrations	*vii*
	Prologue	*ix*
I	This Coveted Land	*3*
II	Getting Set	*17*
III	Boomer Bastion	*30*
IV	Bound for Utopia	*44*
V	Exodus from Arkansas City	*58*
VI	South from Caldwell	*71*
VII	Purcell Passage	*81*
VIII	A Land Surrounded	*90*
IX	The Insiders	*101*
X	To Jordan by Coach	*115*
XI	Harrison's Hoss Race	*124*
XII	Guthrie and the Eight O'Clock Crowd	*136*
XIII	The Grab at Oklahoma Station	*151*
XIV	New Empire	*164*
XV	The "Bubble Towns"	*180*
XVI	Land Fights at Oklahoma City	*187*
XVII	The Sooner Cases	*195*
XVIII	Other Sooner Cases	*211*
XIX	Eighty-Niners—I	*223*
XX	Eighty-Niners—II	*236*
	Notes	*247*
	Bibliography	*265*
	Index	*276*

Illustrations

The Unassigned Lands	2
Boomers and soldiers	10
Blue-shirted soldiers	21
Relay house between Oklahoma Station and Fort Reno	33
First post office at Oklahoma Station	36
Oklahoma City before the land run	42
A boomer camp at Purcell	52
A tent city in Kansas	59
Salt Fork of the Arkansas	76
Purcell, Indian Territory	82-83
A boomer's dugout	87
Wagon crossing on South Canadian River	96
Camp 5th U.S. Cavalry near Guthrie	109
Red Rock Station	121
Rush for the "Promised Land"	126
Guthrie Post Office	140
Guthrie Land Office	143
First train into Guthrie	145
Surveying crews at Guthrie	146
First bank in Guthrie	148
Oklahoma City days after the land run	157
Oklahoma City four weeks after the opening	162
Terrain near Cimarron River	183
Oklahoma City	196
Oklahoma City intersection of Main and Broadway	199
Oklahoma City Post Office	202

Prologue

ON the morning of April 22, 1889, thousands upon thousands of Americans from over the entire nation lined up on the borders of what was then known as the Unassigned Lands of the Indian Territory, or the "Oklahoma country." They came in covered wagons, buggies, and many other conveyances, by horseback, and on foot to wait with strained anticipation until high noon when the blue-uniformed cavalry troops facing them across the line would give the signal loosing the horde of mankind and horseflesh to make a great, wild dash for 160 acres of free government land. Thousands of others climbed aboard and atop railroad trains headed for Oklahoma from Arkansas City, Kansas, and Purcell, Chickasaw Nation. The springtime beauty of the day, with the lush, green landscape lying ever so serenely under a cloudless sky, would long be remembered as the setting for this moment of history as men and women rushed forward to claim the virgin land.

This, essentially, is the way the Run of 1889 has been recorded, and it is a valid picture so far as it goes. But there was so much more to this significant event, so much more that has never been told. . . .

The Run of 1889 into the original Oklahoma lands was one of the most unique social phenomenons of American history. Its magnitude in terms of participants and land area involved, its indefinite rules which allowed wide interpretation without the benefit of precedent, its peculiarities as a way of occupying a new country, all combined with the insatiable American passion for free land to produce a chaotic, picturesque, and dramatic occurrence unlike anything in man's previous experience.

It was an event of vital consequence to those who participated, yet it was couched almost as a sporting contest. It concocted a situation where honesty was discouraged and dishonesty encouraged. It offered reward to connivance, opportunism, political favor, and sometimes the brute force of arms. Even with these things to one side, the Run of 1889 predicated a major prize of society upon the speed of a person's horse!

At the worst the run can be viewed as an act of conglomerated human greed, where citizens dashed frantically about to grab land that had once been faithfully promised to the Indian forever. At the best it can be seen as a fulfillment of God-fearing citizens who wished to build homes for themselves and for future generations. In truth the Run of 1889 was much of both.

Many of those making the run were sincere, honest people who abided by the rules in good faith and refused to enter the Oklahoma country until the appointed hour. There were those who cheated badly, some of them succeeding but many losing their claims in the thousands of "sooner" cases which filled the courts following the run. And there were those otherwise honest people who, upon seeing so many others crossing the line early, did likewise for fear of losing out completely in this "game" which meant so much to themselves and their families.

While the law clearly gave citizens of all races the right to make the Run of 1889 and to claim land in the Oklahoma district, in fact the rush for homes was predominantly a white Caucasian event. Contrary to common belief, very few black people participated in the actual run on April 22, unquestionably intimidated by racial modes of the day, though many came in later and can justly be counted among the pioneers of Oklahoma.

April 22, 1889, was one of those days which divided history. It would be difficult to find another single day's event which more strikingly reflected the end of the Old West in Oklahoma. When the crack of pistols and carbines and the boom of the Fort Reno cannon echoed across the rolling hills of the Indian Territory, they sounded the death knell to frontier life. They also heralded the beginning of towns and a new rule of law and order over the land. Never in the history of America had such change occurred with such suddenness. A bevy of new towns sprang into existence all in the breadth of a single day's time.

Other land rushes would follow until the government would finally turn to a lottery system of opening public land. None of the other runs would be so wild, so grand, or so glorious as that first rush which in the vernacular of the time became known as "Harrison's Hoss Race."

It is the intention of this book to present the central facts of the Run of 1889 fairly and fully and to avoid the misrepresentations which are so often made by glossing over the more sordid aspects of this historical event, though it must be recognized that the full truth of the Run of 1889, particularly just who was in early and who was not, will never be known.

This book is based upon four principal areas of research, each of which offers its own special perspective. There are the government reports and records, which offer primary information concerning who claimed what tract of land as well as investigative data. There are the many newspaper accounts, often repetitious but still revealing a view of the Run of 1889 which could not otherwise be found. There are the personal reminiscences, which sometimes contain errors because of natural slippages of memory but which give us a personal look into participant experiences. And there are the sooner cases, a vast body of testimony and countertestimony of the land offices and courts which fill in many details of what really happened on April 22, 1889.

The sooner cases, now located in the townsite files of the National Archives, have been retrieved in copy form for the Oklahoma Collection of the Central State University Library for on-site use by scholars of Oklahoma history. Some of the testimony and opinions rendered by the Land Office officials, as well as investigative data, can be found in the Harn Papers of the Oklahoma Historical Society and in the early newspapers of Guthrie, Oklahoma City, and Kingfisher.

The Oklahoma Land Rush of 1889

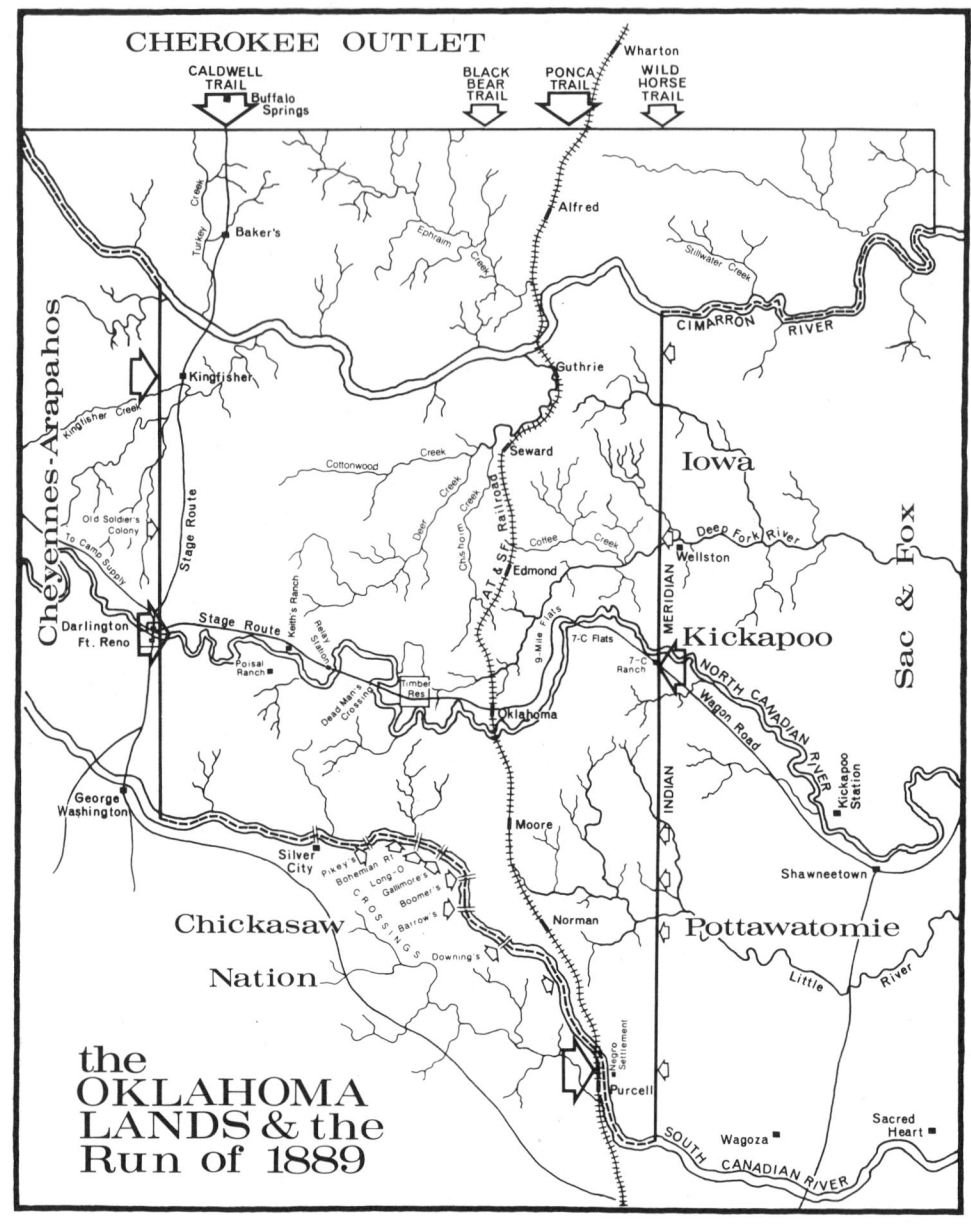

Map of the Unassigned Lands, known as "Oklahoma," on the eve of April 22, 1889. Arrows indicate the major and minor sites from which the Oklahoma run was made. (Courtesy Stan Hoig)

CHAPTER I
This Coveted Land

Ille angulus placet miki praeter omnis.—*That little corner of my neighbor's land pleases me better than all my vast estates.* Congressional Record, *July 26, 1888.*

LONG had the white man coveted this land, and now it would be his. When the Indians of the South had been removed to this then-remote part of Western America beyond the Mississippi River, President Andrew Jackson had promised that their new home would be theirs for "as long as the grass grows or the water runs, in peace and plenty."[1] But following the Civil War, white men began looking to westward expansion, and numerous bills were submitted to Congress to make a state out of the Indian Territory.

Leaders of the Civilized Nations of the Territory had effectively resisted these moves through the decades of the 1860s and 1870s. But it was one of their own, Colonel Elias C. Boudinot, a Cherokee lawyer and railroad lobbyist, who first publicized the significant fact that some two million acres of land had been left unassigned to any Indian tribe following treaties between the United States and the Creeks and Seminoles in 1866. It was this area located at the very heart of the Indian Territory which now came to be known popularly as the "Oklahoma country."

In the spring of 1879, Colonel C. C. Carpenter, a Kansan who affected the long curls and buckskin modes of Custer and Hickok, was encouraged by the *Kansas City Times* to promote the invasion of the Oklahoma country. Though Carpenter himself remained safely in Kansas, a small intrusion did take place in May 1879. Settlers from Kansas and Missouri reached the North Canadian River of the Oklahoma country before being removed by U.S. troops. Carpenter, when confronted by Indian Bureau officials and threatened with imprisonment, quickly went into hiding and forsook his invasion scheme.

It was left to Captain David L. Payne, an early Kansas pioneer, politician, and soldier, to ignite a continuing "Oklahoma boomer" movement to invade and colonize the Oklahoma lands. From 1880 until his death in November 1884, the hard-drinking ne'er-do-well of the frontier led settlement intrusions from Kansas and Texas into the Oklahoma country despite strong federal opposition and continued removal by U.S. army units. Payne recruited followers, agitated in the press and at public meetings, fought his battle in the courts, and lobbied in the halls of the Congress with great persistency until the Oklahoma movement had become a national issue.

Following Payne's death, the Oklahoma cause was carried on under the leadership of William L. Couch, a former Payne lieutenant. Though Couch led his own invasions of Oklahoma, legal pressures and continued resistance by the U.S. government brought the Oklahoma movement to an impasse by 1886. But it was then a highly significant event took place with the construction of the Santa Fe Railroad line across the Indian Territory from Arkansas City, Kansas, to Gainesville, Texas. This line, which was completed in the spring of 1887, ran directly through the center of the Oklahoma country. The *Boston Transcript* astutely observed: "This will inevitably open up the long coveted Oklahoma land to settlement by whites."[2]

The *Arkansas City Traveler* was also quick to note that the new route offered dual advantages to the railroad and the Oklahoma boomer. Settlement of the Oklahoma land would open new market areas for the railroad. The boomers, by attaching themselves to the railroad grading and construction crews, could gain entry into Oklahoma. The military would have no power to stop them while they traveled "unmolested to the promised land."[3]

Thus during 1887 little was heard from the boomer movement. Construction of the Santa Fe line had kept the "Oklahomaists" occupied and hopeful. Though many on the frontier anticipated speedy legislation to follow completion of the road, the news from Washington remained scant on the matter of Oklahoma settlement. Finally in December, the boomer cry of "On to Oklahoma" was again sounded when a fanciful El Dorado newspaper story told of secret plans of some 100,000 men who supposedly were to make a raid into Oklahoma in the early spring of 1888.[4] Coincident to this came the announcement from Washington that an Oklahoma bill was being prepared and would be presented to the House of Representatives by either General James B. Weaver of Iowa or William M. Springer of Illinois.

The smouldering coals of boomerism were fanned back to life in January of 1888 when a circular was sent out to some 500 men in Kansas, Missouri, Colorado, Arkansas, New Mexico, Texas, and the Indian Territory calling them to a conference in Kansas City on February 8. Leading the move were W. L. Couch, Samuel Crocker, fiery editor of the boomers' *Oklahoma War Chief* newspaper, and former Kansas congressman Sidney Clarke. These boomer loyalists had persuaded a number of important men to sign a circular promoting the meetings, among them being long-time Oklahoma enthusiast Dr. Morrison Munford of the *Kansas City Times*.[5]

The purpose of the affair was to reawaken frontier interest in Oklahoma settlement and to convince Congress of strong popular support for the immediate opening of the Oklahoma lands. Preliminary meetings were held at Caldwell and Arkansas City on February 1 and 3, with Couch and Crocker speaking to turn-away crowds. The boomer leaders were joined on the platform by J. S. Jennings of the *Wichita Republic*, Judge J. M. Galloway of Fort Scott, and Milton W. Reynolds of Gueda Springs. Reynolds, who was well-known in Kansas journalism as "Kicking Bird," had only recently taken an active role in the boomer cause, having spoken to a rally at Arkansas City in late January. The *Wichita Eagle* commented wryly that "Milt Reynolds has 'jined' the Oklahoma boomers. That country will now be opened for settlement."[6]

At Arkansas City, Reynolds had issued the warning that "Congressmen and Senators who heed not the mighty voice of the people might as well at once turn up their Congressional and Senatorial toes to the daisies, for the places that know them now will know them no more forever."[7]

A resolution urging immediate opening of the unoccupied lands of the Indian Territory was drafted at the preliminary boomer convention, to be sent to all the Kansas congressmen. Couch, Crocker, Reynolds, Jennings, and Galloway were elected to represent the meeting at the Kansas City conference. Couch and Crocker, along with the old boomer, the long-haired John Furlong of Wichita, were on the front seats in the Kansas City Board of Trade Hall on February 8 to hear the opening speaker state the boomer theme: "Unless some good reason exists why this country [Oklahoma] should remain a home of savages, and a hiding place for criminals; unless there is a good reason for it, the people of the neighboring States have a right to demand the opening."[8]

Couch was called upon to speak. He told the conference that while he favored opening the entire Territory to settlement, he supported the Springer Oklahoma Bill because it would meet with less opposition . . . "and then it is only a question of time until the entire Territory is opened."[9]

One of the invited delegates was Chief John Earlie, whose Ottawa tribe resided in northeastern Indian Territory. When asked to speak, the chief walked to the front of the stage with great dignity. He and his tribe, he said, were heartily in favor of opening all of the Territory to settlement. The Ottawas had already divided up their lands, and he thought it would be better for the Indians and cheaper for the government to do away with tribal relations in the Territory.

"I want the Territory opened up," he told the white audience, "the Indians to mix with the whites, the whites with the Indians, and the Indians to become more and more like the whites."[10]

When the speech making was done, convention delegates drafted a resolution to Congress calling for the speedy opening of the Territory. A delegation which included Couch, Crocker, Clarke, and Munford was elected to carry the resolution to Washington and present it to Congress.

Following the convention, the delegation headed for Washington. Munford, who was personally acquainted with President Grover Cleveland, secured an audience with the chief executive for himself and Crocker.[11] The two discussed the Oklahoma question with Cleveland and then made arrangements for the entire delegation to meet with the President. Sidney Clarke did the talking for the group and presented Cleveland with a copy of the "Kansas City Interstate-Oklahoma Legislative Memorial."[12] This done, most of the members of the delegation left Washington; but Couch, Crocker, and Clarke remained behind to assist in advancing the Oklahoma Bill in the House.

There had been several bills for the organization of Oklahoma Territory, as well as numerous petitions and protests, submitted to the first session of the Forty-ninth Congress when it had convened in December 1887. One had been authored by Weaver of Iowa, another by Richard W. Townshend of Illinois, one by Bishop W. Perkins of Kansas, and still another by Senator Charles H. Van Wyck of Nebraska. But it was the bill introduced on January 6, 1888, by Springer of Illinois that was initially debated by the House of Representatives on February 25 and 28.

One of the opponents of the bill, Representative George T. Barnes of Georgia, complained of "secret societies with signs and grips and passwords organized for the purpose, ready to rush in as settlers."¹³ He also described the Indian who, with his ear to the ground, listened with dread to the sound of the advancing hosts.

Indeed, the Indians of the Territory were listening, and they by no means all agreed with Chief Earlie. On January 31, a delegation of Indian leaders and their attorneys appeared before the House Committee on Territories, which was chaired by Congressman Springer. The spokesman for the Cherokee Nation read a protest against the authority of the United States to enact any kind of legislation relating to the Indian Territory.¹⁴ Following him was Colonel G. W. Harkins, representing the Chickasaw Nation. Harkins, a man well educated in Eastern schools, eloquently made the point that if the government could throw open Oklahoma then it might well take on itself to do the same for the entire Indian Territory. He told how he had been taken from his wigwam as a boy and sent to one of the white man's colleges. There he had been initiated into book learning

> I read in a note to Virgil's "Aeneid" or somewhere else, of the sharp Yankee trick played by the Phoenician Princess Dido on the Choctaws and Chickasaws of the north of Africa, thousands of years ago. She bought, it is said, as much of their land as a bull's hide would cover, and then adroitly cut up the hide into strings so fine that it encompassed the site of ancient Carthage, twenty-three miles in circumference... If Congress to-day holds the power to throw the boundary lines of the Territory of Oklahoma around any part of the land staked in by the first section of this bill, what power is restricted to a little patch of land in the northwest corner [of the Chickasaw Nation] as insignificant in comparison with the whole of the inclosed area, as was Dido's bull's hide compared with the Punic City? That little patch is the bull's hide in this case. It is the pretext which covers, on paper, large tracts of land wherein the Cherokees, Creeks, Seminoles, Chickasaws and Choctaws

have rights which you can not wrest from them unless you have power to rescind solemn treaties of the United States.[15]

But Harkins's argument failed to deter the committee. On June 25 Springer introduced a revised bill which received a favorable recommendation by the Committee on Territories and went to the House floor for debate. These discussions were held from July 26 through August 30. General Hooker of Mississippi opened with the argument that the bill was in violation of treaty stipulations and that Congress had no power to create a territorial government over any part of the Indian Territory.

"You ceded this land west of the Mississippi to these Indians," he contended. "You ceded it to them under the most sacred obligations which could bind the conscience of man or nation, and yet now the proposition is made and offered here to make a Territory out of land to which the Government of the United States does not own the title to an acre . . ."[16]

Perkins replied to Hooker by countering in part ". . . those people for whom I speak ask, not as speculators, not as 'boomers,' not as 'lawless trespassers,' but as honest, industrious settlers, and law-abiding American citizens . . ." that barriers be removed and they be permitted to occupy the lands under the public-land laws and with appropriate legislation of the Congress. "They do not ask that the Indians be wronged or that they be driven from the lands they occupy, but they do ask that these vacant and unoccupied acres be given to them under the appropriate legislation, and that the Indians be fairly paid for any claim, legal or equitable, they may have to the lands thus opened to settlement."[17]

Stockdale of Mississippi said he had examined the bill carefully and found it to be just to the Indians and equitable in all its provisions, that the supporters of the bill were the true friends of the Indians. The refuge of criminals and barbarism, he said, was proposed to be opened to a Christian civilization, and it was impossible and impolitic to attempt to arrest the march of empire.[18]

Boomers and soldiers, a reocurring confrontation while Congress debated whether or not to open the Unassigned Lands to settlement (Harper's Weekly).

White of New York, Peel of Arkansas, Cannon of Illinois, and Perkins of Kansas spoke for the bill on July 28. Perkins argued that the poor people of the country, the pioneers of civilization, needed this land for homesteads and insisted they ought to have it.[19] Cobb of Alabama spoke against the bill. Three amendments to the measure were voted down by a strong majority.[20]

On the twenty-ninth, Payson of Illinois offered an amendment to the bill whereby the Oklahoma lands would be open to settlers only under the Homestead Act rather than requiring payment of $1.25 an acre in four installments over a period of three years as required in the original bill. Springer and boomer leaders saw this as a pretext to encourage many to vote against the bill on economic grounds, since the Payson amendment could cost the treasury an estimated $30 million. Anderson of Iowa wished to amend the bill so that every honorably discharged Union soldier could have his land free.[21]

The argument over payment continued on the thirtieth with Representative Samuel R. Peters of Kansas contending that under homestead laws speculators could pay their two dollars for land office fees, hold the land for six months or longer, and then sell it at a profit. Nelson of Minnesota issued a warning that the government was being too extravagant with the public domain. The rapid settlement of the Western lands, he said, had enhanced their value, and $1.25 was little enough for anyone, however poor, to pay.[22]

Despite all the discussion and debate, the Springer Oklahoma Bill failed to receive action before the legislative session ended. Disappointed but as determined as ever, the boomer leaders headed home, Couch going by way of Iowa to assist General Weaver with his campaign for reelection. It was necessary now to work out new plans for keeping the Oklahoma issue alive and heated in both Kansas and Congress. No one knew better than Crocker how to do that. He persuaded Marsh Murdock, Payne's old nemesis at the *Wichita Eagle* who had now swung over to the boomer side on Oklahoma settlement, to call another interstate Oklahoma convention for November 20 in Wichita. The biggest names in the Oklahoma movement were brought forth to give the meeting special drawing power—Springer of Illinois, Mansur of Missouri, and Weaver of Iowa.[23]

Hundreds of delegates from over Kansas and surrounding states arrived at the Wichita train depots and later filled the Crawford Opera House "to suffocation" to lustily cheer their congressional champions and boom Oklahoma settlement. In the afternoon, Springer addressed the convention. He said there were two main barriers to the settlement of Oklahoma. One was the complications growing out of Indian titles to the land, those being of a "very shadowy and unsubstantial character." Since the government had declared its intention of settling friendly Indians on those lands, Springer felt it was of utmost importance for early passage of the Oklahoma Bill before "complications and embarrassments . . . will confront us."[24]

Springer, who had never been to the Indian Territory, then spoke of the great cattle syndicates who leased some six million acres of the Territory's grazing lands. "The time for their occupancy is short," he insisted, "and the cattle kings must go." But the main thrust of his oration was that "There is an irrepressible conflict between barbarism and civilization. The result of that conflict is not a matter of doubt. No portion of this continent can be held in barbarism to the exclusion of civilized man."[25]

Weaver told the crowd that he had long since decided that white men had rights as well as black or red men and insisted that the interests of both Indians and whites demanded passage of the bill. Mansur pointed to over 365 murders which he said had been committed in the Indian Territory during the past year, concluding that a sort of sentimentality in the East and South against the bill was evaporating in the light of such facts. A resolution was drafted calling upon the President of the United States to exercise his authority in support of opening Oklahoma.[26]

Once again Couch, Crocker, and Clarke were appointed to go to Washington and present the document in the interest of the bill. "Oklahoma Harry" Hill, an original Carpenter and Payne boomer and now a successful Wichita horse and mule trader and stage line owner, and H. L. Pearce of Wichita were named to raise the $1,500 required to defray the expenses of the committee.

Not mentioned at the Wichita convention but of great significance to the cause of opening Oklahoma to settlement was a measure passed by the legislature of the Creek Nation in late October approving the sale of their interest in the Oklahoma lands. Such a sale would do much to clear away the last vestiges of Indian claim to the contested area.[27]

While the boomers were adamant in their charges of a cattle syndicate lobby in Washington, the cattlemen claimed otherwise, insisting that they had no lobby there at all. The Cherokee Strip Live Stock Association listed a number of cattle companies, however, in which congressmen were known to hold an interest. Lobby or not, there was always the noticeable presence of cattlemen on Capitol Hill whenever the Oklahoma Bill was being debated.

There was no question about the lobbying efforts of the

boomers. The delegation chosen at Wichita entrained immediately for the capital in order to be there when Congress reconvened in December 1888. Their efforts were rewarded on February 1, 1889, when the Oklahoma Bill was passed by the House of Representatives with a 147 to 102 vote.[29] It was not an easy victory, however, for opponents of the measure fought back with every parliamentary device they knew to delay the final vote. Weaver and Springer were given much credit for their floor fight, while Couch, Crocker, and Clarke "labored in and out of season for the advancement of this great measure."[30]

But the fight was far from won. The Springer Bill now went to the Senate where it was debated on February 5. Senator Chase of Rhode Island immediately branded the bill as "a well laid scheme to encroach upon Indian rights and rob them." Senator Morgan of Alabama defended the bill as going further in recognition of Indian rights than was justified by law. Morgan also brought forth a new argument in favor of opening Oklahoma. He charged that a "very reprehensible and dangerous state of affairs existed under the communistic system of the Indian Territory and that a Federal court was needed to restore law and order within the Territory."[31]

The Springer Oklahoma Bill was referred to the Senate's Committee on Territories, while the Kansas boomers and the pro-Oklahoma congressmen held a strategy meeting at the Territorial Committee room of the House on February 12. All were anxious that the bill be returned to the Senate in time to make arguments for it.[32] But the boomers and their friends in Congress could but sit and fume while the cattlemen and their lawyers thronged the Senate Public Lands Committee in their efforts to defeat the bill.[33]

Milton Reynolds and other Kansas supporters arrived in Washington to help as best they could. Finally on February 18 the Committee on Territories reported the Oklahoma Bill to the Senate favorably without amendment. There was a minority report, however, and rumors circulated that a substitute bill would be submitted by the opposition. Even as the bill was waiting to be called up, cession agreements with the Creek and Seminole Indians were being considered by the House Indian Affairs Committee. Both of those tribes had indicated they were willing to sell their remaining rights to the land to allow Congress to use it for purposes other than for settlement by "other Indians or freedmen," as their 1866 treaties had specified.[34]

Another mass convention of Oklahoma boomers was held at Arkansas City on February 20, 1889, and a resolution was drafted and wired to senators John J. Ingalls and Preston B. Plumb of Kansas, urging them to use every effort to secure the speedy passage of the Oklahoma Bill. But in Washington it appeared that opponents of the bill would be successful in delaying a vote until Senate adjournment. Proponents now decided upon a clever counteraction.

The annual Indian Appropriations Bill was being considered in the House. Representative Samuel W. Peel of Arkansas, chairman of the Committee on Indian Affairs, on February 27 submitted an amendment—Section 12—to the appropriation bill which provided $1,912,952.02 to pay for final rights to the 2,370414.62 acres of land ceded by the Seminoles and Creeks. Springer then added Section 13, authorizing the President to open the lands to settlement through issuance of a proclamation. Representative Thomas Ryan of Kansas added another clause authorizing the establishment of two land districts and offices within the cession area.[35]

These House-inserted clauses were defeated in the Senate, however, and it was necessary to order a joint Senate-House conference on the matter. There Senator Bishop W. Perkins of Kansas made a determined stand for the amendments and succeeded in getting them restored to the bill, which now passed the Senate. Thus the Oklahoma lands were finally placed into the public domain preparatory to a presidential proclamation opening them to settlement.

The successful passage of this historic rider, however, depended upon some practical action outside of Congress, as it happened.[36] When the rider clauses were finally drafted in makeshift form, approved by the Senate-House committee, and ordered printed, General Weaver came to Crocker and asked how quickly he could get the bill additions into print. They were running out of time. The *War Chief* editor took a glance at the handwritten riders.

"Well," he said, "if I don't have too far to go to find a printing office, and with enough help, I can have this bill printed and in your hands in an hour. How far away from here is the printing office?"

Weaver told him that it was nearly a mile down Pennsylvania Avenue from the capitol where they were. Crocker took the bill, promising to get it printed and back just as fast as he could. An attorney for the Santa Fe Railroad was standing with the two men, and he handed Crocker a dollar for fare on the horse-drawn streetcars of Washington.

"Now, Mr. Crocker," the lawyer said, "fetch that bill to us as quick as you can. Chairman Springer wishes to introduce it before adjournment."

The portly Crocker hurried out and caught the first streetcar to the printing office. There he quickly explained to the printer the importance and urgency of getting the bill printed immediately, suggesting that it be divided among a number of compositors in order to expedite that phase of the procedure. This was done, and the entire manuscript was soon set in type and on the press.

Grabbing the pile of printed pages, Crocker ran out of the printing shop to catch a streetcar back to the capitol. But when he reached into his pocket for the dollar bill given him by the Santa Fe attorney, he discovered that he must have lost it in his rush. Crocker dug frantically through his pockets and finally came up with a nickel for his fare, allowing him to make it back to where Weaver and the others were waiting impatiently. The makeshift bill was introduced and successfully passed, being signed into law by President Grover Cleveland on March 2, 1889.

The riders to the Indian Appropriation Bill did not provide for the establishment of a new territory or even mention the name of "Oklahoma." As an expedient it merely provided that the lands ceded by the Seminole and Creek Indians should be considered as public domain and be opened to settlement on a date to be set by a proclamation of the President of the United States. This action would be left to the newly-elected President, Benjamin Harrison, who was to take office on March 4, 1889.

And so it had finally come to pass. It had taken a full decade of intrusion, agitation, promotion, and political maneuvering to bring it about. The movement for which Boudinot had first voiced the premise, which the *Kansas City Times* and Carpenter had launched in the spring of 1879, which David Payne had taken up as his life cause in 1880, and which W. L. Couch had carried on after Payne's death in 1884, had been crowned with success. The first land of the Indian Territory—and no one had any doubt that it would be only the first of such openings within this country which had been promised so faithfully to the Indian—would soon be settled by non-Indians.

CHAPTER II
Getting Set

"It is an astonishing thing," an observer of the day commented, "that men will fight harder for $500 worth of land than they will for $10,000 in money." New York Herald, *April 14, 1889.*

OLDTIMERS compared it to the stampedes to California in '49, to Pike's Peak in '58 and '59, and to the Black Hills in '75 and '76. Each of these national crazes had seen Americans by the multitudes rush headlong across the West, all burning with expectation and possessed of a determination to let nothing stop them from getting their share of the national wealth. Then it had been gold they sought; this time it was *land.*

Lying at the heart of the Indian Territory were over two million acres of land—known popularly as the "Oklahoma country"—which the government had purchased from the Indians and was now making available for homestead claim. In this year of 1889, free land was a national passion. Typical was A. C. McCord, the old Payne boomer who operated the Santa Fe House at Purcell. Every night when he went to bed, he said, and every morning when he arose, he enjoyed looking across the South Canadian into the promised land of Canaan.[1]

But a 160-acre homestead was by no means the only reason why men would hurry so feverishly to Oklahoma.

Many of them were not farmers at all and had no intention of breaking the soil for a livelihood. Some sought to locate themselves in some new town community as merchants, professional men, laborers, or capitalists to profit from the cornucopia of opportunity which the opening of Oklahoma promised. To some, town lots were far more valuable than 160 acres in the country. Virtually all were driven by an even deeper impulse to take part in a final adventure of the nineteenth century on the American frontier where the Indian and the cowboy still held forth.[2]

Many of the old boomers who had marched with Payne and Couch had not been content to sit along the border in Kansas and wait. A good number had gone into the Oklahoma country as members of the work crews of the Santa Fe Railroad when it constructed its line across the Indian Territory in 1886 and 1887. They had remained inside the disputed area under one pretext or another—some as railroad workmen, some as freighters hauling supplies for the government, some as wood cutters for the army, and some who simply squatted in a tent or a dugout and lived off the land.

The newly-created frontier community of Purcell, located in the Chickasaw Nation just across the South Canadian River at the southern tip of the Oklahoma district, had become a rendezvous for many of the Couch group of boomers. These men had already selected and staked choice homestead claims, mostly in the vicinity of Oklahoma station on the Santa Fe line, with hopes of retaining the land after the opening by virtue of the traditional "squatter's rights" claim. Other late-comers had also drifted into the area from parts of the Indian Territory, some slipped across the borders of Kansas and Texas, and others simply purchased tickets on the train and rode happily past the U.S. troops patrolling against settler intrusion.

In January the military began a step-up of its efforts to keep intruders out of the Territory. On the fifteenth of that month Captain A. L. Woodson left Fort Reno with fifty-two horse soldiers of Troop K, Fifth Cavalry, two six-mule and one four-mule teams, and marched by way of the Guthrie station to Chilocco Creek just south of the Kansas line. There Woodson established Camp Price where the railroad crossed the border. His assignment was to keep a lookout for intruders into the territory and turn them back. Locating his second camp on the Chikaskia twenty-three miles to the west, Woodson sought to cover all the boomer trails leading out of Arkansas City, Hunnewell, and Caldwell. He soon found that every traveler intercepted had the excuse of some legitimate business or was on his way to Texas, the Chickasaw Nation, or any place other than Oklahoma. Those who gave the appearance of being boomers were turned back, nonetheless, and escorted across the Kansas line.[3]

In Wichita, Kansas—the city from which Payne had first launched his campaign to open Oklahoma to settlement—business leaders had become concerned that the border towns would beat them out as an outfitting and trading center during the anticipated rush to Oklahoma. In December 1888, the Wichita Board of Trade had written a letter to Major Gordon W. Lillie, the "Pawnee Bill" of the Pawnee Bill Wild West Show then stranded in Philadelphia without funds following a rainy, disastrous season. Lillie had once lived on the Pawnee Indian reservation of the Indian Territory where his father was employed as a teacher.[4]

The membership of Wichita's Board of Trade included some men who had known David Payne well. Oklahoma Harry Hill, who had been chief guide for Payne's first expedition, was now the owner of the Wichita Horse and Mule Market as well as a stage line operator. Marsh Murdock, the red-headed editor and publisher of the *Wichita Eagle* who had been an early settler of Wichita along with Payne, had fought the Oklahoma movement with hard-hitting editorials. Judge H. C. Sluss, Payne's old political foe, was now an avid "Oklahomaist." These men and others looked to the enormous trade potential that would come with the opening of the Oklahoma country. The Board decided upon a movement to draw the boomer attention and trade to their town.

Wichita, the letter to Lillie said, needed a man of Pawnee Bill's type to lead the boomers to Oklahoma. They offered him a salary to do so, and the showman quickly accepted the opportunity. He was facing financial ruin, and this would provide him a chance to return west and regroup. Bringing with him his entire entourage of clowns, trapeze artists, sideshow entertainers, trick riders, and circus animals, Lillie entrained for Wichita. He was met at the depot by Murdock, Hill, and others who escorted him to an open carriage and paraded him to his hotel behind a brass band—much as the boomer faithful had done for David Payne on occasion.[5]

A banquet was later held in Lillie's honor to kick off the "Pawnee Bill Colonization Company." Calculating that the only thing Payne had lacked was a good press agent (he calculated incorrectly for Payne had been an excellent publicist for the Oklahoma cause), Lillie immediately began sending out press releases. Form letters were printed in newspapers by which settlers could enroll in his colony for one dollar. Like Payne, Pawnee Bill sought to make the cattlemen and the U.S. army appear as villains to the public interest. He charged that reports of soldiers arresting people in Oklahoma were being issued by the cattle kings of the Territory in an attempt to frighten away settlers.[6]

By the middle of January 1889, the showman was releasing promises that he would lead some 4,800 people into Oklahoma by February 1 "or bust." The Arkansas City merchants were especially indignant over Lillie's activity. Newspapers there scorned "Pawnee Bill and his few lawless followers," who they claimed had been hired for the purpose of "assembling a large crowd at Wichita as an advertising scheme and nothing else."[7] At Gueda Springs, Milton Reynolds also heaped ridicule on the "long-haired idiots" who contemplated a raid on Oklahoma and surmised that "If Pawnee Bill or any other sweet William wants to court positive failure, he can learn in forty-eight hours that the thing cannot be done." The *Topeka Journal* derided Lillie as an ignorant, long-haired cowpuncher who

Blue-shirted soldiers spent many hours on the trail chasing the determined army of invading boomers (Harper's Weekly).

---

sought to make himself a hero or martyr by invading Oklahoma.[8]

While Lillie was busy recruiting a following of settlers at Wichita, W. L. Couch had been in Washington, D.C., working for passage of the Springer Oklahoma Bill. Couch and other boomer activists deeply resented interference and presumption of leadership by Lillie. Interviewed in Washington, Couch had assured the press that "no person with such a blood-curdling name as 'Pawnee Bill' has ever been associated with the Oklahoma movement."[9]

Couch quickly fired off an urgent wire to the Wichita Board of Trade demanding that they have the showman desist from his public threats to invade Oklahoma. Couch argued that if Lillie continued he would jeopardize the bill then before Congress.[10] The Board of Trade directed Oklahoma Harry Hill to contact Lillie, who had already departed Wichita with his colony and was at Hunnewell on his march toward Oklahoma.

Hill arrived at Hunnewell on February 2 and talked with

the showman. Together the two men rode to the Kansas-Indian Territory border where they witnessed the troops stationed there under Woodson. The presence of the soldiers convinced Lillie that any effort to cross the border with a large number of people would be futile and injurious to the Oklahoma Bill—if not to Lillie himself. Furthermore, news arrived informing them that the Oklahoma Bill had passed the House. With Hill having withdrawn the support of the Wichita Board of Trade for his operation, Lillie accepted an offer from the Caldwell Board of Trade to move with his followers to the Caldwell fairgrounds to await further developments in Washington.[11]

When the Indian Appropriation Bill was signed into law, people in Kansas went "wild with enthusiasm." Settlers shouted and fired off their shotguns, and some oldtimers did jigs for joy. Men in the boomer camps huddled about in small knots to talk and speculate as to when the new President, Benjamin Harrison, would issue his proclamation. That night bonfires of celebration were put ablaze, "ratification meetings" were held, and prominent citizens made speeches. In Caldwell money was raised to purchase Senator Perkins a gold-headed cane for his efforts in behalf of Oklahoma settlement.[12] Some settlers felt they should rush right on in, but others cautioned against it, citing Section 13 of the Indian Appropriation Bill, which clearly stated that no one would be permitted to claim land who had entered Oklahoma ahead of the time set by the President.

The Kansas press now became filled with reports, some false, of the invasion of the Territory. The *Kansas City Gazette* reported that a group of settlers on Chisholm Creek inside the Territory had called for Oklahoma Harry Hill to find the best way into the country for settlers. People all along the Kansas border, the paper said, were clamoring for Hill to take them on in ahead of others.[13] From Oklahoma station came reports of a spreading rumor that Hill was on his way from Kansas at the head of 400 men. He was to be joined there by several hundred more under the direction of E. C. Cole, a Kansas real estate promoter who had made a couple of excursions into the Oklahoma country in 1884 and had co-authored a somewhat misinformed book on the area. He also had become a town company organizer.[14]

Harry Hill did, indeed, go to Oklahoma on March 13, but by train and not as the head of any invasion group. Traveling with him was a correspondent for the *Wichita Eagle* who penned an account of the trip and the people he encountered at this pre-run point of history. Hill, the reporter noted, was on his way to Purcell to confer with Couch and other boomer leaders. He had also heard that his old claim below Oklahoma station on Crutcho Creek was being taken over by intruders, and he wanted to see about it.[15] There was still another reason for his trip—Hill, the businessman, wished to look into the possible establishment of a stage line connecting the future towns of Oklahoma.

All along the route between Wichita and Arkansas City white-sailed boomer wagons could be seen moving toward the Indian Territory as the men rode southward on the train. One outfit of special notice consisted of two cows, a mule, a yellow dog, and a young couple who proudly shared the space of their wagon with a Cottage organ. Just below Arkansas City the train passengers could see a large encampment of boomers, "evidently awaiting for something to turn up that will let them into the promised land."[16] Two of Woodson's troops stood guard on the railroad bank where a plank-on-a-fence-post sign reading "Indian Territory" marked the border.

A strict demarcation in the countryside was visible at the border. On the Kansas side were farms and houses and cultivated fields; on the Indian Territory side the unbroken fields of prairie grass stretched to the horizon in all directions. To the west, standing just south of the line, were the stately buildings of the Chilocco Mission School for Indian children, which the government had built in 1884.

The first stop beyond the border was at Willow Springs, consisting of a station house and two one-story frame buildings, all painted the dark red of the Santa Fe company. Large haystacks stood surrounded by wide double furrows to protect them from prairie fires, many of which were set off by the sparks from the train locomotive. One such fire was later encountered near the Salt Fork of the Arkansas River. Great clouds of smoke billowed skyward, and the red line of flame extended for some ten or more miles.

As the train passed through the Ponca Indian reservation, little white-washed houses could be seen dotting the prairie, some with tepees standing beside them in token symbol of the old and the new in the Territory. A young Indian woman near one house ignored the calls and waving of handkerchiefs from passengers of the train. A second stop was made at Ponca station, another collection of small red buildings, and then the bridge over the Salt Fork was crossed. About a mile to the east could be seen the houses, school, and steepleless church of the Ponca agency.

Beyond the Salt Fork the country became more heavily treed in contrast to the bald prairie behind. When Red Rock station was reached, the train was boarded by a Pawnee Indian, "a big overgrown boy with a strong inclination to be always smiling," wearing a strange combination of Indian and white man's garb. He showed the conductor his Indian agency pass and forked up two bright silver dollars for his fare to Oklahoma station. At the next stop, Mendota, another Indian stood ready to board the train. He was Cheyenne. Anyone aboard who knew of the long tradition of bloody warfare between the Pawnees and the Cheyennes might well have feared the worst.

But when the Pawnee left the train to visit the water tank at a stop, passing the Cheyenne, there was not so much as a glance between the two. Later, aboard the train, the Pawnee went back and joined the Cheyenne, the two talking in sign language. Harry Hill, who knew some hand talk, promoted his entry into the conversation with a package of cigarettes. The Pawnee told Hill that he had a wife and two children. Hill joshed the boy by pointing to the correspondent and saying that the man had three wives. The Pawnee threw up his hands in horror and thereafter eyed the reporter with suspicion.

Past Mendota the train crossed the line separating the Cherokee Strip from the Oklahoma country. At Alfred station, the first stop inside the Oklahoma lands, were to be seen several boomer wagons with children and dogs playing about them. In addition to the wagons, there were a number of tents and sod houses, indication that the boomers had been there for some time.

Now the country became rougher as the breaks of the Cimarron River were approached, and the soil had turned to a rusty, brick color. The Cimarron was crossed by a long trestle railroad bridge, and just below was a ford for the wagon road which followed along the west side of the railroad all the way from the Kansas border. Beyond the bridge, near the junction of Cottonwood Creek and the Cimarron, was Guthrie station. It consisted of a small depot, two section houses, and a water tank—all painted the Santa Fe red. During the water stop of the train, the reporter learned that large amounts of stock feed were being unloaded at Guthrie for the horses of soldiers who would patrol the northern part of Oklahoma—a sure sign, the reporter thought, that the government was making plans for the country to be opened to settlement soon.

Edmond station, some fifteen miles south of Guthrie, was reached at dusk—a section house containing a telegraph office, a water tank, small pump house, a thirty-foot diameter well with a conical cover, and a two-story coaling barn that straddled a side track. Near the barn stood a small cattle-loading chute. On either side of the tracks could be seen the flickering lights of boomer tents and wagon homes as darkness settled in. It was at this stop that ten young men, all well armed and equipped with camping gear, disembarked from the train and disappeared into the night. No one knew if they were hunters or land seekers.

At Oklahoma station the train was met by some 200 people who crowded the platform eager to buy newspapers from the newsboy on the train. Everyone was anxious to know the latest on the opening, and they pressed Hill regarding his plans. Hill, however, refused to divulge his reasons for being in Oklahoma.[17]

Only the lights of the few houses and boomer camps could be seen by passengers as the train moved on southward. At Verbeck station—soon to be renamed "Moore"—extensive grass fires were again visible to the west, making "a grand and striking sight and illuminated the prairie on every side for miles and miles."[18] Norman station, little more than a section house and box cars, was passed; and soon the South Canadian River was crossed, the train then speeding on the five miles farther to Purcell. Here another large crowd was waiting to meet the train and devour the remaining newspaper supply. Harry Hill, the *Eagle* reporter, and their luggage were loaded into a four-horse bus and driven up the steep bluff to the Clifton Hotel.

The railroad station lay between the bluff and the South Canadian, but the town itself was perched up the side of the hill. It was comprised mostly of lumber structures with canvass or straw roofs, though there was one brick building then under construction to house a bank. The city had been built upon land owned by a Chickasaw citizen named Robert Love, who collected twenty-five dollars a year for the lease of business lots and twelve dollars for residential lots. Merchants talked of moving the town across the river after the opening of Oklahoma to avoid the fees.[19]

To the north of town, looming even higher than the bluff of the business district, was a red-rocked, red-dirted eminence which had been aptly dubbed "Red Hill." The hill provided a commanding view of the surrounding countryside, particularly to the east where the railroad line, the wide bed of the South Canadian, and the unoccupied acres of the Oklahoma country could be observed for miles around. The Catholics had erected a mission atop Red Hill, its bell providing a civilizing tone to the community.

Purcell was a rowdy, frontier-style village, however. Gambling was openly conducted on the streets as well as in its four poker houses. Though federal law prohibited the selling of liquor on the Chickasaw lands, bootlegging was a thriving business at hotels, livery stables, and other places. The conductors on passing trains kept the place well supplied. Almost everyone carried guns or wore them strapped to his waist. Indians, half-bloods, outlaws, and all the tough elements of the frontier mingled with settlers of every description who were pouring into the town daily. The western sport of shooting up the town was still practiced by drunken cowboys on occasion.

There were no sidewalks, and the only lights were those shining forth from the hotels and dance halls. The flickering lights accentuated the rifles, shotguns, and revolvers the men carried; but the atmosphere was relaxed and happy, and the sounds of revelry filled the night air. During the day the town fairly hummed with wagons, horses, and people. The surrounding countryside was dotted heavily with cabins, dugouts, tents, and covered wagon homes. Estimates of the number of people in Purcell at this time ranged from 2,000 to 10,000, all of them ready to move into Oklahoma at a moment's notice. The *Eagle* correspondent was sympathetic of the frontier flotsam which he observed:

> Some are poor, indeed, and their garments show the effect of sun, storms and rough usage. Their unkempt hair and rough beards show a most reckless disregard of conventionalities. Their rattling old rigs and rattling piles of bones that draw them are well in keeping with their appearance. Such, however, are not all of them, for many have fine times and outfits. Some have their homes upon wheels ready to move at the word. One man camped on the South Canadian has a sawmill which he will move upon his claim.
> Then the building of the Santa Fe railroad has greatly changed the means of entrance and now over the iron trail the most enthusiastic arrive at Oklahoma City and Purcell unmolested by the soldiers. They stop at the Clifton or other of the good hotels here keeping them always full; take teams and wagons and scour the country to see it and learn its advantages for themselves.
> One thing quite certain, there is no diminution

of interest nor dropping off in numbers. The white covered wagons are rolling in from every direction; from the trains daily alight the fortune hunters in this new El Dorado.[20]

Not long after Hill had checked into the Clifton upon his arrival, the clan of original boomers began showing up to hold a conclave on the matter of protecting their interests in Oklahoma once it was opened. W. L. Couch, smallish of physique but possessing a determined demeanor that was enhanced by a bristling mustache, and the roundish, balding Samuel Crocker had arrived back from Washington. John Furlong (who after the Run would become a "miracle water" merchant and healer), hair down to his shoulders in frontier style, was there along with the old Payne follower, A. P. Lewis, who now operated the sawmill on the South Canadian. Congressman Charles H. Mansur of Missouri, an Oklahoma promoter, was a visiting dignitary.

Of special concern to the boomers was the exclusion clause of the new law, Section 13, which read in part: " . . . but until said lands are opened for settlement by proclamation of the President, no person shall be permitted to enter upon and occupy the same and no person violating this provision shall be permitted to enter any of said land or acquire any right thereto."[21] If this limitation was applied to the opening of Oklahoma without exception, almost all of the oldtime boomers stood to lose the choice homestead claims they had long since taken. But the only hope was that the long-honored frontier preemption or "squatter's rights" would prevail. The boomers felt very strongly that the homesteads they had claimed were justly theirs in consideration of the effort, time, money, and suffering they had applied in booming the country for settlement.

The discussion continued most of the following day, and it was finally decided that legislation could be pushed to remedy the exclusion clause. The boomers also gave consideration to a plan whereby all the old boomers would congregate upon one section and from there control, without occupying, the land they expected to take. An old boomer named Snyder was named secretary of the group and charged with keeping a list of members and their claims. All were sworn to the protection of one another's homesteads.[22]

During the following day a news reporter for the *Kansas City Gazette* found Harry Hill and asked what advice he had for the hordes of anxious people waiting to plunge ahead into Oklahoma. Hill said that he thought they should go in only as peaceful, honest settlers. Later that day, in response to pleas for help, he sent a telegram to President Harrison. It read:

> President Benjamin Harrison: The situation in Oklahoma is critical. It is a Western necessity to have some action at once on Oklahoma. If the thousands of honest settlers clamoring for admission are deprived of their right to settlement till too late to make a crop it will not only be a disappointment but will cause actual starvation on the borders. Very respectfully, Harry L. Hill[23]

CHAPTER III
Boomer Bastion

Not far from the depot at Oklahoma Station, two gamblers operated a faro game in a tent. The word was out that boomer Tom Ward had lost his all there—his entire sixty-five cents.
Wichita Eagle, *March 22, 1889.*

ON the morning of March 15, Harry Hill and the *Eagle* reporter caught a train back to Oklahoma station, able now with daylight to observe the boomer dugouts and cabins on both sides of the South Canadian and the numerous covered wagons moving along the traces of the old Arbuckle Cattle Trail, which followed along the course of the railroad. Herds of cattle grazed contentedly on the rich grassland around Norman and Verbeck [Moore] stations. The weather had turned cold and raw, and the Oklahoma station platform was deserted except for a soldier and two or three railroad employees.[1]

Prior to the arrival of Payne's first expedition in the spring of 1880, the site of Oklahoma station, about a half a mile up on the north bank of the North Canadian, had been distinguished only by the Star Mail Route from Vinita to Albuquerque and by the Arbuckle Trail crossing of the river a short ways to the east. From 1880 to 1885 Payne and Couch had led numerous groups of boomers to this site. None of their settlements survived, however, and it was not until the graders for the Santa Fe arrived during the fall of

1886 that the first permanent structure was raised at the place that is today downtown Oklahoma City.

This first building was erected by trader William Decker, who had followed the progress of the railroad south from Red Fork station with his "Seymour" post office and trading store. For a short time the location was known as Seymour, but in July 1887 the Santa Fe Railroad Company used the name of "Oklahoma" in its station application to the government, and an official post office was designated under that name.[2] Hopeful of continuing his trading business, Decker constructed a one-and-a-half story lumber building and a small stockade-style corral in November 1886. Located just west of the scheduled railroad depot, the store was well marked by a stand of several tall cottonwood trees. For a short time this store and post office, surrounded by tents, grading equipment, and mule teams, operated for the benefit of advance crews of the railroad. But the government refused to renew Decker's trading license, and he sold the building and corral to another Darlington agency trader, J. S. Evans.[3]

The grading crews moved on across the river and southward, and in March 1887 came the rail-laying gangs and the carpenter crews who erected a section house, wooden loading platform, pump house, and water tank for the railroad. Another crew began digging a well at the station site. Just to the east of the rail line, the Quartermaster Department of the U.S. Army built an eight-room house for their forwarding agent, C. F. Sommers. It was there during the last of February 1888 that Eva Sommers became the first child born at the site of Oklahoma City.[4]

By mid-April 1887 the Santa Fe line was open from Arkansas City to Oklahoma station for both passengers and freight. Squatters had already begun to make themselves at home in the area, for a *Topeka Commonwealth* correspondent visiting the location told of a raid made by Lieutenant S. E. Adair and a detail of Cheyenne scouts from Fort Reno to clean out the boomers: "Uncle Sam has destroyed the town and the only remnants are the half-burnt poles of sod houses and the stumps from which the trees were cut . . ."⁵

Oklahoma station—already referred to on occasion as "Oklahoma City"—quickly became a central freighting point for goods to and from Fort Reno, the Darlington agency, Fort Sill, the Sac and Fox agency to the east on Deep Fork, and other points. Freighting outfits with their high box wagons and long mule teams now cluttered the area, and the cottonwood trees quickly lost their bark to ever-hungry mules. Evans died shortly after purchasing the building and corral, and the structures were sold to C. F. Sommers and C. B. Bickford, the latter having secured a government transportation contract. Bickford put up another stockade fence beside the old one. His freighting operations were handled by a man named George W. Gibson, who returned from a visit to Arkansas City one day with a new bride and began offering meals at his place.⁶

Gibson was also the station agent for a stage line which now extended from Oklahoma station along the north bank of the river to the Council Grove area, where the government had established a civilian wood-cutting operation to supply Fort Reno and Darlington. The stage route crossed the river there at what would later come to be known as "Dead Man's Crossing,"⁷ recrossing the river to a relay station near the present town of Yukon, and from there going on to Fort Reno, Darlington, Anadarko, and Fort Sill.

In December of 1887 Samuel H. Radebaugh, an old Payne boomer, was appointed as postmaster at Oklahoma station. He arrived the following February to take up residence in a two-story frame house built for him by another boomer of the past, P. M. Gilbert, who had once been a strong Payne supporter and who was now connected with the government wood camp at Council Grove. Gilbert built the house, which was located due west of the depot and a short distance north of the Decker building, out of a carload of Texas lumber which had been wrecked there.⁹

Radebaugh did more than run the post office, causing him to be charged by the military with operating a trading

The relay house on the mail route between Oklahoma Station and Fort Reno near present Yukon, was one of few structures in the Unassigned Lands before the land run (Harper's Weekly).

---

post without a license in league with Gibson. Sommers, too, was accused of carrying on a trade in grain.[10] Not having the protection of government employment as did Sommers and Radebaugh, Gibson was told to leave Oklahoma station. Aboard a train from Kansas, Gibson complained to a reporter that "he was making too much money, fell from the grace and was froze out, and was obliged to sell to a friend that was more in favor with the powers that be . . ."[11]

Gibson was still there, however, feeding and housing muleskinners and others in the Decker building when A. W. Dunham arrived at the station one cold night in April, 1888, to take over as the Santa Fe agent. "This building," Dunham wrote, "was made from rough lumber, a story and a half high, and had two or more sleeping rooms upstairs. The cracks were not closely battened, and the biting wind found its way through in unstinted measure. We knocked at the door, and soon made it understood who we were and what we wanted. George Gibson came down holding a coal oil lamp, to which was attached a tin reflector."[12]

There were others who had located at Oklahoma station for one reason or another. Ben Miller, likable rancher and former president of the Cherokee Strip Live Stock Association, was there as an agent for the Indian Bureau. He and his wife lived in a small house near the Sommers residence. George Thornton, part-time freighter and part-time deputy U.S. marshal, had a one-room shanty not far from the station pump shack. In addition, the Santa Fe kept two section gangs at the location.[13] A meat hack from Silver City on the

South Canadian made regular visits to supply the small-but-growing community.

Joseph C. Chrisney visited the station in the spring of 1888 and wrote a number of exuberant descriptive articles about the Oklahoma country for his newspaper at Chrisney, Indiana. In one he surmised: "This is a grand, natural townsite, with beautiful country surrounding it. The river on the south affords an abundance of water; the second bottom for the town proper and the elevation for residences, colleges, and the Capitol buildings. I never saw a prettier country, nor a prettier town site."[14]

James McGranahan bought out Gibson for $250 and took over as agent for the stage line, soon after becoming postmaster in replacement of Radebaugh. McGranahan was no newcomer to the territory. He had been a freighter with Sheridan and Custer during their winter 1868-69 Indian campaign, had freighted at Fort Sill, and later served as stage line agent at Bullfoot Ranch on the Fort Reno-Caldwell route and at the relay station between Oklahoma station and Reno. His wife Sarah came with him.[15]

In August 1888 the editor of the *Purcell Register* made a train visit to Oklahoma station, reporting a population of about fifty people.[16] But his count may well have been on the short side for a good number of boomers were beginning to accumulate just outside the station. Radebaugh, his wife, and three daughters had remained on in their building, which had now become a headquarters for the boomers who had seeped into the area. Among them was the old Emporia boomer, T. W. Eckelberger, who had been one of Payne's top lieutenants.[17] By the last of 1888 a sizeable group had accumulated around the station, their tents pitched or dugouts built well back in secreted places.

On November 30, following a warning from the military at Fort Reno to leave, a meeting was held among the preemptors to discuss their claims and situation. It was generally agreed that all would abandon their claims and improvements until the land was officially opened.[18] A few of the squatters returned to Kansas, but it was not really expected that many would leave permanently. A good number were still in the area in late December when Lieutenant A. C. McComb put himself on friendly drinking terms with the men there. He met with the squatters, "quietly sympathizing with the boomers and telling them they are all right."[20] Still, he said, they must obey orders, and when the troops came around with instructions to serve there must be no hard feelings. The officer set up his headquarters in a large tent that served as a makeshift city hall and cheerfully read his orders to anyone who requested it. This charade was accompanied by "intelligible winks that were translated into Oklahoma vernacular and meant that they could just make a move on or before the third day thereafter, come back or do what they liked, as that would relieve the officer of his 'painful duty,' and he would, you see, stand in with them on the deal."[21] Thus the squatters and the military could work for each other and give good entertainment to the public at the same time.

The boomers talked the matter over at length, then they decided the thing to do would be to skip the area for a short time in order to protect the lieutenant. Some caught the train to Kansas, some moved south to Purcell, and others took refuge "among the oaks." However, when one boomer who was chopping wood was invited to leave the country by McComb's Cheyenne scouts, he refused and asked to "see the papers" which the officer had read with so much sport. The man got a smash to his head with a rifle butt instead, reinforcing the complaint that the Indian scouts took entirely too much pleasure in bossing the white men around.[22]

McComb returned to Oklahoma station in February, finding a number of boomers still there. Among them was a Wichita man named T. C. Eggleston, who claimed the title of President of the Oklahoma Co-Operative Townsite and Homestead Company.[23] He carried about a large plat of the North Canadian valley which was filled with the names of settlers and railroad employees who had joined the company for a fee of two dollars as a sort of mutual protection

The first post office at Oklahoma Station, was constructed by Postmaster Beidler from an old chickenhouse (Harper's Weekly).

---

agreement. When McComb and his men arrived, Eggleston had hidden out behind the post office building. Later that night, when the scouts were "doing up the town" at the station, Eggleston was noticeably absent. Presumably, the other boomers noted with some humor, the townsite developer was out showing a claim to a client.[24]

When Hill and the reporter arrived from Purcell, they went to Radebaugh's hotel where they found a group of men seated around a good fire discussing the matter of when Oklahoma would be opened. "It was one of those subjects that the longer they discussed it the less they knew about it."[25]

Five wagons stood fully loaded with supplies and other goods that were headed for the Darlington Indian Agency. The teamsters, Cheyennes and Arapahos who were paid by the government for hauling their own annuity goods from the depot to their agency, were laughing and joshing one another in good fun over the predicament of their wagon being stuck in a puddle of mud.[26]

Making friends with Radebaugh, the reporter persuaded him to hitch up his wagon and take him on a tour of the area surrounding Oklahoma station. Following the road of the old Star Mail Route eastward along the North Canadian, the two men forded the river at the Arbuckle Trail crossing. They toured past the hilltop site of Payne's original townsite of Ewing two miles south of the river, then visited the remains of the Wantland Crutch-O Ranch log hut and corral on Crutcho Creek where Harry Hill had first spent the winter some ten years before. Blessed with a two-acre lake and trees, the site had once been a camping ground for Indians on the move through the country.

Boomers were camped in the brush and woods, hiding out until the day of the opening. One old boomer named Bruce, it was told, had built a house next to the Wantland place, which was claimed by Harry Hill, but a company of Indian scouts had burned the house and driven the old man off. The boomer's daughter, Nellie, a school teacher from Kansas, had arrived just recently and vowed to work the claim herself. Supposedly, she went out to the tract, dug a house in the side of a hill, and held forth with the support of a dog, a flock of chickens, and a Winchester. She was the toast of the boomers at Oklahoma station.[27]

The reporter was led far out into the brush to one well-concealed boomer camp in the center of a thickly wooded area near a small lake. From there he was escorted across the dividing ridge between the North Canadian and the Deep Fork, finding prairie chicken, quail, wild turkey, deer, and honey bees to be plentiful in this virgin resort of the boomer. After enjoying a hearty evening meal at the camp, the reporter returned to the station. There the boomers were highly disturbed over reports that a large party of soldiers was on its way from Fort Reno to clear out the squatters again.

A meeting was called for eight o'clock that night at a driftwood point on the north bank of the North Canadian a half mile below the station. A fire was built and guns fired into the air to announce the meeting. Within a few minutes a large number of men—the reporter estimated the crowd at 500—had suddenly appeared. They sprawled on the ground, leaned against wagons, smoked, chewed, argued, and talked about how earlier in the month they had hanged and burned Kansas Senator Preston Plumb in effigy for his lack of support in opening Oklahoma.[28] Finally the meeting was called to order, and Eckelberger was elected president of the affair. The old boomer, a confirmed proponent of squatter's rights, insisted to the crowd that they should stick fast because the military had no legal right to throw them off their claims. When he announced that Harry Hill was present, a general cry of approval went up.

Hill was ushered to a wagon bed while a newly appointed secretary was given a smoking lantern by which to record Hill's speech. Hill told the boomers that he was against their coming in early, but since they were already there he felt they should work their claims and try to raise enough food to keep them during the coming winter. Soon, he said, they would be reinforced by thousands of others. The boomers cheered him enthusiastically. Hill climbed down from the wagon, and within five minutes the site was deserted, the boomers having faded into the darkness to return to their tents, dugouts, and wagons in the woods. In the morning they would begin erasing the tracks and trails leading to their encampments as best they could.

Present at the station at this time was a young photographer by the name of Kid Hamill, who added to the historical record of the day by photographing the boomers assembled in front of Radebaugh's place and again at the driftwood site on the river, plus other pre-run views of Oklahoma station.[29]

On the morning following the meeting, March 16, a freighting wagon arrived from Fort Reno, and the drivers confirmed that the soldiers were, indeed, on their way. The military unit, a force of about seventy-five soldiers and Indian police, arrived at two o'clock that afternoon. They were under the command of Lieutenant John M. Carson, Jr., a young West Pointer who had been given strict orders to remove all unauthorized persons. He was determined to do so, accepting no excuse that was not bona fide.

Carson and his detail found some forty men idling around the depot. He immediately ordered his men to begin tearing down all the boomers' tents and dugouts they could locate and ordered everyone except government and railroad employees to leave by nine the following evening. The same order was issued to Radebaugh, despite the ex-postmaster's plea that he needed time to settle his affairs with the post office authorities and locate a new home for his family.[30]

When Carson learned that Eckelberger had been telling people that the troops were acting illegally and advising them to stay put, the officer hunted him up and ordered him to leave on the next train. Eckelberger did so, though he would soon return. Four men claiming to be railroad employees on a few days' leave were ordered to move out by the next day. Dismounted patrols were sent to scour the brush along the North Canadian in both directions, and a unit of Indian scouts was directed to search along Mustang Creek south of the North Canadian to the west.

Taking a force of six men, Carson scouted four miles east of Oklahoma station where he found the claim of an old Civil War veteran named W. A. Arnold on Crutcho Creek. Arnold lived in a tent, but nearby was a half complete dugout, chicken coups, corn bins, a plow, and a wagon with a team of mules. Both Arnold and another man named Patterson refused to leave their claims. Arnold even stampeded his mules to prevent Carson from impounding them. He declared that it would take brute force to remove him and that he would die first right where he was.

Wishing to avoid conflict if possible, Carson decided to leave and return the next day, giving the boomers a chance to leave on their own. Though Patterson was gone when he came back the next morning, Arnold was still on the grounds and as determined as ever not to leave. Now joined by four other men, the old veteran armed himself with a stick and put up a stout resistance against the soldiers.

When Carson stepped between the combatants, Arnold swung the stick at him. The officer warded off the blow, grabbing the old man and holding him until a trooper used a pistol butt to quell him. Carson suffered a badly sprained thumb out of the fracas.[31]

The other squatters dashed for the woods, and a warning shot to stop only added to their speed in the other direction. Arnold was bound and tossed into a wagon with all his moveable effects and taken off to the soldiers' camp. His improvements were all destroyed.[32]

While some of the boomers left on the train for Purcell and Arkansas City, most of them simply took to the woods again until the military was gone. A few others besides Arnold were found and brought into camp, however. Among them was a Negro man found at a wood-cutting camp and an elderly black woman who was living in a dugout, her husband being away at the time the soldiers came.

On March 21 Carson broke camp at Oklahoma station and headed for Purcell with his prisoners, hauling their goods in two wagons. He left the woman, Mrs. Smith, behind to await the return of her husband. On the way to Purcell the troops garnered in another party of seven men and three wagons. Arnold and the others were sent across the South Canadian into the Chickasaw country with orders not to return to Oklahoma.[33]

Harry Hill having come and gone, Oklahoma station now became host to some other boomer celebrities. No sooner had the troops ridden off than the boomers began coming out of their hiding places. On the day following, the twentieth, W. L. Couch and Congressman Weaver arrived by train from Arkansas City. The boomers had already planned a big dance for that night at the Radebaugh house, celebrating the departure of Carson, and the two boomer leaders were invited to attend. When they arrived, they were cheered long and loud—"some old campaigners howled themselves hoarse hurrahing for Captain Couch."[34]

Weaver made a speech, saying that all good citizens would wait until the President had issued a proclamation before entering upon the land, though they might pass through and look it over. He knew that those present would do that. He predicted that Oklahoma would be a state within two years. When the two visitors had departed, the boomers held long discussions again on the subject of pre-entry. The oldtimers argued strongly that since they were on the land prior to the passage of the law, they could hold their claims on the grounds of squatter's rights and could not be ousted.[35]

Weaver, having visited Purcell, was back at Oklahoma station again on March 25, telling all to mind the law. He told the boomers that he knew those who came on the day of the run would not disturb the claims made by the original boomers. He was so confident of this that he himself selected a beautiful high meadow a mile and a half northeast of the depot as a claim for himself. He put up a stake with a note which read: "B. Weaver, of Bloomfield, Iowa, wishes to take this quarter section when he can lawfully do so."[36] That done, the lawmaker caught the train to Arkansas City where, not to be outdone by Caldwell, local citizens presented him with a gold-headed cane.

Though publicity of a directive to the military to start making a list of names of those found inside Oklahoma had somewhat stymied the influx of people, Oklahoma station was still being visited by land speculators and business men looking for profitable business locations. A carload of lumber and household goods was unloaded for a Chicago man. By Tuesday, following his release on the Friday previous, boomer Arnold was back at Oklahoma station saying that he held no ill will against Lieutenant Carson.[37]

Couch was in Purcell on March 27 when he received a telegram with electrifying news. President Benjamin Harrison had finally signed the proclamation which had been on his desk since March 20. At long last it had happened! The lands known as Oklahoma would be opened to settlement!

The news spread quickly, and settlers all over the frontier went wild with joy. At Guthrie and Oklahoma stations men

Oklahoma City before the land run, a scruffy collection of tents, log cabins, shacks, cattle pens, and Santa Fe depot (Harper's Weekly).

---

and women swarmed out of their hiding places in the woods and rushed up to passing trains to get confirmation and any bits of additional information they could about the great event to come.[38]

What they learned was that President Harrison had signed his proclamation on March 23. It defined the lands recently purchased from the Creek and Seminole tribes and declared them to be open to settlement under the laws of the Homestead Act, expressly warning once again that "no person entering upon or occupying said land before said hour of 12 o'clock, noon, on the 22nd of April A.D., 1889, hereinbefore fixed, will ever be permitted to enter any of the said lands or to acquire rights . . ."[39]

The proclamation further reserved two acres of land for government use, one near Guthrie station and another near the old stagecoach relay station known as Kingfisher, which consisted of a picket house plastered with mud, a picket stable, a wire-fenced garden, and a haystack.[40]

These two locations were soon named as land office sites

by the Commissioner of the General Land Office, Kingfisher serving the Western District and Guthrie the Eastern. These two districts were divided by the line between Ranges 3 and 4 and constituted about the same number of townships. Altogether there were some 10,000 quarter sections of land to be had, all freely granted.[41]

A big celebration was held by the boys at Oklahoma station on the night of March 28, and they were still sleeping off their hangovers when quite unexpectedly Lieutenant Carson and his troops rode back in at midnight. He and his men had marched back along the south bank of the North Canadian until they reached the railroad track and turned north to take the boomers at Oklahoma station completely by surprise.

In compliance with his new orders to take down names, Carson compiled a list. On it were W. A. Arnold, arrested this time a half a mile east of the railroad driving a team and wagon; Mrs. Smith, still where Carson had left her waiting for her husband; T. C. Eggleston, who now claimed to represent a newspaper called the *Oklahoma Times* (then being published in Wichita); Sam Loo, a Chinese man from Wichita who was at the station to see about starting a laundry there; J. D. Eades, alias "Kiowa," a well-known gambler; Radebaugh and his family; and more than sixty others rounded up in the sweep from Fort Reno.[42]

Only a few days later, in early April, a reporter for the Chicago *Daily Inter-Ocean* arrived at the depot. He found that the North Canadian bottoms, which had been filled with squatters a short time before, were now virtually deserted, though at night the boomers "still come tumbling out of their holes. They gather on the depot platform, and as the train comes in they eagerly push forward to buy their favorite paper, and thus get the latest news." He found that some were well dressed and happy-go-lucky people, but most of them were poor devils who had nothing on earth except "a ragged suit of clothes, a mule team, a covered wagon, a dog, and a tattered tent, and still, in their own way, they are happy."[43]

CHAPTER IV
Bound for Utopia

"A young man from Missouri, whose soft felt hat flapped up and down in the wind like wings of a wild turkey, said that he did not suppose that Oklahoma was any better than any other place, but that he was going there merely for the reason that everybody else seemed to be going." Harper's Weekly, May 4, 1889.

EVEN as the old boomers and the squatters at Oklahoma station and elsewhere were attempting to consolidate their holds on preempted claims, a mighty invasion force of land seekers was beginning to move toward Oklahoma. Harrison's proclamation, plus the resulting publicity that filled the newspapers throughout the country, touched off a surge of excitement and brought people hurrying forth by train, wagon, horseback, and on foot. They came from all parts of the nation and from other countries such as Canada and England. The Oklahoma excitement was cited as the cause of a large increase in the number of emigrants booking steerage passage from Liverpool—10,000 in the week before the run—as well as from Bremen, Hamburg, Antwerp, and other ports.[1]

Reports of the old boomers' efforts to protect their claims through the formation of secret leagues caused much concern. Of special impact was a story which surfaced to the effect that the boomers had concocted a scheme to burn the railroad bridges leading into Oklahoma. The reports deterred only a few, but they did cause brisk sales in Winchesters.[2]

As early as April 2, a colony of thirty Mormons, said to be the advance of a much larger group in Utah, arrived at Arkansas City. There they tried to purchase tickets to Guthrie station, but the Santa Fe agent already had his orders not to sell tickets to points inside the Oklahoma country. After considerable argument the Mormons were forced to buy passes to Purcell instead, though they angrily declared their intentions of getting off at Guthrie anyhow.[3]

A few days later a delegation of fifty men from Sacramento, California, was also refused passage to Guthrie. Two families arrived at Arkansas City on a large flatboat loaded with household goods, livestock, and agricultural implements. They had floated down Walnut Creek, they said, and planned to travel to Oklahoma by way of the Arkansas River, if there were not too many sand bars.[4]

Another report, apparently concocted by a fiction-bent correspondent, appeared in newspapers around the country and overseas. Four Hoosiers, it was claimed, were camped near the Antelope Hills in western Indian Territory (then still raw Indian country), and they had with them a hot-air balloon. Supposedly, they planned to make an ascent on the morning of April 22, float over Oklahoma ahead of everyone else, then descend upon their claims at noon. In air-minded France, *Le Figaro* newspaper was very annoyed that the American reporter had not given the names of the brave "aeronauts."[5]

From all corners of the country now came reports of building interest in Oklahoma. In Chicago the Chicago Oklahoma Colony Association met 200 strong and listened to accounts of a man who claimed to having traveled all through the territory. Among the crowd were youthful adventurers, tradesmen of all sorts, speculators, farmers driven to the city by adversity, clerks yearning for the free life of the frontier—tenderfeet all with their "short hair, button shoes, 'biled' shirts, stiff hats and other articles of apparel..."[6]

F. R. Robinson, passenger agent for the Santa Fe, was there to encourage the would-be settlers, promising them a special train with special rates and reassuring them that they had nothing to fear from the old boomers already on the border. The Chicagoans also heard a native of Fort Gibson, Indian Territory, Frank Touse, say he thought it was useless to go unless they had money enough to carry them through the first six months.[7]

In New York City an advertisement appeared in the *Times*, reading: "Wanted—100 men to go to Oklahoma, I.T. You must have some money to pay your expenses; every citizen of the United States is entitled to 160 acres of land. If you wish to join the party call at once and register your name; this party must reach Oklahoma on April 22, the day the land is open to entry. D. Grauman."[8]

In virtually every major city of the country, people began to hold meetings to form Oklahoma colonies and make plans for taking part in the run. At Sherman, Texas, Captain D. L. Parker claimed an enrollment of about 200 men, all ready to leave at a moment's notice. Captain S. H. Scott of Fort Smith, Arkansas, organized a large colony and planned a townsite near the Kickapoo reservation. A prominent merchant of Conway, Arkansas, passed through Fort Smith with a large, well-armed, and belligerent group on a special Missouri Pacific rail car.[9]

It was reported that "Oklahoma fever" had also broken out among the black people of Little Rock, and a large number of Negroes were expected to join the rush under noted black politician W. R. Furbush. A party of North Carolina Negroes, headed by planter George Ingram, arrived at Fort Smith even as a group of fifty Fort Smith blacks were on their way to Oklahoma with Guthrie as their destination.[10]

At Topeka the Oklahoma Capital City Town Site and Improvement Company announced that it was ready for business and was selling shares at ten dollars each. From Springfield, Illinois, home of Senator Springer, came word that General David T. Littler, already rumored as a favorite choice for governor of Oklahoma, had left that town with other colonists. Word circulated of an advance guard of old soldiers from Ohio, Maryland, and West Virginia which was moving west.[11]

Townsite companies sprang into being throughout Kansas. There was the Southwestern Kansas Immigration Society; the Oklahoma Colony of the Real Estate Homestead and Emigration Association for the State of Kansas; the Fuller-Russell Town Site Company of Arkansas City, Kansas, Guthrie, and Oklahoma City, Indian Territory; the Wellington Consolidated Land and Town Company of Oklahoma, whose object was to combine all the capital of southern Kansas speculators into one large town site company instead of many small ones; the first Oklahoma Town Company of Meade Center; and numerous others.[12]

In Omaha, Nebraska, some 200 men gathered and smoked as Captain Jesse G. Smith, who claimed to be an old Payne boomer, described the wonders of Oklahoma. Eventually the group organized, then split into two factions, one hiring Smith to lead them and the other expelling him. It was decided by one group of old soldiers to send emissaries on ahead with their power of attorney to file soldiers' declaratory claims for them, though some still had reservations about the "Hanging Gardens of Oklahoma," as pictured by Smith.[13]

When the Chicago group of Oklahoma colonists met a second time on April 12, Touse had become considerably more enthusiastic about Oklahoma, having prepared a table of sections best suited for farming there. He was now willing to sell cards on these sections for fifty cents each, with the purchaser signing an agreement to pay him another $4.50 when possession of the land had been made.[14]

There were three separate colonies in Chicago: the Bergs Colony of about sixty people; the Winter and Townsley Colony of the same number; and the Chicago Colony of about fifty members. Most of those signing up to go to Oklahoma were single men who were out of work and "ready for any scheme afloat."[15] Some of the Chicagoans were concerned about the "ferocious cowboys and Indian killers," but others claimed to feel no special concern even though they were armed to the teeth.

"We are going with Winchesters and double-barreled shotguns," said a Mr. Summerfield, president of the Chicago Colony, "and will stand as good a show and better than those who have been waiting around the borders for months."[16]

At the final meeting of the Chicago Oklahoma Colony on April 18, both Robinson of the Santa Fe and an agent of the Wabash line were present, and the two became engaged in a wordy war over which company could best serve the cause of the colonists. In a standing vote, the Santa Fe won, and plans were made for the departure of the colony by train on the night of April 21.[17]

Longtime boomer George W. Cooper arrived in Kansas City on April 16 to arrange for transportation for his colony at Emporia. Cooper, who had been with the Santa Fe for eleven years, laid claim to an inherited leadership of some 20,000 boomers (actually the number was more like 200) and said he would need forty cars at Emporia to carry his people to Oklahoma. Cooper was secretive about his plans, but he stated that he had first gone to Oklahoma in 1866, had ever since longed to settle there, and did not intend to be left out in the rush.[18]

The Walden Colony of Kansas City, an early competitor to Payne's Oklahoma Colony, had resurfaced, claiming that its now-deceased president, W. B. Walden, had originated the Oklahoma boom in 1879. It would make no united effort to enter Oklahoma, though it claimed to have founded an original townsite on the south side of the North Canadian some twelve miles east of Kickapoo station.[19]

The Kansas City Union Depot became a funnel through which much of the Oklahoma migration poured. Every train brought in colonists by the hundreds from all parts of the North, East, South, and Midwest for transfer to the Santa Fe and Rock Island trains, which went out loaded to the platforms for either Caldwell or Arkansas City. One reporter observed a striking similarity to most of the men headed for Oklahoma—they were all well armed.[20]

Another apparent similarity was that each and every one

had a ravishing appetite for any information about the Oklahoma country. Any book, newspaper, pamphlet, map, or other item containing anything at all on Oklahoma sold quickly. Conductors on the incoming trains complained of being worn out trying to answer a wide and endless variety of questions about the country by gun-toting passengers. Newsboys on the trains were reaping big profits from selling blank affidavits and notices of preemption which claimants could file at the land offices.[21]

A parade of American types of the day passed through the Kansas City station. From Pennsylvania came thirty miners, including women and children, who said they were tired of mining life and were anxious to find work in "God's sunlight" as farmers. They carried long sheaf knives. A party of lumber raftsmen from Michigan were dressed in picturesque costumes and caught the attention of all. They were reportedly led by Richard O'Rourke, better known as "Stage Line Dick" from having driven stages in western Kansas. He wore a small felt hat, a shirt made of bright line woolen material, and his trousers were held up by a worsted belt. A man from Maryland wore a fancy corduroy suit and carried a rifle in a new leather case. He had purchased the gun especially for the trip to Oklahoma, he said, and admitted that he had never fired a rifle in his life.[22]

A group of Illinois colonists arrived by the Rock Island, their women wearing calico dresses and poke bonnets and carrying enormous baskets filled with edibles. From New York, Massachusetts, Illinois, and Pennsylvania came a concourse of pharmacists, butchers, tailors, and blacksmiths. Fifty-six bricklayers from Fort Wayne, Indiana, passed through the Union Station bound for Guthrie. Seventeen tall mountaineers from Peach Gap, Tennessee, transferred to the Rock Island for Caldwell. Two deserters from Fort Leavenworth were arrested as they tried to board a south-bound train. Thirty Italians from Castle Garden, New York, came well armed and ready for any emergency. From Memphis came a large colony of Tennesseans accompanied by Alabamians, Mississippians, and Georgians—tall, tough-looking men who wore pistols about their waists and seemed to feel no need for the rifles which others carried.[23]

A party of Missourians won center stage by virtue of their leader's unique appearance. The man was tall and lank and had a thin face covered with scrubby chin whiskers. Over his rough clothing he wore a pair of overalls made of bunting and stamped with small American flags, his pantaloons being striped in red, white, and blue. He carried a long rifle of ancient pattern and wore a brace of "cannon-calibred Navies," which was accompanied by a large knife. He had been to Oklahoma before, he said, and was now leading a group of followers back. Asked if he were looking for trouble in Oklahoma, the Missourian replied, "Ain't lost any."[24]

A thirty-man colony from Terre Haute was comprised of members wearing long yellow slickers and carrying large white canvas valises. They were the proud possessors of a huge American flag, which they said would be hoisted at the center of their claim in Oklahoma.[25] From New York City came eighty men carrying Winchesters and tools. They were the group headed by D. Grauman, a railroad ticket broker who had run the advertisement in the *New York Times*. The group—comprised of doctors, lawyers, surveyors, engineers, clerks, bakers, and others—planned to preempt a townsite two miles from Guthrie station on the Cimarron, then elect a mayor, marshal, and councilmen.[26]

There was one family which had come directly from Scotland to make the run into Oklahoma. Forty-five colonists from Lafayette County, Missouri, arrived carrying tents, light poles, and complete sets of cooking utensils. One man carted a bundle of oil cloth signs which read: "This claim preempted. Papers filed with Register." They had cost him six cents each, he said, and he planned to sell them for a dollar apiece at Guthrie.[27]

A party of twenty Swedes, none of them naturalized citizens, passed through the Kansas City station, stirring up some resentment among other rushees. There was a group of heavily armed black men who passed through, also, and a special emigrant train with fifteen coaches bearing a group from Iowa.[28]

The station at Kansas City became a mecca for sharpers of all kinds. Land sharks stood beneath huge banners selling town lots in the future "Oklahoma City, Texas," a spot on the map in the Texas Panhandle. The lots sold at two dollars each, with a one dollar fee for recording the deed. Close by was another group engaged in selling lots in the "City of promise, New Oklahoma," a few miles south of the other. Both groups denounced their competitor's scheme as a fraud, but both were doing a brisk business.[29]

The station platform swarmed with confidence men, swindlers, and pickpockets. A man from Vermont was taken by a swindler who gave him a $750 bogus check to hold as security for a loan of $20, which was supposedly needed for a freight bill. A man from Iowa on his way to Oklahoma to establish a saloon complained that his ware—several jugs of whiskey, rum, and brandy—had been stolen.[30]

One operation involved three or four sharpers who would board a train, win the confidence of a car load of settlers, and suggest that the organization of a colony be made for the mutual protection and benefit of all. The schemers would produce their pocketbooks and contribute to a common fund to encourage the others to follow suit. If the common fund failed to develop, it would, nonetheless, give the sharpers a chance to size up each man's purse and its place of concealment. Usually they would have their prey fleeced within 100 miles or less.[31]

Not everyone was eager to face the wilds of the new land, however. In Milwaukee an Oklahoma-interested citizen advertised for followers and had some fifty responses. He was highly disgusted when only one man, a miller who hoped to establish a mill on the South Canadian, and his son turned up. The recruiter blamed the "blood-and-thunder and the cock-and-bull story yarns" which the old boomers

A boomer camp along the southern border of the Unassigned Lands, where hopeful homesteaders waited for the fateful announcement of the land run (Harper's Weekly).

---

had fed the newspapers for scaring the Oklahoma fever out of people.[32]

The Omaha group under Captain Smith arrived sixteen strong, claiming to represent a colony of 518 and to hold the power of attorney for 117 old soldiers. Smith said that the colony planned to locate eighteen miles southeast of Fort Reno and establish a town to be named "Thurston."[33] Even as the Omaha group headed south, a party of seven boomers returned to Kansas City disgusted and downhearted after advancing some forty miles into the Cherokee Outlet.[34] They claimed the crowd was much too large and the land too poor.

Four boys, age thirteen to fifteen, caught the Oklahoma rage and started for Oklahoma in a spring wagon, armed with shotguns. But on the first night out, some ten miles from Kansas City, their camp was hit by a drenching rainstorm, and the boys gave it up and returned home.[35]

Still the cloud of homeseekers continued unabated. The crowd at Union Station on the night of April 21 was the largest yet, and the Santa Fe and Rock Island trains were comprised of from two to three sections with as many as fourteen cars per section. Every train was crowded to the maximum, and railroad officials estimated that from Monday evening to Saturday night nearly 10,000 pilgrims had passed through Kansas City on their way to make the big run for free homes.[36]

In Chicago a reporter visited the train station to see off the Chicago Colony as it departed for Oklahoma on the evening of April 21. His description was colorful:

"Board for Utopia!"

"Where?"

"Utopia."

"No; I want to go to 'Klahama."

"Same place—where's your certificate?—all right—this car's full—take next one."

"All right. Rah here, Bill. Le's take these 'ere seats and keep 'em till we git to Whotopia, or whatever that feller with the lantern said."

Bang went the seats and down into them sat a quartet of Oklahoma boomers. The Santa Fe train was made up of seven coaches and was about to leave the Dearborn Station for the land of—see railway guide for particulars.

At 11 o'clock last night there were but few of the 200 boomers to be seen about the station. But the interior of the coaches resembled St. Louis during a Democratic convention. Formality was thrown aside, so was everything else except shirts and trousers. It cannot be said that the air was strictly Oriental in its fragrance; at any rate it was too complicated and powerful for the truly cultured and artistic smeller. But the negligee of the boomers would at once appeal to the lover of the unconventional.

The man from Saginaw rested in a quicker-the-dead position in the immediate vicinity of him of the Hoosier State. The Town of Lake had its delegate there also. But the man whose system was completely saturated with content was he of Peoria. There was a far-off look in his eye and a pint bottle of cemetery promoter in his lap, and he murmured softly to himself, saying, "I'm from the town of Peoria, State of Illinois, and I want a 160 on the southeast quarter, northwest half, Township 4, Range 13 west, b'gosh."

Each boomer had a general store with him—frying pan, tin plates and spoons, iron knives, "spuds," sugar, flour, and what not wrapped in blankets and tied with a clothesline. Near by, too, lay the trusty Winchester with which to bring to earth the festive sagebrush hen and other game of the Far West. The seven-shooter was not an entire stranger to the crowd. The men were of all sections, creeds, denominations, and politics—men past the 50th milestone in life's road; men young, vigorous, and tinged with romance; others tried and found wanting in vocations; others ambitious to grow up with the great Southwest—all dissatisfied with civilization, all hankering for the free life of the frontier and 160 acres of Uncle Sam's property.

"Give me the frontier and you may have all the cities in the world," said an old rounder as he lay down his pack and began to add materially to the specific weight of the atmosphere, assisted by a small but robust pipe.

"Ever been on the frontier?"

"Nowhere else for the last twenty years. All through Manitoba, British Columbia, down into Washington Territory, all over. I tell you there's nothing like it."

"Much money?"

"Like dirt. Why, up there in Manitoba I got $375 a month and didn't do anything either. No, didn't stay because—"

"Board for Oklahoma," shouted the conductor, and the train moved away to the land where land may be had for asking for it and retained at the muzzle of a Winchester.[37]

It was reported that a wagon train of 485 vehicles containing colonists bound for Oklahoma from the Salt Lake valley of Utah and points in Colorado had passed six miles west of Wellington, headed south.[38] A reporter for the *Wichita Eagle* visiting the Kansas border declared:

> Boomers, boomers everywhere. The white tops of their wagons or tents appear upon every available camping ground. On all the highways leading southward are seen their wagons. Yesterday the actual number of wagons that passed down one street of Arkansas City alone was 247 and today as the time for the opening approaches the number increases. From Winfield down to Arkansas City the road lies near the railroad and salutations are almost continuously exchanged between the boomers aboard the train and the boomers in their wagons.[39]

Trains were arriving at the border fully loaded, most of the passengers disembarking there but some traveling on to Purcell. Train travel through the Territory had suddenly become very heavy, not only from settlers but from sightseers as well.

Colonies and townsite companies abounded, and they appealed to a great many people who sought the welfare offered through organization and numbers. Some of these groups would play key roles in the run and the founding of early cities; some, however, would suffer from bad planning or meet misfortune and lose out. By either count, though, they were the vehicle by which a great many people entered the Oklahoma lands.

Pawnee Bill and his group of mostly old boomers, estimated at some 300 wagons, were settled in at the Caldwell fairgrounds waiting for the time to move. In Wichita there were two old soldier colonies organized and gaining members daily from the flow of G.A.R. veterans from the eastern states. On April 16 it was reported that an advance guard of an old soldiers colony from Ohio, Maryland, and West Virginia had reached Wichita, then moved on to Wellington.[40] Still another veterans group, numbering 150, was organized into a colony at Arkansas City under Al Mowrey as president.[41]

In early April, Dr. J. M. Minick, an old soldier himself, requested and received permission from Captain Woodson to make a reconnaissance of the Oklahoma country. Taking two companions with a light wagon and a team of horses, Minick traveled down the Caldwell-Fort Reno road, sport-hunting and examining the country. The men did not find any land that suited them until they reached the North Canadian valley near Fort Reno.

Moving on down the North Canadian, Minick and his men visited Oklahoma station, then drove north to Edmond station and from there out west to Deer Creek and Cottonwood Creek. From what he had seen of Oklahoma, Minick said in a letter to the *Wichita Beacon*, only about one-sixth of it was fit for farming, though some of the valleys were, admittedly, very beautiful and fertile. Game, especially deer and turkey, was plentiful.[42] Minick declared that his colony of 500 was fully prepared to defend itself with rifles and revolvers against either Indians or claim jumpers.[43]

The other old soldiers colony in Wichita was headed by E. C. Cole, who claimed an enrollment of 3,000. Cole, too, went into Oklahoma country, visiting the Kingfisher station area, which he had seen before and liked. Cole purported to be in good with the government and maintained that he could get in ahead of time. He also told everyone that he was a favorite of the Rock Island Railroad, which would extend its line from Pond Creek to wherever he chose to locate.[44] There was talk, also, of a Cole plan to take possession of the Cherokee Outlet by force with a body of men numbering five thousand.[45]

In early April, a large number of Winfield and Cowley County, Kansas, men had hired N. A. Haight to go to Guthrie station and survey off a town plat. The soldiers at the station, however, refused to let Haight get off the train, and he was forced to draw up a plat based on his view of the location from the train and from notes made when he had helped survey the area in 1873. Some 200 members of the group each contributed ten dollars to defray expenses, and each was permitted to select a lot from the plat in the order that their fee had been paid.[46]

Another important group was organized as the Oklahoma Town Company, an unincorporated body of individuals from different towns in Kansas. Because it was formed at Colony, Kansas, which supplied a good number of members, it became known as the "Colony Crowd." Leaders in the company included Dr. Delos Walker and the Reverend James Murray. This colony laid plans to go to Purcell by train, shipping their horses, wagons, and other goods by freight car and making the run from the South Canadian River above Purcell. Their ultimate destination was Oklahoma station.[47]

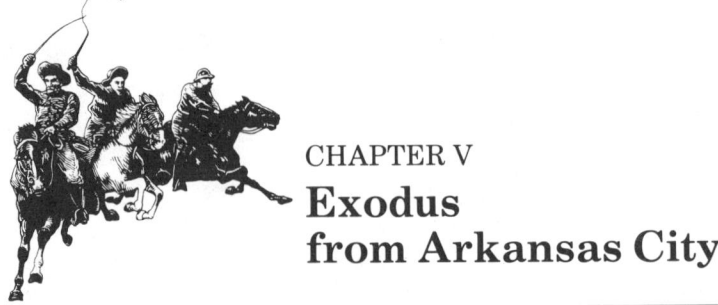

CHAPTER V
Exodus from Arkansas City

> *A minister felt the call to distribute religious literature to the wagons as they struggled through the thick mud in leaving Arkansas City. When he offered a printed piece to one sweating, swearing driver, he was told none-too-politely to keep it. "My friend," the reverend asked, "don't you want to go to Heaven?" "That's just where I'm headed," the driver answered with a crack of his whip. "And if I can cross the Cimarron, I'm bound to get thar."* St. Louis Republic, April 22, 1889.

FOR years the small corps of destitute families had clung to the southern border of Kansas, clustering in makeshift camps on the outskirts of Caldwell, Winfield, Hunnewell, and Arkansas City. These were the impoverished loyalists who had followed Payne and Couch on their excursions into the forbidden country. They had endured the privations, the hardships, and the forced removals and had known the bitterness of defeat at the hands of the military. For almost ten years now they, or others like them, had waited for the day when the government would allow them to cross the border and settle on what they had long contended was free public land.

By 1889 Arkansas City had become the prime staging point for the invasion of the Indian Territory from the north. It had won out over the other contenders by virtue of its location. Situated just three miles north of the Indian Territory, Arkansas City was the last major rail station on the Santa Fe line leading into the Oklahoma country. Moreover, the wagon road which followed along the railroad was the shortest route to Guthrie and Oklahoma stations. Thus the town became the principal point of embarkation for the majority of those wishing to make the run from the north.

A tent city appeared on the Kansas side of the Oklahoma border as land-hungry pioneers gathered at towns such as Arkansas City (Harper's Weekly).

By April 15, a week before the fateful day, Arkansas City had mushroomed into a gathering place for thousands who intended, in one fashion or another, to enter Oklahoma on April 22. Described by a reporter as resembling Leadville during the height of the Black Hills excitement, the small town daily became more and more crowded, its streets, hotels, and stores swarming with newcomers. Cot hotels, saloons, and gambling places sprang up in tents on vacant lots. Every street corner was occupied by hucksters who sold everything from packages of prize soap to patent medicines guaranteed to cure almost anything, including snake bites. And there were always those who had maps of the Oklahoma country, showing the choice locations for settlement.

The "brethren of the green cloth," gamblers, were *en force*. Every saloon and tent gambling house operated stud poker games and faro. These did a thriving business, their tables constantly surrounded by large crowds. The hotels and rooming houses had long since filled far beyond their normal capacity. When night came, those without quarters unrolled their blankets wherever they best found a spot, including even the saloons and tents where the "clink of glasses and the rattle of chips is mingled with the long drawn snore of some boomer who had stretched out beneath a table or in a corner to snatch a few hours' rest."[1]

But, despite the extensive gambling and drinking, there was very little drunkenness. Virtually everyone carried a rifle or shotgun or wore a handgun strapped around his waist, and there were plenty of tough-looking characters around. Thus a natural caution was exercised by men who realized that if they permitted themselves to become drunk, both their pocketbooks and their personal safety would be endangered.

From the town proper could be seen the myriad of camp fires of the boomer camps along the Arkansas River and Walnut Creek. The main boomer camp was situated in a large grove of trees along the Walnut Creek bottom. As newcomers arrived, the camp spread out wider and farther along the creek. Only a few days earlier, 258 prairie schooners had arrived, bringing over 500 more persons to join the nearly 10,000 estimated to be already there.[2]

Reporters, along with artists and photographers of Eastern journals, visited the camps, interviewing the boomers, writing stories, recording scenes for their publications and for history: the white tents, wagons with their battered canvas tops, grazing stock, camp fires with bonneted women bending over cooking kettles, laughing children scampering about the stern-faced men who had brought their families from all parts of the nation to gamble their welfare and, perhaps, their lives on the chances of securing land in Oklahoma. Practically every state and territory in the Union was represented in the Walnut Creek settlements.

Some of them were the old Payne-Couch boomers, who held a natural feeling of earned privilege over those who had only lately arrived. Though the mood of the camp was congenial and free of trouble, there was a mood of suspicious restraint against friendly involvement with others who in a few days would be competitors for government land.

The camp was heavily armed, every man wearing one or two revolvers about his waist, while in most wagons close at hand and loaded was generally a double-barreled shotgun or Winchester rifle. As new wagons appeared daily to increase the size of the boomer camp, the competition factor and the tension of the camp grew. On the night of April 16, a fierce wind and rain storm struck the camp, blowing away the canvas coverings of some of the wagons and soaking those huddled there. There was much suffering, particularly among children of the camp.

But, almost as if the reward was timed to follow this incident, on the following morning the wonderful news was announced through the camp that the settlers would soon be able to move out. The Interior Department had decreed that at eight o'clock on the morning of April 19, a Friday, the boomers would be allowed to cross the Kansas border into the Cherokee Outlet and advance to the Oklahoma district line preparatory to making the run on April 22. The news was received with great jubilation, and the settlers fell to the task of preparing to move out.

The original order allowing the settlers to enter the Outlet on the nineteenth was later revised to permit entry on April 18 instead. Not all of the boomers learned of this change, however, and some remained in their camp until the morning of the nineteenth. Though this gave a small advantage to some, it did prevent what would have otherwise been a chaotic situation and permitted a more orderly exodus from the area.[3]

All during the day of the seventeenth and far into the night, the boomers were preparing to break camp. Harness was checked and given final repair. Wagon wheels were greased, and their iron rims tightened. Camp equipment was packed away in the wagons, water barrels filled, and last minute purchases of foodstuff made in Arkansas City. It was late when the camp finally settled down to rest. In the darkness before dawn the men and boys began rounding up the stock which grazed outside the camp area. A final camp fire breakfast was had, and then the camp equipment was packed away in the wagons and the younger children stowed in the crevices between.[4]

Even before dawn had broken, the long whips began to crack over the heads of the many teams. With milk cows and riding horses hitched in tow behind and faithful dogs trotting dutifully alongside, the wagons began pulling into line. Drivers whooped at their animals as the women and children called out their final farewells to camp neighbors and friends. All were eager and pleased to be on their way, but still there remained an underlying feeling of uncertainty about moving off to a strange and unknown land.

The seemingly-endless procession of boomer wagons began filing down Summit Street leading south out of Arkansas City, the road bounded on one side by a wire fence and on the other by a hedge. It was a narrow passageway and also a very muddy one due to the recent rainstorm. A huge traffic pileup resulted when some of the wagons became stuck hub-deep in the black mire. All the day long, teams struggled against their harnesses while drivers shouted and cursed and both men and women heaved to at the wheels to move the wagons onward. But had the mud been twice as bad, it would not have stopped the determined settlers.

It was estimated that on the morning of the eighteenth, some 400 wagons crossed the Arkansas River bridge while some 600 more struggled along the way behind. A large number of onlookers had come out from the town in carriages and on horseback to watch the event of the boomers crossing the line into the Indian Territory. The Chilocco Indian School, located just across the border, also came *en masse* as spectators.

The instructions from Captain Jack Hayes, now commanding the Fifth Cavalry troops at this point, had been for the boomers to be started across the line at eight o'clock. An orderly was to give the signal. But as the long-awaited moment approached, the orderly had not arrived, and the settlers were growing increasingly impatient. Finally a Kansas City man, who was there merely as a spectator, stood up in his carriage and shouted, "Why should we wait any longer? A few minutes makes no difference. Follow me."[5]

He then drove his carriage across the line, causing a great

roar of approval from the crowd. All along the line now the others followed suit, and soon 1,000 or more covered wagons lumbered over the line and, with delight, headed on their way across the Cherokee Outlet some sixty miles to the northern border of the Oklahoma lands.

The prairie, green with the first grass shoots of spring and virtually dustless because of the recent rain, seemed to turn white with schooners. At their lead was the wagon of Dan Sikes, an old veteran. Perched on a cracker box for a seat, the oldtimer unfurled a huge American flag, and for two miles along the sweeping line of settlers, patriotic hails resounded for Old Glory. Another boomer wagon stood out among the hundreds of others. The owner had built a regular house up from the floor of the wagon, complete with shingled roof and protruding stove pipe.

All day long the wagons, led by Hayes's troops, moved down what was known as the "Ponca Trail" to the south. Camp was made that evening at Willow Springs, and the camp fires which lighted the bowl-shaped area around the springs seemed to reflect the excitement that the boomers all felt in this unique adventure.[6]

It was fourteen miles from the Kansas border to the Salt Fork of the Arkansas. The river was in flood stage from recent rains, rendering it a formidable barrier. To many of the ardent Bible readers among the invasion, the Salt Fork symbolized their "River Jordan" on the march to the "Promised Land." Two men had been permitted to come ahead to build a temporary bridge across the river; also Hayes had made plans for an army pontoon bridge.

When the first wagons arrived, however, they found the temporary bridge in precarious condition. The danger presented by the rampaging water was fully recognized when a part of a boomer wagon was seen to pass under the bridge, causing speculation that a family had been lost upstream. An old ferry boat which had once been in use there was placed into service by a Winfield outfit on Thursday evening. A rope was put across the river, and by the light of torches and lanterns wagons were taken apart and ferried over. The horses and mules were made to swim. After numerous hairbreadth escapes in the frothing waters, the Winfield group made it across by two o'clock in the morning. Then, laughing derisively at those behind, the men cut the rope and rushed on ahead toward Oklahoma. When Hayes learned of this, he sent a squad of cavalry after them. The soldiers galloped through the night to Ponca station, boarded railway cars with their horses and arrived at Red Rock station ahead of the Winfield men, who were ordered to hold up and wait for the others.[7]

Other settlers now set about to build a raft; but Hayes declared both it and the temporary bridge unsafe and issued orders that neither could be used. Instead he put his troops to work building a larger, safer raft and installing a pontoon bridge. By placing mooring stakes across the river, the troops prevented the bridge from washing away. Despite these efforts, one impatient boomer left his wife and children behind and swam the river with his horses. Another man attempted to cross with his family with him. He made it, but his family and team were swept away. One newspaper reported that two families were lost trying to make the ford.[8]

The four-span Howe trestle railroad bridge which crossed the flooded Salt Fork was the best answer and the strongest temptation to the settlers. One boomer ventured to force his team across, only to have an invaluable animal fall between the ties and break a leg. The railroad officials on hand refused to allow use of the bridge, offering instead to transport the settlers' household goods and other property across at $4.80 per carload. Even if the boomers were willing to pay the price, this would mean a delay of up to forty-eight hours. A large crowd gathered at the bridge and began making suggestions and demands for use of the bridge. One plan offered was that the tracks be torn up on either side of the bridge to halt the trains, then tear down a building on the Ponca Agency a mile away to get lumber with which to cover the bridge.

Hayes telegraphed the general superintendent of the

Santa Fe, saying that he could not be responsible for the railroad's property unless the boomers were allowed to cross on the company's bridge. He was immediately advised to act at his own discretion and prevent harm being done to the railroad property. Accordingly, Hayes ordered planking taken from the platform of the Ponca depot six miles away and laid down between and beside the tracks crossing the bridge. The boomers and soldiers worked all the night of April 18 accomplishing this task.[9]

Soldiers with red flags were posted a half mile above and below the bridge to signal trains and prevent them from crossing until the bridge was cleared. Then, at a toll fee of twenty-five cents per team, the boomers began crossing the bridge . . . "At 8 o'clock in the morning the first wagon crossed, dragged by willing hands, the horses being led behind . . . At the other side a rough road was thrown up to the steep embankment of the track, and the wagons were let down, tongues manned by volunteers, half a dozen keeping hold of the wheels, others hanging on behind."[10]

A long line of teams formed on both sides of the tracks. Men were organized into three squads of ten each—one at the north end, one at the center, and a third at the south end of the bridge. A driver would unhitch at the north approach, lead his team across, and be ready to hitch up again as soon as his wagon appeared at the south end. Signal men on both the north and south would notify the men at the bridge when a train was coming. The men would remove the lumber to let the train pass, then replace it and resume their work of moving the animals and wagons across the bridge.[11]

For mile after mile, the boomers waited in line for their turn to cross. Some 7,000 men, women, and children and over 2,000 teams, horses, mules, and cattle crossed the bridge during a twenty-four hour period. The toll fee was divided among the men who had worked hard all night to prepare the bridge for crossing.[12]

A reporter described the scene: "Little girls leading blind horses, aged men, paralyzed, seated in the homes on wheels; horses scared and frightened by open approaches;

men ordered to stand in line to make a living wall to prevent the frightened beasts from going over and carrying their owners with them; officers, correspondents of journals and boomers carrying children and babes, and leading fearing, helpless women."[13] Also present was Arkansas City photographer W. S. Prettyman, who caught the drama of the crossing on his glass plates.[14]

Some of the animals in the boomer caravan refused to cross over the bridge and were forced to swim. A spirit of willing cooperation was prevalent among the settlers, though at one point some men pushed their way to the front and crossed out of turn. Hayes made them come back and go to the back of the line. By five o'clock the majority of the settlers were across the Salt Fork; all of them by nightfall. Many went into camp there, but some hurried on southward. It was felt that their impatience would be in vain, for a bridge would likely be needed for crossing the Black Bear as well.

During the first day of the exodus, a warm sun had helped the boomer cause by drying out the roads. Also, the flood waters of the streams of the Outlet had begun to recede, and some of those who had pushed on ahead found it possible to cross the not-wide but steep-banked Black Bear. Still it was necessary for the troops and settlers to make a corduroy bridge of trees, limbs, and brush with dirt piled on top and to cut down the banks of the river so that the army of homesteaders could cross.[15]

It was at the Black Bear that an incident took place which challenged the abilities of command of Lieutenant Fred W. Foster. The young officer and ten of his men had accompanied the lead wagons from the Salt Fork. Upon reaching the Black Bear, a number of the settlers wanted to continue on ahead rather than go into camp as Foster had ordered. A group of about sixty men banded together against Foster, displaying their weapons and insisting that he had no right to stop them.

Foster ordered his men into a line with carbines at rest, fully loaded. One of the settlers, assuming a spokesman role, stepped forward to argue with the officer. Foster remained adamant in the face of the other's demands.

"The next thing we know," the man said insolently, "you'll be objecting to my taking my shirt off without permission."

"No objection to your taking it off," Foster answered calmly in good humor, "if you wear a clean undershirt."

His words broke the belligerent mood of the crowd, who enjoyed a good laugh on the spokesman. Someone shouted, "He's right; only doing his duty." Others agreed that Foster was right, and the crowd dispersed in an agreeable manner.[16]

After crossing the Black Bear, the boomer caravan divided into three main segments, the main body continuing on down the Ponca Trail along the railroad, one group veering off to the east to the headwaters of Stillwater Creek on what some knew as the "Wild Horse Trail," and a group under Foster turning southwestward on a route known as the "Black Bear Trail."[17]

The vanguard of the boomer invasion along the Ponca Trail reached the Oklahoma border at sundown on April 20, Saturday; "The first glimpse of a harbor light was never more welcome to a storm-tossed sailor than was the rolling green plain of Oklahoma to the hardy crews of the white-topped prairie schooners."[18] Near the railroad the line was marked by a barbed wire fence, but otherwise only by occasional piles of stones. Though most of the boomers halted there, it was estimated that some 500 men rushed on into the forbidden territory, each with his own particular plan for grabbing a choice claim.

One settler bragged how he planned to dig a hole and hide in it until the hour of twelve noon arrived on the twenty-second, then jump out and take his claim while his wife was coming with their wagon. Another openly admitted that he and six others had already been into the Oklahoma country and had staked their claims, rationalizing that "to all intents and purposes" they had not entered until the proper time.[19] Each would witness the other's claim. A Kansas

City cattleman who had just come up from Galveston by train said at Red Rock station that he had counted over 100 boomers in the bushes along the tracks.

Lieutenant Foster and his men had escorted the settlers to the west along the Black Bear Trail and approached the Oklahoma border some ten miles or so west of the railroad north of Skeleton Creek (then known as Ephriam Creek). This was essentially the same point of entry used by David Payne on his early intrusions into Oklahoma.

Leaving a detachment of troops at the Black Bear to assist late-arriving settlers with their crossing, Captain Hayes rode forward to investigate the situation with the main body of settlers at the Ponca Trail crossing of the line where Lieutenant Henry Waite was in charge. Concerned that turmoil and bloodshed might well result when the heavily-armed settlers rushed for land, Hayes on Sunday rode west along the line to where Captain A. L. Woodson was camped at Buffalo Springs. The two officers discussed the matter and considered driving a wagon along the line and disarming the homesteaders. But, realizing the act would not only be a sizeable undertaking but also very unpopular, the officers decided against it.[20]

All day Sunday wagon after wagon pulled up to the line and began fanning out to the east and west. The boomers would cheer and fire volley after volley into the air as they arrived. Some of the more enthusiastic, particularly the cowboys from the Cherokee Outlet ranches who were making the run, spurred their horses across the line, only to be ordered back by the troops. That night a group of old soldiers formed a parade line and began marching up and down the rows of wagons, firing their pistols and singing Civil War songs. A crowd of nearly 2,000 men, women, and children followed after them in revelry.[21]

The unceasing stream of wagons was still stretched all along the forty miles from the Kansas border, the road being lined with wagons and people all rushing pell-mell toward Oklahoma. Some of the wagons were the old style wooden axle relics of past generations, while some were new, well-built Studebakers.[22] The wagons carried a strange assortment of items in addition to household wares: desks, chairs, books, farming implements, grocery stocks, even a well-drilling machine in one instance and a law library in another—some of the things needed to establish a new community in the wilds of the frontier.[23]

Easter Sunday, April 21, was a quiet, happy day along the northern border of Oklahoma. Under clear skies the mood of the settlers ranged from quiet contentment to high glee. Still the reticence against close companionship or confidence in outsiders, which had been so noticeable at the Walnut, had now returned. Every man was concerned that he might lose out in the race and seemed afraid to say anything about his intentions lest someone beat him to his choice of locations. There was concern, too, that the cowboys, hated enemies of the old-time boomer, would be able to outrun the settlers with their faster cowponies. Those boomers who had been able to afford it had purchased race horses ranging in price up to $500.

During Easter morning an old-timer from Ohio held religious services. He had acted as a self-appointed chaplain for the Walnut Creek settlement, calling his flock together each Sunday morning by ringing an old cowbell. Now, once again and for the last time, he stood on his soap box and rang his cowbell to summon his congregation. With his old gray head bowed, he delivered an opening prayer there on the border of what he and his followers hoped would be a new Canaan for them. Across the green wilderness of that quiet spring morning the sound of settlers' voices rang clear as they sang "Nearer My God to Thee." They sang from their hearts, and it was a soul-touching sound that made all who could hear it pause to listen.

Then the old man spoke to the settlers, reminding them of the blessings they were about to receive on the morrow and asking them to refrain from acts of violence.

"I know," he told them, "that things that will arouse your angry passions will happen. I know there will be disputes about land. I know that bitter feelings will be engendered and possibly blood spilled. I ask you all, in the name of Him whose blessings have been showered on us so plentifully, to restrain your passions and bury your arms. Look to Him. Pray to Him, and you shall have protection. Might cannot prevail. You may gain a temporary victory with a six-shooter or a Winchester, but in the end you'll be damned."

Now warmed to his task, the old man changed from the language of the pulpit to that of the frontier.

"You've all been on the border a long time, boys; you've all seen men use guns, but you've never seen a man who was made happy or rich by that. A feller can pink down another with a forty-five and think it's the easiest way to settle a dispute, but I'll give ye a pointer that his conscience will bother him afterward. Settle your fights in the land office. That's the place to appeal to, and you'll all git justice thar."[24]

After a parting prayer hymn the boomers returned to their wagons. By noon the sun had heated the land to summertime temperatures, sending most of the people to shady spots where they could rest up for the coming ordeal. That night the camp fires burned low and not many people moved about. On the morrow it would happen.

CHAPTER VI
South from Caldwell

> *At night the sounds of violins, banjos and accordians could be heard from the boomer wagons and tents at Caldwell. In the town, hotels and boarding houses were full, and merchants were doing a record business in outfitting the new arrivals. The drug stores, particularly, did a large business in whiskey.*
> St. Louis Republic, *April 18, 1889.*

HOLDING a key position along the Kansas border, also, was the small former cowtown of Caldwell, which had the advantage of being at the top of the road and stage route leading across the Cherokee Outlet to the Darlington Indian Agency and Fort Reno. Additionally, it was serviced by three railroads—the Santa Fe, the Frisco, and the Rock Island, the latter of which had already extended its line into the Outlet to Pond Creek, with active plans for continuation on across the Territory. With Kingfisher stage station, which lay directly south from Caldwell, being named as a land office site, it was certain that many people would choose this route by which to reach the Oklahoma country.

When President Harrison issued his proclamation opening Oklahoma, the stage line was obliged to cease its operation between Caldwell and Fort Reno. The Rock Island quickly initiated a final survey of its line southward, following the same general line as the stage route. In order to compensate for its inability to entrain customers at least to the Oklahoma border, the railroad moved to establish emergency stagecoach services from Pond Creek to Kingfisher station for those making the run.

Oklahoma Harry Hill was contracted to provide the stage services. Hill called in fourteen of his retired stagecoaches from different parts of western Kansas, painted them "gaudy, gorgeous" colors and added them to the trail-scarred coaches of the Caldwell-Reno stage line.[1] Another well-known stagecoach personality, Colonel D. R. "Cannonball" Green, whose nickname came from the old Cannon Ball Stage Line out of Kingman, Kansas, immediately began buying up all the horses and mules to be found for the line. On April 18, Topeka sources reported that eight carloads of Missouri mules had passed through that town on a fast Rock Island freight headed for Caldwell.[2]

In addition, the Rock Island sent forward two large boats and 1,000 feet of heavy rope to be used in crossing the Salt Fork and the Cimarron, which were reported to be in flood stage.[3] Plans were made for a large tent hotel to be located at Kingfisher, but it would first go into temporary pre-run operation at Buffalo Springs under the name of the "Rock Island Hotel." Free transportation was offered to teams and wagons of those who purchased tickets from Wichita to Pond Creek, the owners to furnish their own transportation to Kingfisher from there.[4] A group of farmers set up a convoy of spring wagons and guaranteed to take people to Oklahoma as fast as the Rock Island could.[5]

As early as late February 1889, a boomer outfit had passed through Caldwell with several new vehicles, one of them equipped with a sheet iron house with windows built on it and accompanied by a bevy of horses, cattle, chickens, and a goat.[6] Following the issuance of Harrison's proclamation, boomers began accumulating at the Caldwell camping grounds. One group of about 100 wagons located on Fall Creek in early April, and they were joined shortly by a group of old border boomers from Wichita. As each day passed, the camp grew rapidly with rushees arriving by wagon, horseback, and railroad. By April 17, the Caldwell camp population was estimated at 5,000—"The streets are full of people and the white covered wagons dot the hills and valleys."[7]

While some of those camped around Caldwell appeared to be well-to-do, many of them were obviously very poor. During the day the campers could be seen sitting around their wagons reading newspapers or anything else they could find dealing with Oklahoma. As at Arkansas City, while there was no hostility most of the campers remained suspiciously aloof from one another.

Troop K of the Fifth Cavalry, commanded by Captain Woodson, arrived from Fort Reno and took up positions guarding all the roads, bridges, fords, and other avenues of exit to the south of Caldwell. Patrols were constant, and settlers were held a mile and a half back from the border. However, there were many unguarded places along the border where people could slip across and strike for Oklahoma.[8]

Most of the settlers, realizing the great advantage which those on the Oklahoma line would have over those at the Kansas border, felt more than justified in going on into the territory. One train of wagons eluded the Troop K patrols, but its tracks were discovered and soldiers were sent in hot pursuit. The boomers were found snugly encamped on Turkey Creek near Kingfisher station, some already with dugouts built and fences up.[9] The group was brought back to Caldwell where their names were recorded and photographs made for future reference.

As early as April 12 about 100 boomers had held a meeting in the dry creek bed near Caldwell and declared their intentions of leaving their families, stock, and wagons and heading for Oklahoma at least by the eighteenth.[10] The Caldwell city council gave them support by writing to General Wesley Merritt at Fort Leavenworth requesting that the people on the border be permitted to move across the Cherokee Outlet in order to have a fair chance. The matter, however, had already been decided in Washington, the announcement being made on the thirteenth that the settlers on the Kansas border would be allowed to cross the line on April 19. When this good news was received at Caldwell, settlers began preparing their wagons and stock for the three-day journey across the Outlet. Captain Woodson announced that his troops would escort the settlers and then hold them on the Oklahoma line until noon on the twenty-second.[11]

The Caldwell contingent of the march on Oklahoma was considered to be more agricultural than the crowd at Arkansas City, where many more of the town speculators had accumulated. There were also a large number of cowboys from the Cherokee Outlet at Caldwell, men who had quit their jobs to make the run. Most of them hoped to grab some land, sell it for whatever they could get for it, and then be back on the cattle ranges in time for summer roundup. Cherokee Strip cattlemen, whose fences were reportedly being torn down by the invading settlers, had mostly resigned themselves to the opening of the Outlet soon after the run into Oklahoma. They planned to gather up their existing herds, sell them off, and not restock for the winter.[12]

On the morning of the eighteenth, Caldwell buzzed with excitement. "It seemed as though everybody was in search of something they needed for the trip to complete their outfit," wrote the *Caldwell Journal* editor, R. B. Swarthout. "The stores were crowded to overflowing and the buzz and noise of those who were in haste to have their wants supplied reminded us of a visit we once paid to the Stock Exchange on Wall Street, N. Y., when a panic in stocks was at fever heat."[13]

On that same morning, Woodson dispatched a bugler to ride from camp to camp to announce that the settlers would be permitted to cross the border at 10 a.m. At nine o'clock the troops themselves broke camp and passed through Caldwell, "booted, spurred and equipped to march," to where just beyond Bluff Creek the boomers were assembled. "The sight as the troops halted and were drawn up into line, with the ocean of prairie schooners in front of them, was a most magnificent one," wrote Swarthout.[14]

Woodson made a short speech, telling the settlers he expected them to keep in line and expressing his determination to treat all alike. Then sharply at ten o'clock, he gave the order "Forward—March." His bugler sounded the call, and the long procession of cavalry, wagons, and horsemen crossed the border into the Indian Territory. The caravan strung out across the prairie as wagon after wagon crossed the Bluff Creek bridge. A man who lived near the spot claimed that he counted 1,153 teams up to four o'clock the following afternoon.[15]

Some of the settlers rode in sturdy wagons pulled by good, strong stock; others had old rickety wagons drawn by broken-down horses or slow, plodding oxen. There were people in buggies and men on horseback with their camping outfits tied behind their saddles. The day being warm and the pace slow, many people walked at their animal's head rather than ride. The trail was in excellent condition despite the recent rains, and the mood of the procession was as happy and cheerful as the day itself.

Many of the Caldwell rushees were Kansas and Nebraska farmers, and there were also a large number of old soldiers—"... it seems as if half the men on the trail wear G.A.R. badges."[16] A reporter speculated that a long, four-horse train of wagons bearing a sign which read "The Great War Show" would do a good business among the group. One man drove a herd of milk cows for the purpose of starting a dairy near Kingfisher. Other wagons carried groceries, drugs, harness, and a variety of goods with which to start other businesses in the new country. One wagon hauled a large boat that was to be used as a ferry on the Cimarron. Though it was apparent that no one was in the mood for trouble, nearly every horseman rode with a rifle across his saddle bow. Occasionally someone would take a shot at a meadowlark, a jacksnipe, or a prairie dog.

Of special notice was a large, high, old-fashioned buggy which was drawn by two shaggy yellow horses. A gangling colt trotted alongside its mother, nuzzling when it could, and a disgruntled black cow was tied to trail behind. The driver was a woman, a Kansas widow, who drove with one hand and tended a small child with the other. A tow-headed boy of ten followed along at the back, pelting the unhappy

The flooded Salt Fork of the Arkansas was a major obstacle for the army of land seekers crossing the Cherokee Outlet to the Oklahoma country (Harper's Weekly).

---

cow with clods every so often and occasionally stopping to wade in the puddles of old buffalo wallows.[17]

By nightfall the lead wagons had reached Pond Creek; and, as a reporter for the *Kansas City Star* aptly described the scene that evening of April 19, 1,000 camp fires glimmered along the trail from Caldwell to Pond Creek, giving the appearance of a vast army in night camp.[18]

The first serious river crossing came early the next morning when the Salt Fork was reached. Just as it was downstream for the Arkansas City crowd, the river was in flood stage. Woodson's men rode out into the stream and set stakes in the current, military style, for the settlers to follow in crossing. A solid mass of wagons and teams began to pile up on the river's north bank as some wagons became stuck in quicksand and others hesitated to enter the water. But everyone pitched in to help one another, unloading wagons to float some items across on boats, men wading or riding out to help those in trouble, the river full of struggling horses and men—everyone dedicated to the cause of getting wagons, women, and children across the swollen stream.

"That," one witness wrote later, "was the happiest bunch of people I have ever seen in my life."[19]

From the Salt Fork it was on to Skeleton Creek where camp was made the second night, then to Buffalo Springs the third night. Here Woodson ordered the settlers to go into camp until Monday morning. Swarthout wrote of his arrival at the camp site: "What a sight met our eye as we reached the top of the divide. Stretched from the east to the west almost as far as the eye could reach was a solid mass of white covered wagons and tents."[20]

People were taking water from the springs there just as fast as it would come out. The gathering, estimated as high as 10,000 on Sunday before the run, was comprised of a wide assortment of frontier types—farmers, laborers, cowboys in broad-brimmed Mexican hats and wearing spurs and six-guns, women, children, old war veterans, teamsters, the black cavalrymen, and others.[21] Many of the campers slept in their wagons or tents, some in the Rock Island Hotel tent, and some roughed it under the stars. One of those present at that huge assembly at Buffalo Springs later described the scene and events of that Easter Sunday:

> Religious services were held, it is true, and were participated in by an immense crowd; but baseball also furnished attraction for hundreds and horse-racing, foot-racing, wrestling and shooting each had its crowd of followers and contributed to the day's programme. And with these different events all going on at the same time in close proximity to each other the effect was at times ludicrous. Standing between the "church-goers" and the baseball "rooters," one would hear the worshippers, but often broken into by the frantic slide! slide! slide! of the baseball "fans." Those conflicting and discordant sounds could be heard throughout the greater part of the day and a seeming rivalry existed as to which element would ultimately survive. But when the improvised choir struck up singing "I've reached the land of corn

and wine," the church element had everything their own way. The stragglers, horse-racers, foot-racers, base-ball crowd, players and all, joined the congregation in a mighty chorus. The words of that song touched a chord that vibrated alike in the hearts of all.[22]

But while most were playing or singing, some of the settler caravan were tending to more serious business. During the day a group of them met to discuss the establishment of a town site at Kingfisher. George E. Hubbard, chairman of the meeting, was elected mayor of the proposed town. It was further agreed among them that the north half of the section where the land office was located would be the townsite location.[23]

That night at Buffalo Springs was noted by its noise and confusion. Wagons and stages arrived all during the night, their heavy rumbling heard loudly by would-be sleepers whose ears were next to the ground. And then, as occurred in many a frontier camp of the day, someone started up the old army cry of "Oh, Joe! Here's your mule!" Someone nearby would sound the call, and then someone else. All through the night this self-entertaining chant would sound through the dark, giving a sense of companionship among the group of strangers who were camped together in the wilderness of the Indian Territory.[24]

Still another sizeable group of Oklahoma colonists had crossed the Kansas border on the eighteenth. This was Pawnee Bill and his colony which had been encamped at the Caldwell Fairgrounds. Having earlier expressed his intention of starting from the George Miller Ranch in the Outlet, Lillie led his group more directly south than the Fort Reno trail, his 300 or so wagons eventually striking the old Arkansas City-Fort Reno cutoff and following that route to the Salt Fork of the Arkansas some twenty miles south of Hunnewell.

They, too, found the river running high, and the crossing here suffered a tragic occurrence. A man named Freither, daring to take the lead in fording the river, plunged his horses and wagon in ahead. The surging waters caught the wagon broadside, sweeping it, the horses, and Freither downstream. The settler and his animals were drowned in full view of the other colonists.[25] It is possible that this was the same wagon which the Arkansas City caravan saw pass under the railroad bridge downstream.

The incident left the group badly shaken and frustrated as to how to cross the river. Finally it was decided to construct a large raft on which they could float their teams and wagons across without having to wait on the waters to recede. But by morning the river had subsided a good deal and become fordable.

The Pawnee Bill colony joined the Caldwell emigration at the juncture of the two trails just above Buffalo Springs at noon on the twentieth. Upon learning that the troops were holding the Caldwell settlers under restraint at Buffalo Springs and not wanting his colony swallowed up by the larger group, Lillie led them on a course west of the trail to the Big Turkey Creek where they went into camp on the twenty-first.[26]

Another important group in this phase of the Oklahoma land rush was the Wichita colony under E. C. Cole. Cole stated publicly that he and his lieutenants would claim two sections of land and turn them over to the colony for a townsite. He was secretive, however, about the exact location he had in mind, saying that he was in good with the Rock Island and could get in early, and even if he didn't the railroad would come to wherever he had located.[27] The Cole Colony (numbering around 200 rather than the 1,000 Cole claimed) left Wichita for Pond Creek over the Rock Island on the morning of April 20, the railroad giving them and their equipment free transportation.

Buffalo Springs was two miles from the Oklahoma line, and Woodson gave notice that the march to the line would begin at ten o'clock on the morning of the twenty-second. Early that morning the settlers began moving about to have their breakfast and get their outfits in shape so as to find a place at the front. By ten o'clock they were massed and waiting for the bugle to sound.

At exactly ten the bugle blast was sounded and the slow and steady march of at least 8,000 people with wagons and teams commenced. The soldiers patrolled the line in front and kept it even. The sight was grand. No one can describe it in a manner that the reader can comprehend the magnificence of the spectacle. In twenty minutes the line was halted on the line of Oklahoma. Eager eyes looked across the flat of land that stretched forth smooth and level as if provided especially by nature for a race of this kind, in hope of discovering a choice spot where they could head their fleet-footed animal to and secure a homestead.[28]

For a distance of nearly two miles along the line stretched the invasion force of settlers—horsemen, wagons, carts, one or two bicycles, men on foot, some on horses, some on nags or mules. The greater part of them massed near the center of the trail, which was a very poor, badly-rutted road. Heavily-loaded freighting wagons had in wet weather left deep cuts that were hazardous for lighter vehicles as well as for horses.

Now to wait until high noon.

CHAPTER VII
Purcell Passage

> In the Purcell livery stables over two hundred horses were being rubbed down, saddled and bridled for the "biggest horse race ever run in the United States." New York Times, April 23, 1889.

PURCELL was the entry point by which most of the run from the south was made. Most of the settlers who came there were Southerners, and they were just as destitute, if not more so, than the boomers on the Kansas border. Some of those who came to Purcell prematurely were eventually driven to sell their horses, wagons, and camping outfits to buy food. They kept only their guns, feeling that their survival and chances of locating a claim were dependent upon their capacity to defend themselves. "They believe that a six-shooter will improve more Oklahoma soil than a plough for a month or two to come."[1]

During the week prior to the opening, an incident was reported which indicated the readiness of men to use guns to secure land. Numerous accounts of wagons and men crossing the river had reached Purcell authorities. A hunting party returned from Oklahoma to say that large bodies of men moving into the wooded interior had been sighted. One hunter claimed that he had actually come across a man who had already located in a secluded valley and was even plowing his field.

Purcell, Indian Territory, a major terminus for land seekers starting from the South Canadian River side of the Unassigned Lands (Harper's Weekly).

At sunrise on the morning of April 13, a Friday, before the people of Purcell were yet astir, several prairie schooners reportedly hurried across the Santa Fe tracks below the depot and forded the river, the drivers whipping their animals to their utmost speed. But as it happened, one citizen who was up early saw the wagons before they disappeared from sight into the timber on the opposite shore.

Feelings against the early entrants ran high in town as the news spread, and before noon that same day an "indignation meeting" was held, during which a number of fiery speeches were made. That afternoon Deputy U.S. Marshal Joe McNalley crossed the river with a posse of thirteen men and easily picked up the trail left by the wagons. The pursuers followed the trail at a gallop. When about four miles from the river, they suddenly came onto four parked wagons with five men sitting around a camp fire having their lunch.

The invaders were ordered to hitch up, and they were escorted back to the river under guard of a deputy. The remainder of the posse advanced onward on foot as skirmishers. A volley of shots rang out, knocking one of the deputies to the ground. The marshal and his men pressed forward, pouring a heavy fire from their Winchesters into the underbrush. As they advanced down a ravine, the lawmen came onto a barricade. Heavy fire from the position

forced the posse to retreat. McNalley divided his forces, sending one group around to flank the barricade. In doing so, the flanking party found itself in a position to pour a heavy fire down upon the barricaded men, who were virtually unprotected from that angle. After several moments of firing by the lawmen, one of the invaders shouted, "We surrender!" The man stood up with blood pouring down his face. Twenty-five additional prisoners were taken, several of them seriously wounded—or so claimed the wire service story that appeared in newspapers all around the country.[2]

The captives were all Southerners, mostly Texans. The leader claimed that they were only the advance guard of a much larger group from Texas, and he threatened revenge if harm were done them. Since the officer who had been wounded had only been creased slightly, it was decided that the only charge against the group would be resisting arrest. Though their wagons and personal property were confiscated and the men held for a short time in a makeshift prison five miles southwest of Purcell, they were eventually released and allowed to make the land run.[3]

The guarding of the border at Purcell fell entirely upon the deputy marshal and his men—a force entirely too small to patrol the long stretches of border along the South Canadian River and the western line of the Pottawatomie reservation. The impossibility of the task increased as the day of the opening approached and the number of settlers escalated. It was estimated by some that as many as 10,000 people passed through Purcell during the pre-run period, a good many crossing the unguarded river well ahead of time.

For a number of years there had been a black settlement on the east bank of the Canadian just across from Purcell. Forced to evacuate the Oklahoma country prior to the run, the blacks formed a colony inside the Chickasaw Nation with the intention of establishing a town site somewhere in the southern part of Oklahoma near the Canadian. A number of black men came from other parts of the country to join the colony in its camp near Purcell.[4]

Many of the new arrivals at Purcell were so destitute that some turned to begging on the streets. A large number lived in dugouts cut into the sand banks of the South Canadian, subsisting on whatever they could find to eat. One family was discovered living on Walnut Creek (Purcell had its Walnut Creek just as did Arkansas City). Their home was a squalid tent of canvas and oil cloth. Inside were a man and three children, all hollow-eyed from hunger and lying on an old quilt on the floor while the mother hovered over a skillet of wild mustard greens—the only edible food in sight. They were provided some help by the people of Purcell.[5]

The old Payne-Couch boomers were generally much better off, having part-time employment with the railroad or being otherwise established. These men knew far more than others about the country of the Oklahoma district. They had long since selected their choices for claims and staked them off. Though prevented from settling on the claims and forced to make the run with the others, the old boomers determinedly proclaimed their rights to the land they had preselected. They also declared their willingness to fight for it.[6]

For some time it had been rumored around Purcell that the old boomers led by Couch had formed themselves into a secret organization to protect their claims. Some parties, particularly the townsite speculators who were busy selling lots at Oklahoma station and other locations, attempted to discredit the existence of such a group. But on Easter Sunday morning, cards appeared around Purcell. They read:

FAIR WARNING
Late Order Made at Regular Meeting of Oklahoma Legion:
Resolved
that We Protect OUR BROTHER MEMBERS in their Long
Respected Rights on Selected Claims, and that
ALL TOWNSITE SHARKS AND CLAIM JUMPERS
Shall be Dealt with
in a Summary Manner[7]

It was a direct threat, and the new settlers resented and feared what they considered to be an attempt to intimidate them and their chances at securing land on equal footing with the old-timers. Many who had the money to do so turned to the townsite companies, paying from two dollars to ten dollars for over 300 lots in the proposed Oklahoma City townsite company. Such companies, of which there were as many as seventeen doing business at Purcell, were extra-legal, but the rushees had little idea as to what was legal and what was not.

In an effort to answer many of their questions, a meeting was held in Purcell's public square at eight o'clock Sunday morning. As the soft peal of the bells of the St. Augustine Catholic Mission sounded, a large throng of settlers crowded the square to hear several prominent men speak. One of them was a Judge Green of Kentucky, the only man in town who wore "store clothes" and a silk hat. He spoke for half an hour on the subjects of town sites, school lands, and other matters. His answers seemed to satisfy the crowd, though it was suggested by some that his talk gave proof to the suspicion that he was involved with the townsite schemers.[8]

Sunday evening was a wild one in Purcell. Cowboys and boomers alike rode the streets, firing their revolvers and passing the word that no one had better try to stop them when they crossed the river. Nearly everyone was in the streets, leaving even the gambling houses empty.[9] Just before dark four deputy marshals rode into town with two horse thieves in tow. They had captured the pair after an eight-mile chase. When the marshals passed through the crowded streets, they were immediately surrounded. A cowboy hollered out to "Hang the horse thieves!" The crowd moved forward, but in the tradition of the old West, the marshals drew their guns and announced that the first man who tried to harm the prisoners would be filled full of holes. The crowd immediately subsided, and the captives were placed in jail under heavy guard.[10]

On the same evening, Lieutenant Samuel W. Adair and a troop of Fifth Cavalry arrived at Purcell with orders to guard the main ford a mile north of town and the river bridge five miles north of Purcell until noon on the twenty-second.[11] Posting a guard at the Santa Fe bridge, Adair took twenty troopers and patrolled the river bank, beating the brush for settlers. Several men were captured, but five outfits that were thought to have crossed during the past three days were not to be found.[12]

Below the railroad bridge the river made a wide bend, and it was known that the quicksand was very dangerous there. The waters of the South Canadian, which had been in or near flood stage, had now subsided. As the troops passed the location, they came onto the body of a young boy lying on the sand. He was dead; and his eyes, ears, and nostrils were filled with silt. Investigation revealed wagon tracks leading from the river bank to a point about forty feet from the boy's body. They did not emerge on the other side. Only the body of the poorly dressed, freckle-faced boy was to be found, leading to the speculation that a boomer family had tried to cross the river and had gone down, wagon and all, in the quicksand.[13]

Even before dawn had come on the morning of the twenty-second, wagons and horsemen were moving toward the river, most to the main ford. From the west and north they came by the hundreds, and the road to the river soom became blocked. When a group of about fifty wagons moved to the point along the river which was known to be impassible, Lieutenant Adair ordered them to move elsewhere. But all along the west bank of the Canadian the wagons and horsemen began arranging themselves for the great rush

A boomer's dugout along the banks of the South Canadian River, a crude shelter which protected one destitute but hopeful family while they waited for the run (Harper's Weekly).

into Oklahoma. Many boomers planned to pull their wagons across the railroad bridge by hand and let their horses swim the river.[14]

Purcell itself was a scene of great activity and excitement. The eating houses were jammed to the brim, with long lines of people waiting for a final solid meal before dashing off into the wilderness. Men with camping gear on their backs poured down the sides of the bluff toward the railroad station. On the streets the gamblers kept their games going until midmorning before packing up to head for Oklahoma or Guthrie station with the rush of their customers.

At the livery stables every man groomed his animal and tended to the girth, strap, bridle, and bit with loving care.[15] Most of the horsemen would take up their position a half a mile south of town where there was a wide stretch of sand but only a short span of water. They formed a line there and began their wait for the moment of departure.[16]

The Santa Fe station, where the railroad crews were working busily to make up trains and load some fifty freight cars with household goods and merchandise for stores, including fence poles and barbed wire, was the scene of great activity. There was one car from Fort Worth loaded with spades. A carload of beer was sidetracked in compliance with the order against selling ardent spirits within the Indian Territory. People crowded the ticket office, which had been busy for several days, and there was more baggage piled on the railway platform "than would be seen in any union station in the country."[17]

Everyone crowded forward to board the earliest train. But when the first train of eight coaches pulled into the station from the south, it slowed but did not stop. The crowd howled with dismay and anger as it moved on, its every entrance posted with guards to prevent anyone from boarding. The howl would have been even louder had the people known that this regularly-scheduled north-bound passenger carried surveyors for the Seminole Townsite and Improvement Company. The surveyors would lay out townsite plats at both Oklahoma and Edmond stations and give the Seminole group an inside to the choice property at those locations.

The first special train appeared at the station soon after. It was a long one of twelve coaches. Within minutes a thousand or more settlers had crowded into the coaches, filling them beyond capacity, and the train began moving down the switch. As had been the case at Arkansas City, the first car behind the engine was reserved for newspaper correspondents, among them being Nanitta A. H. Daisey, representing the *Dallas Morning News*.

Another train of equal size was brought up, and it, too, was immediately filled. As the trains awaited their appointment with history, a fight between gamblers broke out in one of them. A deputy marshal on board drew his gun, it was reported, and nicked the ear lobe of one man, the other man disappearing during this action. The two trains were eventually joined together as one behind two engines to produce what came to be known as the "boomer train."[18]

Virtually everyone in Purcell not making the run had

located himself either on top of a house or found a perch on Red Hill north of town. Red Hill offered a perfect vantage point from which to witness the historic event unfold. One person to take advantage of it was a correspondent for the *New York Times*, who with field glasses at hand could view the panorama of Oklahoma for miles. It is doubtful that anyone had a better view of the Run of 1889 than did he.

Twenty minutes before high noon the engines of the long special train sounded their whistles and began moving slowly down the tracks along the river toward the bridge. A great chorus of shouts and the popping of pistol shots rang out as the train headed around a bend. Now every eye along the river turned toward the bridge where Lieutenant Adair sat his horse calmly, watch in hand. Except for the train, all movement and life seemed to hover in suspense as the great wall of humanity along the river waited impatiently for Adair's signal.

CHAPTER VIII
A Land Surrounded

"The country ain't fit for nothing only Horned Frogs and Prairie Dogs and in 3 or 4 years the people who try to stay will starve out and the country will fall back to its proper owners—Frogs, Dogs and Cow-Boys." Letter, Indian Citizen *(Atoka), June 18, 1889.*

THE Arkansas City and Caldwell migrations from the north, which comprised the largest group of people to make the Run of 1889, massed principally on the approaches to Guthrie and Kingfisher. There were those more independent-minded rushees who pulled off from the main crowd to the areas between the two points or off to the outer flanges of the seventy-eight-mile north line where there would be no troops to monitor entry into Oklahoma. Still the troops spread themselves across as much as possible of the line between the Santa Fe rail line and the Caldwell-Fort Reno trail, and the crowd control was better here than at most other places along the more than 300 miles of border surrounding the Oklahoma country.

Actually, the north line was the farthest from the most desired locations—Guthrie, Kingfisher, Oklahoma station, and the North Canadian valley east of Fort Reno—most people preferring to locate near a potential population center. Owning a distinct advantage over the northliners were those who came to the line west of Kingfisher station. At this point the border was less than two miles from the designated land office site, while the north line was some twenty miles distance. From the east line to Guthrie was nine miles; from the north nearly twenty.

At the point where the west boundary was crossed by Kingfisher Creek, a good-size crowd accumulated during the week preceding the run. Some of them were refugees from the drought-stricken areas of the country to the west, and there were some of the Caldwell crowd who had seen the advantage of the west line and drifted on down away from the others who were being escorted by Woodson. In addition, there were a number of cowboys from the Cherokee Strip ranches who were there simply for the sport of it. They were joined in this by others of the frontier who loved nothing better than a good horse race. A *Chicago Tribune* correspondent told of an innovation which was introduced on the line west of Kingfisher station:

> All along the line to the west as far as the eye can reach the boomers with their fast horses are ready. In the hands of most are long sticks that look like fishing rods or lances. They are peeled willow rods, pointed at one end, with the owner's name, and the words on most are "Soldier's claim." The intention is to rush their horses at their highest possible speed and as they reach the border of their land to stake their claim pole in the ground while going at full jump by a quick motion of the hand. The desirable claims will be dotted with sticks.[1]

The reporter also noted that on the evening of the run, people on the west line were getting nervous and were slipping across the border under the cover of darkness. Troops under Captain W. C. Hall of the Fifth Cavalry guarded the line due west of Kingfisher, but settlers had scattered on down the nearly-twenty miles of the west line from Kingfisher Creek to Darlington and Fort Reno. None of this portion of the line was guarded.

It was along here that the old soldiers colony under Dr. Minick camped prior to the run. Having traveled down from

Caldwell to Buffalo Springs with Woodson, they managed to slip away from the others and swing on across the northwest flank of the Oklahoma country and move southward, going into camp below Kingfisher Creek at noon on April 21. The plans for this maneuver had been carefully laid.[2]

The colony of veterans had gathered on a Wichita street on the morning of April 18, lining up their wagons in single file. Eighteen wagons had arrived at ten o'clock when Minick stood up in his buggy and gave them parting instructions: "I want you to camp sixteen miles from Fort Reno on the night of the twenty-first," he told them, "and on the morning of the twenty-second I want you to go with an Indian guide I have engaged to the land and ten minutes after twelve o'clock on the twenty-second I want every man on his claim and prepared to hold it.

"I know your histories during the years of 1861 to '64, and I believe that if any crowd attempts to cross the Canadian River and to jump the land that you are to take that you will show the timber there is in you and show that you are really old soldiers."[3]

The troops still in garrison at Fort Reno had enough to do just to patrol the North Canadian valley in the Darlington-Fort Reno area, which had become an important staging area for the run, drawing a large number of the impoverished farmers of the Texas Panhandle, No-Man's Land (today's Oklahoma Panhandle), western Kansas, and southeastern Colorado. That future dust bowl of the 1930s had been hard hit by drought, grasshopper swarms, and crop failures for three seasons preceeding 1889, and the people there looked with prayerful hope at the promise of the Oklahoma lands.

Fort Reno had been the center of military operations for this section of the Indian Territory since it was permanently established in 1875. A neatly arranged post built around a central compound where soldiers drilled daily, Fort Reno dominated the North Canadian valley from a point just west of the border of Oklahoma. To here hourly came the hard-riding couriers carrying dispatches from various field commands. Possessing a military telegraph, Reno was important as a communications center, and some of the news correspondents had hired cowboys as their own personal couriers to dash accounts of the land run activity to the fort telegrapher.

Across the river to the north was the Darlington Indian Agency, its small cluster of buildings surrounded by teepees and dominated by the large three-story brick building used as a commissary for the agency. Nearby was the Indian trading store of Major Barker where older Indians lounged about wrapped in their blankets and shawls. A government school operated for the benefit of Indian youths, while the Mennonites conducted a school for the younger children. During play hours, troops of little Indian boys and girls waded in the clear waters of the North Canadian or played in the sand along the river's bank.[4]

Toward the second week of April, the first of the would-be Oklahoma settlers began arriving at Fort Reno, going into camp on the land between the fort and the agency and the Oklahoma line. At first, agency officials tried to have them moved, but the matter was mediated and the settlers were permitted to stay.[5] As the day of the run approached, more and more wagons rattled through the dirt streets of Darlington and on to the boomer camp, their canvas covers tattered and torn, some of them pulled by plodding ox teams, all loaded to the brim with household goods, plows, and other paraphernalia and trailed by emaciated livestock and starved-looking dogs.

On April 18, it was reported that some 500 wagons were headed for Fort Reno down the old Cantonment Trail along the North Canadian. They were described as carrying extremely destitute families who were coming in hopes of getting loans against the land they would claim. This belief was held despite repeated warnings that it would take nearly six years to prove up on their claims so as to borrow money against them, veterans excepted.[6] Some of the settlers were very dismayed and angry when Indian scouts intercepted them and diverted them from the Fort Reno road toward Kingfisher.[7]

Another news account told of a colony of 150 men who had arrived at Fort Reno. They were from Denver, and all were well armed. They had surveyors among them who were ready to mark off the claims that they had already selected.[8]

During the days preceding the run, the covered wagon settlement on both sides of the North Canadian at Fort Reno grew to a sizeable proportion, the camp crowded with people, horses, oxen, cows, sheep, chicken coops, barking dogs, and scrambling children. The settlers spent their time fixing saddles and bridles, mending harness, repairing their wagons, hobbling stock to graze, and watering them at the river. In between the men gathered in groups to talk about the forthcoming event. During the evenings, the same cry of "Oh, Joe! Here's your mule!" circulated the settler camp.[9]

Most of those making the run seemed interested in joining a town company. But getting into one was much like joining a secret society. It was necessary to be vouched for by someone already in the company. An applicant stood well if he were already a member of the Odd Fellows, Masons, or some other such organization. If he were to become a member, he would have to take an ironclad oath not to divulge the plans of the company in any way, supposedly under penalty of death. Settlers besieged the telegraph operator at the post with questions concerning the correct astronomical time, everyone feeling that their fortune and future might well hinge on the matter of a single minute.[10]

Everyone was up very early on the morning of April 22, getting breakfast, saddling their horses, harnessing teams, and making all the last minute adjustments. The morning was barely under way before the crowd began moving toward the starting line. At Fort Reno, orders were issued for every soldier who could be mounted to report to the Oklahoma line to help monitor the movements of the settlers. Some of the married soldiers indicated that they, too, had plans to make the run and take up claims.[11]

At the line everyone stirred about in confusion and excitement, jockeying horses into position and backing wagons about in an attempt to get their "toe on the line." As far as the eye could see to the north and to the south there was a continuous line of horses, wagons and buggies. Facing the teeming line of settlers was a thinly spread picket of blue-uniformed soldiers, stationed in places to be visible to all across the North Canadian valley. At Fort Reno the artillery primed its howitzers to be fired at the moment of high noon to signal the start of the run. Long before the appointed time, settlers pressed against the starting line, the soldiers having difficulty holding them back. Finally at ten minutes of twelve, the soldiers began yelling, "Everyone on the line."[12] Those making the run braced themselves for the start, while those who were simply spectators fell back to watch as their husbands, sons, fathers, and friends made their dash to win a new home in Oklahoma.

From Fort Reno the western border extended on south another fifteen miles to the South Canadian River, whose meandering course formed the southern boundary of the Oklahoma country. The South Canadian was a wide-bedded stream lined with cottonwood, willow, and dogwood. Normally its clear, mild channel wandered back and forth among the sun-bleached sands of the river bed. But when in flood stage, the river was Mississippian, a broad expanse of surging, frothing red water which swept soil and uprooted trees eastward downstream. On the evening of April 22, the river was just receding from a flooding, its current still very brisk and the channel deeper than usual. It could be crossed by horse and wagon, but at some risk for caution was required to prevent being caught by the force of the current. Ropes were needed for a safe crossing by wagons.

South of the Canadian lay the sparsely-settled lands of the Chickasaw Nation. Across from the southeastern corner of the Oklahoma country was the cowtown of Silver City,

One of the many wagon crossings along the unguarded South Canadian River (Harper's Weekly).

originally a trading post of the Abilene Cattle Trail established by Montford Johnson in 1879.[13] Johnson's ranch butted up to the South Canadian at this point, as did W. T. Peery's Long-O Ranch just to the east and others along the river. The scattering of people who lived south of the river had in time found the best places to ford the South Canadian in going north, and these crossings now drew small crowds of rushees to them.[14]

The Silver City crossing lay just north of the town, while four miles to the east was Pikey's crossing. Opposite the mouth of Cow Creek and a mile and a half north of the Long-O ranch house was the Long-O or Peery crossing. On downstream in order were Gallimore's or Jenkins's crossing, the Boomer crossing, Barrow's crossing, Downing's ford, and the Foster or "Old Santa Fe" crossing. There were others, but it was mainly to these that the settlers came in wagons, buggies, and on horseback, most of them moving upriver from Purcell.

Some of the rushees stopped at camping places such as Downing's Grove or at Barrow's farmhouse to wait for the appointed time. However, there were a great many who took advantage of the completely untended border to slip across and locate a claim and return or to hide out in the brush within Oklahoma until the time of the run. Even so, on the morning of April 22, each of the crossings drew its own group of 50 to 150 settlers.

On the evening of April 21, a group of Bohemian settlers arrived at the Long-O crossing, some twenty-five or more of them in several wagons. Here the river channel divided into two streams, forming a long sandbar which was nearly 200 yards long and 100 yards wide in places. The Bohemians drove their wagons across to the sandbar and went into camp. On the morning of April 22, a large crowd of settlers gathered on the south bank of the river, becoming increasingly agitated by the forward position taken by the Bohemians.

One of the men on the south bank stepped forward and called to the group on the sandbar to come over. A small party of the Bohemians led by Captain Anton Caha mounted horses and rode across to the south bank. They were asked by what authority they had crossed the line into Oklahoma. Caha's response was that numerous authorities— he cited Senator Weaver and the governor of Nebraska among them—had said publicly that a man could enter Oklahoma just so long as he did not occupy a particular tract he wished to claim ahead of time.[15]

The Bohemians returned to their camp, and later in the morning they were seen to hitch up their wagons and continue on to the north bank of the river. The settlers on the south bank now began to move their wagons across to the sandbar, some of them plunging on into Oklahoma well before noon and others arguing and debating whether or not to go ahead or to wait until high noon and have the law definitely on their side.[16]

At Gallimore's crossing another large crowd accumulated, becoming increasingly impatient as the morning wore on. Several men avowed their intentions of entering early, and they would have done so had not one man held them back with threats and persuasion. A similar situation developed at Barrow's where a man stood up in his sulky, saying that he had just come from Purcell where he had set his watch by meridian or railroad time. Still the crowd could not be restrained entirely, many of them crossing their wagons to a sandbar and some going on into Oklahoma well ahead of noon.[17] A number of important "sooner" cases would stem from these early South Canadian entries, some involving the Bohemians and some involving men who arrived upon the choicest Oklahoma claims early.

The run from the east line was equally shrouded with clandestine entry and controversy. No reporters are known to have been anywhere on the east line, nor were there any military stationed there to monitor entry. A military detachment was active on the morning of April 22, scouring the area along Soldier and Crutcho creeks east of Oklahoma station; but the unit was hardly effective in restraining people from entering Oklahoma at will.

The eastern border of the Oklahoma country followed the western boundary of the Pottawatomi reservation from the main Canadian to the North Canadian, a distance of some thirty-five miles. William Greiffenstein, former Indian trader and a founder of Wichita, Kansas, who was married to the daughter of Pottawatomi chief Burnett, operated his UF cattle ranch in the southern portion of the reservation east of Purcell.

A mile or so below where the east line crossed the North Canadian River was the ranch house of William H. McClure's 7-C cattle operation. McClure grazed his cattle on both sides of the North Canadian and into the Oklahoma country. The Shawneetown Road ran past his place between Oklahoma station and the settlement of Shawnee Town some fifteen miles down the south bank of the river. Nearby, on the river's north bank, was the Indian village known as Kickapoo station. In the far south of the Pottawatomi reservation on the north bank of the South Canadian was the Catholic Sacred Heart Mission. It was reported that both Shawnee Town and Sacred Heart had jumped from 150 inhabitants to 3,500 in the week preceding the run.[18]

From the North Canadian the east boundary followed the Indian Meridian another ten miles northward along the border to the Deep Fork, where the Indian trading post of Wellston was initiated in 1880 by C. T. Wells. Here the Kickapoo country butted the Oklahoma border, while north of the river was the Iowa reservation. Eddy B. Townsend, an ex-Indian agent with connections in Washington, D.C., and his partner C. C. Pickett operated their IOA cattle ranch on the Iowa land. From the Deep Fork, the Oklahoma boundary continued northward another twenty-two miles to the Cimarron, then followed the winding channel across the northern boundaries of the Iowa and the Sac and Fox reservations until it cut back to the north line.

It was a long, impossible border to guard, and there is no evidence that the government or the military made any effort to do so. Thus the eastern border of the Oklahoma lands, like the southern border, was wide open for early intrusions by settlers who were left to their own judgment and consciences as to when to enter. Evidence indicates that there was a great deal of premature entry made all along the eastern line.

It was at the border near McClure's 7-C ranch house that the largest crowd developed on the east line. On a direct route Oklahoma station was only twelve miles distant, but the land between was cut by streams and gulleys and heavily cluttered with brush and scruboak which made travel difficult and slow. For this reason, the Shawnee Town Road followed inside the northward bend of the North Canadian, an area known as the "7-C Flats," crossing from the south bank to the long stretch of land between the North Canadian and the Deep Fork which had come to be known as the "Nine-Mile Flats."

Crowd estimates at McClure's ranch vary. One witness put it at 1,000, and another said he counted 360 wagons in the vicinity. But one thing that most accounts do agree upon is that a great many people did go across the border early there. To many, the east line was known as the "Pott Line," since it was also in part the border of the Pottawatomi land. One man later told of talking with another who had slipped across the border early. The "moonlighter" (as an early entrant was first called instead of "sooner") insisted that he had, indeed, made his start at noon from the "pot line," that is, a rope hung between trees in his camp having some pots strung on it.[19]

There were, of course, rushees scattered all along the east line from the South Canadian to the Cimarron, mostly in small groups such as the ones which gathered at the Deep Fork east of Edmond station, the Winfield colony which crossed the line well ahead of time east of Guthrie, and the crowd which made its dash at high noon to the city of Lexington. History must record that it was, indeed, a grossly unfair situation for those people who were being restrained on the north and west.

CHAPTER IX
The Insiders

> *"More or less, injustice was inevitable,"* wrote an investigator a short time after the opening, *"but it is a melancholy truth that United States deputy marshals and deputy collectors caused more trouble, more friction, and perpetrated more wrongs calculated to disturb the public peace than all the other citizens of Oklahoma put together."* Harn Collection.

IN commenting on the reaction of citizens in Wichita at the time of President Harrison's proclamation opening Oklahoma, the *Eagle* noted: "Some favored going soon and others sooner."[1] It was a prophetic choice of language, for later when the run was over the word "sooner" would become the common cognomen for those who entered the Oklahoma lands ahead of time in order to grab a choice location.

But those hiding out in the bushes and gullies of the Oklahoma country prior to the opening were not the only early entrants. There were a number of others who managed to get into the area through either legitimate reason or pretext. Most of them were government officials or employees, lawmen, or railroad employees. Many of these men took advantage of their privilege to grab claims ahead of those making the run from the Oklahoma borders. The most controversial of these were the men appointed as special deputy U.S. marshals or deputy tax collectors.

Two U.S. marshals held jurisdiction over the Oklahoma country. Marshal William C. Jones of Kansas had responsibility over a portion of the Indian Territory, including

101

Oklahoma. Jones, a Civil War veteran and onetime warden of the Kansas State Penitentiary, had been a Democratic appointee. With the election of Republican Benjamin Harrison as President, Jones's job came under fire from those who wished to see him replaced by a Republican.

On March 1, 1889, a new federal court had been established at Muskogee, Creek Nation. Thomas B. Needles, former state auditor of Illinois and a Republican, was appointed to the post of U.S. marshal under the court. His area of authority also covered the Oklahoma district, making it overlapping with that of Jones's. There is no doubt that the Republican administration preferred to rely on Needles during the land run.[3]

On April 10, Needles was authorized by Attorney General W. H. H. Miller to appoint as many deputies as he felt he might need for service in Oklahoma. Jones automatically assumed the same privilege. On April 15, Jones entrained for Arkansas City where he proceeded to appoint deputies to serve at the Guthrie and Kingfisher land offices and other locations. He felt that the main conflicts would take place when rival claimants met at the land offices.[4]

The men appointed by Jones were mostly established lawmen who had already been serving as his deputies in Kansas, Texas, and the Indian Territory. Captain O. S. Rarrick, a grizzled old lawman with a superb physique for his age, was placed in charge at Guthrie. Serving with him would be Charles Collins, Ransom Payne, J. O. Stevens, Captain W. J. Weaver, M. J. Keyes, John Patterson, and Asa Jones, brother to the marshal. John Walters, Captain D. F. Wyatt, and newcomer Ed Madden were assigned to Kingfisher. Old frontiersman Jack Stilwell, who had been with Forsyth at the famous Beecher's Island fight in Colorado in 1868, remained at Fort Reno and Darlington.

J. B. Koonce, Asa Jones, and Ewers White were sent to Oklahoma station. R. L. Cox and J. P. Jennings, two experienced deputies from West Texas, were placed at Alfred station, where they had been sent earlier to catch horse thieves plaguing the area. Additionally, Jones responded to a Santa Fe request and appointed as deputies eight conductors of trains passing through Oklahoma as a precaution against lawless acts enroute.[5]

Marshal Jones wired Rarrick his instructions: "Proceed to Guthrie and take charge of matters there. Don't hold or attempt to hold any Oklahoma land. Arrest all disturbers."[6]

Marshal Tom Needles arrived at Arkansas City on April 20, where he met with John I. Dille and Cassius M. "Cash" Barnes, who had just been named as Register of Deeds and Receiver of Moneys, respectively, at the Guthrie Land Office. Both Dille and Barnes requested that Needles appoint and assign men they knew as deputies for their office. They recommended B. J. Turner, J. H. Huckleberry, and O. E. Mohler as men they personally knew and had confidence in. Their requests seemed logical to Needles, who issued commissions for the three and ordered Dille and Barnes to have the trio sworn in before a U.S. commissioner. Needles later insisted that he did not know and had never met these men.[7]

Additional appointments by Needles included W. W. Ansley and Ed Collins, who were assigned to Kingfisher; John Varnum, T. J. Mitts, Temp Elliott, Thomas Taylor, Daniel Hay, Smith Winters, W. H. H. Clayton, and John C. Bell at Guthrie; Jacob Wheeler and George L. McDonaugh at Edmond; W. J. Wilkins at Norman; and Thomas Wright and Jasper Reece at Oklahoma station.[8] The appointment of deputies by Jones was deeply resented by Needles, who told a *New York Times* reporter that "Mr. Jones' appointments are in clear conflict with my authority."[9]

Responsible for even more appointments than either Jones or Needles, however, was Internal Revenue Collector Nelson F. Acres of Kansas. Instructed by the Internal Revenue Service to designate a list of names from which special agent George R. Clark could select deputies, Acres appointed a large number, none of whom had ever reported to Clark before. These were deputies only "to the extent of having authority to enter the territory" before noon on April 22. Investigators after the run, however, were never able to obtain a list of the tax collector deputies, though one was known to exist.[10]

On the evening of April 20, a party of seven men disembarked from the train at Oklahoma station, all carrying deputy marshal papers. This was the Springfield, Illinois, party headed by General Dave Littler, which had obviously made contact with Marshal Jones when passing through Arkansas City. A reporter at the station described them as a strange looking assortment of men—one was a man of around seventy years of age, wearing a fine broadcloth suit and carrying a gold-headed cane. The group indicated that they planned to form a town site there.[11]

"It is thought that there are over thirty 'deputies' now in and about Oklahoma," commented a *St. Louis Republic* correspondent, "who, at noon tomorrow, will turn in their resignations and accept it all by themselves, each individually, and turn private citizens. They will then bounce claims."[12]

The deputies at Oklahoma station were mostly Jones's men. It was rumored that Marshal Jones was in league with Dr. Munford of the *Kansas City Times* in a townsite manipulation, having first considered Guthrie station as their site but having changed to Oklahoma station instead because of less competition there. Lieutenant Adair and Corporal O'Brien, Fifth Cavalry, claimed that altogether there were thirty-two deputy U.S. marshals who arrived at Oklahoma station by rail, twelve of them holding commissions from Needles and the rest from Jones.[13]

After the opening the courts would struggle to determine the truth concerning who had entered the Oklahoma country legally and who had made claims in violation of the law. In doing so they would throw much light on the questionable activities of many of the deputy marshals, tax collectors, and government officials involved in the settlement of Oklahoma. Cornelius MacBride, Interior Department investigator, summed up the situation that developed at Guthrie: "The atmospheric condition of things here on and before the 22nd day of April seemed to impel men, heretofore honest and honorable, to grab, catch and hold everything in sight."[14]

This was not to say, of course, that all of the public officials and others who entered Oklahoma early acted dishonestly. But even some of the carpenters sent in to erect the land office buildings at Guthrie and Kingfisher could not resist the temptation of their advantage. Two of them were said to actually be lawyers who had hired out as carpenters purely for the purpose of working until noon on the twenty-second, then resigning and locating claims for themselves.[15]

John A. Pickler, inspector for the Public Land Office, had been assigned to the task of procuring land office buildings for the two sites by Secretary Noble. Pickler arrived at Arkansas City to discover a fact not so apparent in Washington, D.C.—there were absolutely no materials or workmen at either the Guthrie or Kingfisher locations.

Pickler wired Noble that he could contract for the preconstruction of both buildings in Arkansas City at a cost of $1,075. Noble gave him the go-ahead. At first Pickler planned to construct the buildings in sections and ship them to the sites; but in the end he shipped two carloads of lumber on a special train to Guthrie along with seventeen carpenters who worked with the contracting firm. By April 19 the carpenters had erected and roofed an eighteen by thirty foot building on the hillside east of Guthrie depot. On that date thirteen of the carpenters loaded the extra lumber onto wagons and drove across country thirty-five miles to Kingfisher, where they erected a second building, working by lamplight after dark to complete the outside framing.

On the morning of the twenty-first, five of the carpenters started back to Guthrie to pick up a wagon bed left there, according to their account. But after going some twenty miles, one of their horses became lame. The men then decided to return to the west line, recrossing it some five miles below Kingfisher. They made the run from that point at "about noon," they claimed, using a stick set in the ground on the south side of a compass to estimate the time of day.[16] Others would charge that the men did not go to the west line at all but instead went directly to their claims. One way or the other, the courts would later rule their action to constitute an illegal advantage.

The officials who had been announced on March 29 by President Harrison included Dille, a forty-five-year-old lawyer from Indiana, and Barnes, an insurance agent at Fort Smith, Arkansas, for the Guthrie Land Office. Jacob C. Roberts of David City, Nebraska, was named Register at Kingfisher, while Jacob V. "Cap" Admire, a newspaperman from Osage City, Kansas, was appointed as Receiver. The two Guthrie appointees visited Washington, where a force of clerks in the General Land Office was busy preparing plat books, blanks, and supplies of all kinds for the Oklahoma offices. The men arrived at Arkansas City on April 16 and were besieged by visitors seeking favor. A rumor surfaced that Roberts had been offered a bribe by a townsite syndicate.[17]

Register Dille caught a train for Guthrie, where he found his land office building nearly completed on April 19. He returned to Arkansas City with a touch of the shakes and looking very bad; he had never been west of the Mississippi before and was not used to frontier life. The officers of the two land offices met and consulted on their operations on April 20. The Kingfisher group left Arkansas City on that same day, being forced to travel by way of Oklahoma station and Fort Reno to reach their destination. The Guthrie men went in on Sunday.[18]

George A. Beidler of Middletown, Pennsylvania, a longtime Oklahoma boomer and a personal friend of Postmaster General Wanamaker, was appointed as postmaster at Oklahoma station in replacement of Jim McGranahan. Beidler, his eleven-year-old son Chase, and his brother R. Linn arrived on April 11, their only reception being a challenge by a soldier as they stepped off the train. When Beidler explained that he was the new postmaster, he was directed to the Sommers's house east of the tracks. Sommers gave them shelter for the night and for several days following.

Beidler found McGranahan willing enough to turn over

the postmastership and duties but not at all willing to give up the seven by nine foot room in his "hotel" where the post office had been located. Nowhere were there any other quarters available at the station in which the post office could be housed. Beidler telegraphed the Post Office Department for authorization to locate and build an office on government land, and he was given the go-ahead. From McGranahan he purchased a picket-style chicken house for five dollars and proceeded to construct a stockade-type eight by ten foot dirt-floored shanty. He secured some corrugated iron sheeting to use for a roof, fitting some boards around the sides as best he could, then raised the United States flag which his wife had made for him before he left Pennsylvania.[19]

From Sommers he secured an old set of pigeonholes, and with scraps of boxes he managed to put the office into working condition. The change of climate plus the damp ground of the little building gave Beidler a severe lung infection. Kid Hamill, the photographer, was still at Oklahoma station on April 21 and took a picture of Beidler, Chase, and Beidler's brother beside the first federal bulding in the Oklahoma country.[20]

Dennis T. Flynn, the first appointee as postmaster at Guthrie, had been editor of the *Kiowa Herald* in Kansas. His appointment had come only after a considerable effort by Kansas Congressman Samuel R. Peters, whom Flynn had given strong political support. Flynn, one newspaper claimed, had looked upon the appointment as a sure ticket to getting rich as it would allow him to enter Oklahoma ahead of others and locate 160 acres squarely within the city limits of the town that Guthrie station was bound to become.[21]

However, when Flynn discovered that he might be restrained by law from making an early claim, he tried to resign the commission. Both Peters and Plumb, who had fought hard to get Flynn the position, refused to accept his resignation. While this was being decided, Flynn waited around Arkansas City, finally going into Oklahoma on the first train of the run and setting up a tent post office next to the land office at Guthrie. Flynn would later become a congressional delegate from Oklahoma Territory.[22]

Previous to the President's proclamation opening Oklahoma, the region had been under the military jurisdiction of Fort Reno, commanded by Colonel J. C. Wade, Fifth Cavalry. On April 2 Wade went to Oklahoma station, vowing to take field command himself until every unauthorized person was arrested or driven out of Oklahoma. He planned to disperse troops to Purcell, Oklahoma station, and Guthrie plus any other key points, and he called attention to the notices that had been posted by the Santa Fe at its station houses warning that no person should attempt to remain upon the railroad right-of-way as a pretext that they were legally outside of Oklahoma. Anyone wishing to make the run, the notices stated, should go to a point on the border.[23]

On April 16 orders were issued in Washington, D.C., directing Brigadier General Wesley Merritt, commanding the Division of the Missouri with headquarters at Fort Leavenworth, to go to Oklahoma and issue "such orders to the troops as any emergency may require."[24] Merritt, Sheridan's Chief of Cavalry during the Civil War and later a commandant of West Point for a time, was also directed to have such forces available as would be sufficient to preserve the peace. Accordingly, all but one company garrisoning Fort Leavenworth was placed under arms to be ready to move out at a moment's notice. As Merritt prepared to leave for Oklahoma, he announced that he was going there with "unlimited discretionary powers."[25]

But the question of employing martial forces to police citizens inside the Oklahoma country had become a serious concern to President Harrison and his cabinet. The matter was discussed several times, and on April 18 a meeting was held on the subject at the White House among Harrison, Secretary of the Interior Noble, Secretary of War Redfield Proctor, and Attorney General Miller. After the meeting, Proctor sent instructions to Major General J. W. Schofield at his home, who in turn sent a carefully worded telegram to Merritt on the following morning.

A camp of the 5th U.S. Cavalry at Taylor's Springs near Guthrie, where part of the small peace-keeping force was garrisoned (Harper's Weekly).

Merritt, who had already entrained for Oklahoma station, was ordered to "act in conjunction with the marshals of the United States courts having jurisdiction in the country opened to settlement," and to use his troops to aid the marshals in executing warrants, making arrests, and quelling riots or breaches in the peace.[26]

On April 19 four companies of infantry marched from the post at Fort Leavenworth to the train station, their band playing the soldiers' favorite, "The Girl I Left Behind Me." The "dough boys," as the cavalry had irreverently tagged the infantry, loaded their equipage into four baggage cars and boarded as many coach cars to head for Oklahoma. These four companies, under the command of Captain Arthur MacArthur, father of the later-famous General Douglas MacArthur, were under orders for Guthrie station. They arrived there that same day, going into tent camp near the depot and assuming guard duty at the station against unauthorized entrants.[27]

Already parked on a side track at Guthrie was a Santa Fe director's car containing Judge C. G. Foster of the U.S. District Court at Topeka; Judge John Guthrie, Santa Fe stockholder for whom the station was originally named in 1886; and several other Kansans of note. Also arriving at Guthrie on Saturday prior to the run was U.S. Commissioner John M. Galloway with his son. Galloway, who had asked for and received special permission to come in early and establish his office, would later be dismissed by Judge Foster for using his official position to preempt choice land at Guthrie.[28]

Two troops of the Fifth Cavalry had arrived at Oklahoma station and occupied the high ground east of the railroad station just north of the Sommers home. On April 18 four companies of infantry from Fort Lyon, Colorado, under the command of Lieutenant Colonel Simon Snyder arrived by train and pitched their camp between that of the cavalry and the railway station. General Merritt had arrived, also, setting up his headquarters in a private railroad car on the station sidetracks.

Other troop movements were taking place. All of the infantry in garrison at Fort Supply and Fort Elliott, Texas, left those posts by rail on April 18, the cavalry units marching overland. On the same date, troops H and K, Seventh Cavalry, left Fort Sill headed for Purcell. Altogether there were fourteen companies of infantry and twenty troops of cavalry inside Oklahoma as of April 21. Couriers were established between Oklahoma station, Fort Reno, and Woodward railway station in far northwest Indian Territory.[29]

There was little question that this was enough force to quell any disturbance during and following the opening. But many settlers were already inside Oklahoma, and it was much too late to dispose of them.[30]

Not all of the railroad employees who were inside Oklahoma before the run can be accounted for by any means; neither is it altogether clear exactly who was and who was not a bona fide railroad employee, since some claimed that status simply to justify their entry. But the activities of some of the principal railroad officials are known. A. W. Dunham, who had come to Oklahoma station on February 20, 1888, to become agent there, was still too young to take a claim and did not attempt to do so. Instead he took a position atop a box car and watched the run from there.[31]

Andrew Kingkade, station agent at Norman, did not attempt to take a claim, either. But section foreman J. L.

Hefley, who lived in a railroad section house with his sizeable family, did. Hefley watched as the crowd from the Chickasaw country, some three miles away, came tearing up before he stepped onto the land he wished to claim.[32]

John Steen, who lived with his wife and son in the one-room pump house at Edmond station, serviced the water tanks along the route between Arkansas City and Purcell. A few days before the run, Steen had stocked up on hams, coffee, bread, and other foodstuff so that his wife could feed the hungry horde that was bound to descend upon the place.[33] Steen would not try to claim any land, but a section hand at Edmond made an effort that was to become a landmark case.

Alexander Smith, a long-time employee of the Santa Fe, had arrived at the station a few weeks earlier, bringing his family with him and living in a tent on the railroad right-of-way. He had seen the notice posted on the depot shack telling employees to go outside Oklahoma if they wished to claim land, but Smith had no intention of letting it deter him from grabbing a choice claim at Edmond. He would merely move his tent off the right-of-way.[34]

Another interesting situation took place at Guthrie station. For a time there had been only a telegraph operator there, a man named Thompson. When the opening of Oklahoma appeared imminent, Thompson invited his girl friend to come down from Kansas so that they could both make claims before being married. She did so, but in his romantic land-seeking excitement, Thompson slighted his duties at the station. The result was a train wreck between Guthrie and Edmond. Thompson lost not only his job but his girl as well.[35]

At Alfred station, Albert Seeley operated a rooming and boarding house for employees of the Santa Fe Railroad. Upon the advice of an army officer, Seeley went to the north line to make the run, leaving his family behind at Alfred and taking the chance that he would be able to reach the land he desired before anyone else.[36] Zack Mulhall of St. Louis had come to Alfred station as an assistant live stock

111

agent for the Santa Fe. He used his advantage inside the territory to build up a sizeable cattle herd and ranching operation. Though he had been at Alfred to check on his cattle shortly before the run, Mulhall also went to the north border and made the run on horseback from there.[37]

Many of the old boomers were either connected with the railroad in some capacity or pretended to be. They had worked hard, invested time and money, and endured much to boom the opening of the Oklahoma lands, and they felt they had a special claim to the homesteads they had chosen. Their cause seemed so just and their feelings were so strong on the issue that it led them to believe that somehow they would be considered an exception to the law concerning early entry. The result was that most of the old boomers remained inside Oklahoma in order to protect their claims, particularly at Oklahoma station.

Most of the Couch family—William L., Meshack H. (father of the clan), Joseph, and Thomas H.—remained at the station and "ran" from the railroad right-of-way. M. Q. "Quint" Couch managed for a time to convince the courts that on the morning of the run he had left his work at repairing a railroad switch and gone to the Pottawatomi line. His claim would be challenged. Rachel Anna Haines, once the common-law wife of David L. Payne, came to the station a few days before the run, supposedly as a cook for the Couch grading crew. Samuel Crocker arrived, claiming to be timekeeper and bookkeeper for them.[38]

Unquestionably the most important of all the townsite companies, the one destined to play a key role in the opening and in later developments at Oklahoma City and Edmond, was the Seminole Town and Improvement Company.[39] Though the Seminole Company has never been tied directly to the Santa Fe Railroad Company, there is much evidence to establish it as an operation of that Santa Fe department which undertook development along its many lines. Several Santa Fe officials played key roles in the Seminole's activities inside Oklahoma prior to the run, and the company had the obvious help of railroad personnel in its early entry. Furthermore, street names on the original plats of Oklahoma City and Edmond include several Santa Fe officials—*i.e.*, Hurd, Campbell, Ayres, Peck, Noel, and Frost, in addition to Clarke (Sidney) and Sommers. Interestingly, there is a "Littler" Street in Edmond, evidently reflecting a connection between the Seminole Company and Dave Littler of Illinois.[40]

The charter of the Seminole Company was filed with the State of Kansas on April 19, 1889, listing its capital stock at $1,750. Its directors were J. W. Wilson and L. H. Crandall of Topeka; J. A. Hudson of Lincoln, Illinois; Sidney Clarke of Lawrence, Kansas; and W. L. Couch of Douglass, Kansas.[41] In this list can be seen a significant connection between the Santa Fe and the boomer leadership.

Soon after the issuance of Harrison's proclamation, and before the charter was filed, the Seminole Company sent surveying crews down along the line through the Oklahoma country and surveyed a number of potential townsites at the various Santa Fe stations, including Norman, Moore, Oklahoma, Edmond, and Guthrie. Plats of these townsites were prepared well ahead of the run, quite likely in the drafting offices of the Santa Fe headquarters in Topeka. Before the opening the decision had been made to concentrate upon Guthrie, Edmond, and Oklahoma station.[42]

Charles Chamberlain, who specialized in townsite development for the Santa Fe, was in charge of the townsite surveys. J. E. Frost, who worked in the Santa Fe land department at Topeka, was general manager of the Seminole Company in Oklahoma, and the Santa Fe's L. H. Crandall was secretary. Another significant connection of the Seminole group was reflected when Frost, Sidney Clarke, and Marshal Jones departed Arkansas City together by train on April 21 for Oklahoma station, where Littler and other Jones-appointed deputies had already arrived. Frost later said that the company expected to derive its revenue from certificates sold at ten dollars each on some 3,000 lots in the Oklahoma station townsite.[43]

113

Chamberlain also arrived there prior to April 22, and his surveyors were given special entry privilege above that of the public.[44]

On the morning of April 22, the only lumber building at Kingfisher was the land office, then still under construction. The land office officials had arrived the night before and now worked feverishly to install fixtures and get the place in working order. The tent of a reporter for the *Chicago Tribune* was just across the way, and other tents dotted the area around the office.[45]

Infantry soldiers under Lieutenant Coe stood drawn up in line at the land office door, the bright sun glistening off the gold buttons of their tunics. On the twenty-first there had been some 500 people at Kingfisher, but by Monday morning many of these had disappeared, going either across the line or into hiding. Only a mile northeast of the land office, John W. Wood, a government freighter in Oklahoma for five years, was loading wood for the army.[46]

Early in the morning Captain Woodson rode in from Buffalo Springs. In the interest of the settlers under his charge, he requested that the names and descriptions of all persons at Kingfisher station be taken.[47]

There were many others, who for valid reason or subterfuge, were already inside the boundaries of the Oklahoma lands when high noon of April 22, 1889, arrived: cowboys, freighters, train passengers, townsite speculators, families of those living in the area, workmen of all sorts, and many with no special calling. It would be a momentous task to unravel the legitimate from the illegitimate, the legal from the illegal in the years ahead.

CHAPTER X
To Jordan by Coach

> "Oh, Nellie, hurry up the pan cakes;
> Wife, do not be so slow,
> And we will go to Oklahoma
> Where the milk and honey flow."
> Arkansas City Republican-Traveler, *April 25, 1889.*

ARKANSAS City had just seen one grand exodus to the south, that of wagons and horsemen; now it was about to see another by way of the modern railway car. The dent made by the departing settlers on the eighteenth had been quickly made up by thousands of rushees who came in upon their heels. All during Saturday and the little-observed Easter Sunday, trains of the Santa Fe had poured passengers into the small border town.[1]

Made up originally in Kansas City, each train had found hundreds of other people waiting at every depot along its route—homeseekers, speculators, gamblers, thieves, sightseers, journalists, more farmer-settlers, and a "sprinkling of the demi-monde."[2] The stores of Arkansas City had remained open despite the religious holiday, and they did a large business with settlers needing food, clothing, and supplies. Every place was jammed with people. In the lobby of the Gladstone Hotel, where one could barely move about, the conversations centered on "committees," "caucuses," and "officers," indicating that here were men who were looking to the political aspects of the new country.[3]

The horde of mankind was described as a "Wild West show headed toward a new field of enterprise and development, and one who had never seen such a thing in action cannot have the remotest conception of it."[4] Though some 7,000 tickets had been sold to Guthrie and Oklahoma stations on the Santa Fe, not one person could be found who did not expect to go on the very first train.[5]

Long before the first streaks of dawn began lighting the eastern sky on April 22, Arkansas City was awake and teeming with movement. Hundreds upon hundreds of men, and some women, emptied out of the hotels, cot houses, stores, barber shops, and homes of hospitality which had accepted temporary guests overnight. Carrying their grips, knapsacks, bundles, blankets, spades, axes or hatchets, and the inevitable rifle or shotgun, they headed *en masse* through the early morning darkness toward the railroad station where a virtual armada of railroad coaches, box cars, and engines waited in appointment for their historic task of the day. Many more rushees were already there, having slept on the depot docks, in freight cars, or simply having wrapped themselves in their blankets on the ground.

Seventy-five was the number of coaches given by some reporters at the scene, though the *Arkansas City Weekly Republican* scribe claimed there were ninety-three. Estimates of the crowd varied from 8,000 to 25,000. The *Republican* reporter, who counted 143 passengers on one coach alone, estimated an average of 115 people per coach and came up with a count of almost 10,000 people who left the town on trains that day.[6]

Mob-like the crowd descended upon the rail yards where a detail of strong-armed railroaders stood ready to protect the company property. But as men crowded and shoved to gain entrance to the cars, their fear of being left behind grew, swelling into near panic. Windows were broken in some of the cars to permit entrance by those determined to secure a seat. Some of the crowd grabbed onto the iron railings of the railroad cars and had to be pried loose.

"It was in vain for the officials to say the train would run in sections fifteen minutes apart," one observer commented. "Every man there wanted to be fifteen minutes ahead of everybody and not fifteen minutes behind anybody."[7]

During the night, word had leaked out that a special car would be provided for the newsmen and that it would be with the first train to move out. Supposedly only members of the press were to know the location of this special, but by boarding time everyone in the city seemed to know of it. Thus when the car was backed up to a point below the depot, the crowd, many of whom had been following the reporters, charged it and attempted to climb aboard. The railroad guards held them back, and the newsmen were formed into a solid phalanx to push their way bodily through to the rear of the car.[8]

Actually the car was a box car without seats, and, as a scribe put it with some sarcasm, "the standing room was excellent" for the fifty-four journalists who were piled into it. Indeed, some of the cattle cars had been equipped with improvised seats to help make up the numerous special trains which were scheduled to depart Arkansas City that day.[9]

There were a large number of pretenders who sought entry to the press car with phony credentials. Practically every major newspaper in the United States, and many lesser ones, appeared to have someone there to represent them. The proven newsmen were called upon to verify or discredit those in question, and those without proper identification or who could not find someone to vouch for them were forced to withdraw from the car. One of those removed was immediately relieved of his wallet by a pickpocket, who quickly vanished into the crowd some $300 richer.[10]

Despite the competition for admission to the trains, there was little unpleasantness and no fighting as might have been expected. The immense crowd seemed to be in a holiday mood, reflecting the beautiful, sunshiny day. Those who failed to get aboard, though disappointed, took the matter good-naturedly and joined the others in waving goodbye; and finally the first engine, with the newspaper car, nine coaches, and a caboose behind, began pulling out of the station at 8:47 a.m. Passengers waved flags from the windows as the crowd cheered and yelled "Hurrah for Oklahoma!" A few men still ran after the train in the desperate hope of getting aboard, while all along the railroad grade people watched and waved and cheered the first Oklahoma-run train. At the bridge across the Arkansas River, just south of the city, two men climbed onto the cow catcher but were pulled off. One man did manage to crawl up onto the brake rods beneath the press car.[11]

Harry Livingston was at the throttle of Engine 266, though Captain George H. Cooper, who wanted to be able to say that he had led the Oklahoma rush, was given the token honor of pulling the throttle to start the train moving. In the caboose of the first train were a number of Kansas dignitaries. Hamilton Wicks, who had just arrived at Arkansas City from New York and had bribed the brakeman to let him aboard the caboose, found himself in the company of Judge John Guthrie; Colonel D. B. Dyer, former Cheyenne-Arapaho Indian agent who would become Guthrie's first mayor; C. R. McLane, a well known Kansas banker; and a number of other important men.[12]

Once on the way, those on board began to feel a new anxiety. The passengers began to fear that the train, being so heavily loaded, would not make it to the Oklahoma border in time for the run. It was 9:40 a.m. when the train passed the sign marking the border between Kansas and the Cherokee Outlet. It inspired a chorus of wild cheers, starting with the press car and continuing down the settler-packed coaches. Though some of those aboard now settled back and showed little interest, others craned at the windows and doors to spy out the secrets of this mysterious, wondrous land of the Indian. The recent rains had greened the countryside beautifully for spring, and one newsman penned a glowing account of the view:

> Here is a grand and magnificent panorama of nature's own loveliness spread out before the enraptured vision—a grand carpet of verdure—in

broad expanse of blossom and bloom, revealing a picture that can be surpassed in no country or clime.[13]

It had been reported that there would be a large crowd of Indians at Willow Springs station and an even larger group at Ponca station to witness the passing of the boomer train. But the train had passed Willow Springs before the first Indians were seen. Then it was a wagon load of Poncas, through whose reservation the train was passing, who responded to the greetings from the train with angry scowls and gestures of defiance. It had not occurred to the rushees that the Indians of the territory had good reason to mistrust and fear this invasion by white settlers.

Before Ponca station was reached, the man riding beneath the press car was discovered by the newspapermen. When the train stopped at Ponca, the man was fished up into the press car and provided with a stiff drink from one of the many flasks aboard. The man said his name was Saddler and that he was a native of England who had been in America for nine years, most recently at Seattle, Washington Territory. He was on his way to Oklahoma to grab some land the same as all. The press corps immediately elected him as the representative of the *London Times* and as a mascot of the new city-to-be of Guthrie.[14]

Among the reporters on the train was Milton Reynolds, representing the *Topeka Journal*. "Kicking Bird" took a good deal of pleasure in displaying an early membership certificate in the "Payne Oklahoma Colony."[15] Dennis Flynn, Guthrie's newly-appointed first postmaster and a former Kansas newspaperman himself, was brought to the press car where he rode the remainder of the way.

Other journalists there represented a wide variety of newspapers around the country. They included the *New York Herald, St. Louis Republic, Pittsburgh Commercial Gazette, Indianapolis Sentinel, Larned Chronoscope, Kansas City Times, Kansas City Star, Cleveland Leader, San Francisco Call and Bulletin, Kansas City Graphic, Iowa*

State Register, Wichita Eagle, Wichita Journal, New York Press, New York Globe-Democrat, Milwaukee Sentinel, Omaha Bee, Chicago Herald, Iowa State Leader, Las Vegas Optic, Greencastle (Indiana) *Star Press, Harper's Illustrated Weekly,* Chicago *Daily Inter-Ocean, Cincinnati Commercial Gazette, Arkansas City Republican-Traveler, Arkansas City Dispatch,* and the *McPherson* (Kansas) *Freeman.*[16]

H. L. Preston of the *Kansas City Star*, realizing ahead the problem of communication he would face in the Territory where there would be but one telegraph line to serve a multitude of reporters, had concocted a novel method of filing his stories. He hired cowboy couriers, stationing them along the railroad where it passed through the Cherokee Outlet, whereby he could toss his copy out of the car window to them as the train passed by. In turn they would ride hard and fast to the nearest telegraph, which was Arkansas City, and have the stories filed with his paper well ahead of the other reporters. Thus it was that his account of the train ride into the Territory appeared in the *Star*'s April 22, 1889, edition—the same day on which it took place.[17]

The train continued on from Ponca, reaching the Salt Fork of the Arkansas River, where a few days earlier the boomer wagon train had crossed with so much difficulty. A temporary halt was made while the engineer talked briefly with the armed railroaders who were stationed there to guard the bridge against the rumored destruction by the old boomers. From there it was on to Red Rock station, arriving at 11:05 a.m., then across the Black Bear to the final station north of the Oklahoma border at Wharton at 11:50.[18]

Nanitta R. H. "Kentucky" Daisey, covering the Oklahoma story for both the *Dallas Morning News* and the *Fort Worth Gazette*, had passed by Wharton station on the Saturday afternoon previous in traveling from Wichita, where an uncle lived, in an attempt to enter Oklahoma ahead of the run. She had witnessed a unique scene at that time:

> Every train that stops is surrounded by cowboys arrayed in their usual costume and ornaments. All

Red Rock Station, located on the Santa Fe track, was passed at 11:05 by the first rushee-packed train crossing the Cherokee Outlet on the morning of April 22, 1889 (Harper's Weekly).

---

seem anxious to show off their professional skills in racing, betting and swapping horses or recklessly shooting revolvers in dangerous proximity to the car windows. Passengers on the 4 p.m. train Saturday were treated to a scene. One cowboy dressed neater than the rest fired a revolver into the air. At this signal the others sent up a yell, drew revolvers, fired them simultaneously, then surrounded the dude, threw him into the air and caught him in time to save him from breaking his bones. The train passed out of sight before the finale.[19]

The boomer train arrived at Wharton to find two freight cars sidetracked there and the place still swarming with cowboys and would-be settlers. The cowboys were mostly from the Cherokee Outlet ranches, but the others were men who had come in on previous trains and disembarked with the intention of making the run on foot. The opportunity of hitching a ride on the boomer train was too golden to pass up. Men crowded about the coaches trying to get aboard.

When they were prevented from doing so, they climbed up the sides of the coaches to the top. Many jumped aboard the coach tops from the adjacent freight cars. One reported estimated the number of hitch-hikers to be around 200, too many for the conductor to expel or collect fares.[20]

The lead train reached the Oklahoma border a few minutes after 12 o'clock noontime, the reporters varying in their recording of the exact moment. Few of them wished to admit that they had just missed the historic moment of the start. But they did arrive in time to see the great cloud of dust ahead and, with field glasses could view the countryside whose entire face appeared to be covered with riders and wagons. Groups of white-topped wagons stood parked at the line, their teams taken out of the harness to make the run.[21]

As the train advanced it began catching up with the rush. At one point it ran alongside two racers whose ponies were neck-and-neck. Off to one side a riderless horse continued his race alone. From the dust to the east a wagon train emerged onto a ridge, pushing forward as fast as its animals could move. At one point the railroad train passed a homesteader who was seen to have dug a hole at the corner of a surveyor's mark and set his stakes. As the train sped by, the man waved his hat wildly over his head, then emptied his Winchester and his revolver into the air, yelling all the while like a "wild Comanche." The train passengers on that side responded in kind, answering with shots and hurrahs.[22]

Just across the line the train pulled to a halt at a cluster of white tents where Troop D of the Fifth Cavalry under Lieutenant Waite maintained a temporary post. A reporter who had been with the overland group from Arkansas City and had been waiting to catch the train at the camp was astounded by its appearance. "It was difficult to determine what manner of moving object approached. The locomotive was covered with men, and the roofs of the coaches held nearly as many as the interior."[23] Despite this, the reporter found his own roof space. Lieutenant Foster, who had just released a section of the line to the west, also boarded the train with his company of troops to go to Guthrie.[24]

In great impatience, the men on the train whooped and hollered for the engineer to continue his run. Ahead of them, the smoke of camp fires already trailed skyward to tell those aboard that they would by no means be the first to reach the land along the Cimarron.[25] Another annoying halt was made at the Cimarron, the engineer again talking briefly with the armed guards there. Some of the men aboard, as others had already, began jumping off the train to make their run for claims. But soon the train was on its way again, and Guthrie station lay dead ahead.[26]

Behind the lead boomer train in Arkansas City, the other trains had been making up, loading, and moving out. The second train pulled out at 9 a.m., and the eighth left at 12:20.[27] Thus all along the Santa Fe line from Arkansas City to the border of the Oklahoma country, trains with cheering boomers at the windows were leaving their smoke trails against the clear, blue sky of the Cherokee Outlet as they sped southward toward the "promised land" of 1889.

CHAPTER XI
Harrison's Hoss Race

The long row toeing this line is bending forward, panting with excitement, and looking with greedy eyes toward the new Canaan, the women with their dresses tucked up to their knees, the men stripped of coats and waistcoats for the race to follow. And then a trumpet call, answered by a thousand hungry yells from all along the line, and hundreds of men and women on foot and on horseback break way across the prairie . . . Harper's Weekly, *April 23, 1892.*

FOR most of the thousands who lined up at the borders of Oklahoma or boarded the trains at Arkansas City and Purcell to make the run, this would be the most eventful and exciting day of their lives. The suspense and anxiety of the contest, the burning expectation of gaining 160 acres of free land, and the participation in an unusual and significant act of history made this day special above all others. From all over the nation and from all walks of life they came to line up *en masse* to take part in the greatest horse race of all time.

There were eight major points where large numbers of people gathered to await the starting signal: on the north line at Stillwater Creek, the Santa Fe railroad, Skeleton Creek, and Buffalo Springs; on the west line near Kingfisher and at Fort Reno-Darlington; on the south at Purcell; and on the east at the 7-C Ranch on the North Canadian. Though there were many other starting places, none of them drew larger crowds or appear to have had an official starter.

Quite likely the largest group to enter at any one point—one writer estimated it to be five times as many as any other—was the overland group from Arkansas City who entered at the crossing of the Oklahoma border at the Santa Fe rail line. A correspondent who made the trip with the wagon caravan and who arrived at the line just a half hour before noon, found the line marked by a cordon of troops which stretched away to the east and west from a red, white, and blue guidon planted near the tracks. A short distance beyond was the bivouac camp of Troop D. Not less than 1,000 teams and 200 horsemen stood poised for the dash into Oklahoma.[1]

It was a sorely disappointing site in comparison to the lush grasslands of the Outlet. The landscape was slashed by gullies with little vegetation save the scatterings of bunch grass and the rusty, bricklike soil showing through everywhere. Still there was no thought of turning back among the thousands of settlers held in check waiting for the signal. Lieutenant Waite took his position in an open space some distance from his men.

The mounted rushees crowded to the front, while drivers of wagon teams worked the reins in their hands for a surer grip. Those with jaded, worn stock moved back, knowing it would be of no use for them to take the front. Tension began to mount among participants all along the line, and men kept an eye on both the officer and their own watches, most of which had been set with that of the lieutenant. There now developed a silence "that but echoed, as it were, the hush upon the boomer lines."[2]

Finally the hands on the watches overlapped, and Waite turned to signal his buglers on either flank. As the buglers sounded "Dinner Call" the line of troops rolled back, closed up and then swung away like a long gate that was hinged on the railroad. A correspondent wrote:

> Shrill cries rose from the boomers, their whip lashes resounded, the horsemen among them shot forward impetuously, the teams tugged at the rattling harness and the whole motley crowd swept forward with gathering motion. In a contest so wholly one of speed the race was to the swift, and

The rush for the "Promised Land," a wild, headlong race for choice quarter sections or town lots, as seen by a British artist (The London Graphic).

---

the broad line began to straggle, the galloping horsemen disappearing over the forest crest ere the teams in the harness had half covered the ascent or the astonished oxen had responded to the goad.[3]

"I thought hell must have broken loose," an old Missourian later said of the start. "Such running and hollerin' I never heard before. It was the biggest field I ever saw in a race. Wagon poles broke, axles snapped, horses ran away, but fortunately nobody was hurt."[4]

One man dashed forward on his horse for a distance then suddenly pulled up and jumped to the ground at the top of the first ridge. He began driving his stakes while the others went tearing on by, yelling their congratulations. There were some men who had no transportation, and they shouldered their bundles and headed down the railroad tracks on foot.[5]

Some ten miles to the west along the line, Lieutenant Foster had posted his men at the front of another group of rushees, those who had taken the Black Bear Trail. The soldiers held a long picket rope marking the starting line. Foster faced the crowd from 100 yards or so inside Oklahoma, his bugler sitting his horse behind. The officer held his reins in one hand, his watch in the other. Finally the time came, and Foster turned to signal the bugler. Even as the soldier touched his horn to his lips, the wall of settlers surged forward, forcing the troops to drop their rope. The clamorous sound of cheering and yelling broke the quiet of midday, and the race was under way.[6]

The men with expensive race horses, some of the animals purchased for as much as $500 just for this occasion, took the lead. There were those who rode one horse and led another to be used in relay fashion. Behind the horsemen came the wagons, drivers urging their animals to the utmost speed.

At first the racers were in one long mass, but they soon began to fan out in all directions. Some kept on a bee line dead south for Guthrie; some veered to the west and some to the east. The racers quickly outdistanced the wagons, which lumbered on behind determinedly. Hardly anyone was content with the land at the border, feeling it was inferior to that further on. But one old man stopped just beyond the line, struck his tent and, lying inside, waved his hat happily at the late comers who passed him by.[7]

Soon the green land that rolled and stretched southward to the Cimarron River valley was spotted with wagons and men and tents. Some without tents went to work immediately building shelters against the now-hot sun and for the coming night. The smoke of camp fires began rising against the sky. In the far distance, the crawling white form of a wagon train could be seen making its way down into the Cimarron valley.

In addition to the rushees, men seemed to sprout from the landscape as soon as the bugle had sounded. Many of those who had ridden hard and fast from the line would stop to make a claim only to be challenged by another who already had his stake on the tract. Sometimes there would be a standoff, but generally the rushee would simply hurry on to find another spot. One man said that he stopped at seven different locations only to have someone appear to issue his prior claim.[8]

East of the railroad, the Wild Horse Trail contingent had accumulated on the border at the head of Stillwater Creek. Captain Jack Hayes had remained at the rear of the Arkansas City exodus, staying at the Salt Fork bridge until all were across and then moving to the Black Bear and helping settlers there. When the last wagon was across on Monday morning, Hayes struck his tents and galloped on south to the Stillwater.[9]

Here he found a large gathering of settlers in camp at the border. He was greeted by a swarm of angry and distraught homesteaders who said that a number of people had stolen a march on the others and gone on in. The hour was then 10:30 a.m., leaving only an hour and a half until time for the run, not enough in which to round up the miscreants. Instead, Hayes insisted that everyone on the line there give him their names on a list and he would forward them to Washington. This was agreeable to all, and Hayes's troopers went among the crowd collecting signatures and lists in the nose bags of the cavalry horses.[10]

This done, a row some two miles long formed, the mass of covered wagons to the center and riders on the outside. Nearly 300 cowboys from the Territory ranches were on the line east of center, each on his favorite cowpony. Hayes, his bugler, and a sergeant rode out in front of the settlers and faced the line. Wagon teamsters held their reins in one hand, whip in the other. The cowboys leaned forward anxiously on their ponies.

Sergeant MacDonald later described the scene that followed:

> The order was given, the bugle blew the blast—charge—forward. And that line broke with a hurrah and rush, and impetuous onward movement—the cowboys firing their pistols and yelling, making a scene never before witnessed in this or any other country, settling up a country by the aid of a bugle call . . . [11]

Off the multitude raced, the cowboys in the lead disappearing over the green-grassed hills, presently reappearing on a distant rise only to disappear again. One old-timer made his race with a plow hitched behind his horse. He merely crossed the line with the plow and began making a furrow around his claim. "Before the call ceased he was plowing as complacently and business-like as though he had occupied his land for years."[12]

When 10 o'clock came at Buffalo Springs, Captain Woodson ordered his bugler to sound an assembly call for the two-mile march to the starting line. He addressed the huge gathering of settlers, cowboys, and others, thanking them in the name of the U.S. government for their good behavior. Then with the troops in the lead, the estimated 8,000 people moved to the border where some 2,000 wagons and several hundred horsemen comprised a line ten miles in length.[13]

Now began a wait of nearly an hour and twenty minutes, during which time the excitement grew more and more intense. Even the animals there seemed to sense the drama of the hour, their heads jerking at the reins and their hooves pawing the ground nervously. A false start was made when Woodson ordered his bugler to sound the call for his soldiers to mount, and some of those at the line started off in a cloud of dust. These were quickly overtaken by the soldiers and brought back to the line.[14]

Now the troops advanced a few paces from the line. Then after a breathless pause, Woodson signalled his bugler, and the great race north of Kingfisher was on:

> What a sight! The horsemen start in a mad race with one another, leaving the wagons behind. For about a mile they keep together and then first one and then another will swing out to the right or to the left to get away from the rush, or to go to some place already chosen for their homestead. The sound from the earth made by the immense caravan sounds like the roaring of thunder.[15]

Another reporter described it thus:

> It was a thrilling sight. The great prairies, boundless and beautiful, were dotted with covered wagons and they looked for all the world like a fleet of ships upon the undulating sea. The horsemen were soon out of sight and half an hour after the start the wagons were lost to view.[16]

At the signal, the entire line had roared with a loud outburst of cheers. Men on horseback dashed recklessly across the prairie, the wagons and carriages following in confused haste. In the chaos of the start some of the wagons and buggies broke down before they had gone any distance, while others soon cracked up in the gullies and sharp turns required to avoid buffalo wallows and holes. The prairie was soon strewn with wrecks.[17]

About a mile from the line the horse of a boomer from Colorado stumbled and crashed to the prairie floor, falling upon the hapless rider and breaking the man's neck. The accident was witnessed by the troops, who quickly rode out and brought him back to their camp where he died in agony an hour later. Still another fatality occurred when a man in a buggy sought to speed up his horses by firing a gun. The shot struck a settler ahead and killed him. The two victims were buried by the soldiers.[18]

Even as the run was being made from the Buffalo Springs point, another group of settlers was on its way down the stagecoach route to Kingfisher. The Rock Island stage line established by Harry Hill and Cannonball Green had been poised at Pond Creek with forty stages and their teams, ready to go. At eight o'clock on the morning of April 22, the stages departed for Kingfisher, all fully loaded even to the top. The unique caravan of frontier stages, every bit as picturesque as the trains from Arkansas City, was soon strung out along what had once been the Chisholm Cattle Trail, raising great clouds of dust much like the Texas trail herds had once done. The stages arrived at Kingfisher shortly after noon.[19]

West of Kingfisher, the signal for the run was given by Captain Hall and Troop C of the Fifth Cavalry. Like the others on the north line, the signal here was a bugle call, but it found support in the far distant booming of the cannon at Fort Reno. A reporter in Kingfisher witnessed the run from the vantage point of the land office, though he heard the pounding of horse hooves and saw a rising cloud of dust before he spied the riders.

"Presently out of the dust-cloud," he wrote, "the forms of racing horses are seen. On comes the mad crowd of rushing horsemen. The cloud of dust sweeps along. Several riders have fallen and horses generally have stampeded. Nearer and nearer thunders the cavalcade, until at last, straight down Chicago Avenue, a mad crowd of excited men, with teeth set and plying whip and spur, rushes into the new-born City of Lisbon [as the post office at Kingfisher station had been so named]."[20]

Some of the stampeding horses carried their owners on past the claims which the rushees had planned for weeks to grab. "Looking in every direction over the hills and plains, the boomers are thicker than the locusts were in Egypt. Thousands still rush along. The race from the line—one mile and a half—had been made in four minutes, and behind, fast closing up the rear, comes the trailing mass."[21]

A gulley half a mile west of Kingfisher proved to be the Waterloo for many riders whose horses could not master the leap. A number of riders were dumped to the ground there, one reported coming up in a scramble to yell out "My claim! My claim!" A man connected with the Rock Island Hotel was riding a gray mare, which sailed over the gulley and carried its owner safely into Kingfisher ahead of the rest.

The settlers on the Fort Reno-Darlington line crowded forward every bit as tensely and expectantly as any of the others. Then from over the hills to their back came the boom of the cannon. The soldiers on the line fired their guns and shouted "Go!" Simultaneously the long line of humanity and horseflesh surged forward with whoops and hollers, whips cracking, horses screaming as spurs jabbed home, wagons rattling, and those left behind at the line cheering loudly. Horseback riders forged ahead, while the heavy covered wagons lumbered far behind. Buckboards and light spring wagons suffered smashed axles and splintered shafts. Here was a wrecked sulky, there a broken wheel of a surrey.[22]

The frenzied racers disappeared into the woods and hills, and the crowd on the line turned back to their wagons and resting places in the shade to wait. Some were young women, still with blush to their cheeks. Some were weary-faced older women with faded skirts trailing in the dust. Flocks of children romped about without the slightest hint of the concern felt by their mothers as to whether or not this day would produce a home for them. To many of the wives, mothers, and sweethearts this seemed to be almost a last chance in life.

While evidence indicates that much of the run along the South Canadian River was made prematurely, there were those who waited until the legal time to enter Oklahoma. One of these was Edd Childer, who was on the line with his wife Elma and their children. Writing from their claim near present Cashion after the run, Mrs. Childer told of how the start was made at their point along the river in a letter to a friend:

> I do wish you could have seen the race of the 22nd. It was a sight indeed. Everyone was so excited that they couldn't stand still. All of the men along the South Canadian River got as far in the river as they possibly could without sinking in the quicksand and there waited for the hour of noon to come. When it was 12 o'clock, they all gave

a loud cheer and then went like a shot, not quite so fast perhaps but still at the highest speed on their horses.[23]

Red Hill, the precipitous bluff at Purcell, made a grand place from which to view the run. It virtually towered over the South Canadian River, along whose west bank the railroad ran and from where the Oklahoma lands lay like a green carpet beyond. Those not making the run from Purcell that day took positions on Red Hill, the river bank, or atop roofs to view the panoramic scene before them—the springclad valleys and timbered hills stretching away to the east and north, serene and virginal under a clear blue sky—a perfect day for the run, everyone agreed enthusiastically.

Like an actor at center stage, Lieutenant Adair sat his horse in the bed of the wide, sandy stream and waited for the fateful moment. But at 11:30 the wait was interrupted when a trooper spied a wagon crossing half a mile below. He succeeded in heading it off and found it was driven by an old Texan. The old man swore roundly when he was ordered to drive his wagon to where Adair was and wait until after the signal was sounded.[24]

On the tracks near the base of Red Hill the long twenty-coach, double-engined train blew steam while the throng of settlers, estimated at 5,000 persons, crowded the river bank on horseback and in wagons. The rich and the poor, young and old, the old boomer and the tenderfoot were all in the line along the river bank. Many had risked their all, every worldly possession, to make this great race for free land.[25]

At 11:40 the conductor of the train gave a signal to the engineer. The shrill whistle of both engines cut through the stillness of midday, and the train began moving slowly toward the bridge which crossed from the land of the Chickasaw into the country known as Oklahoma. Virtually every man on the train began shouting in anticipation as the train gathered speed. A fusillade of shots rang out as it passed the fording point of the river and headed a bend to approach the bridge.

133

Time seemed to move at a deathly pace during the next twenty minutes. All eyes were on the young officer who sat his horse calmly in the river bed, looking very military in his blue and gold uniform.

> Suddenly he is seen to motion to the soldier near him, and the next moment the cheerful strains of the recall are sounded. In an instant the scene changed. There is a mighty shout, and the advance guard of the invading army is racing like mad across the sands toward the narrow expanse of water. The north and south wings stroke the water together. In they go, helter-skelter, every rider intent on reaching the bank first. There goes a horse into a deep hole, and his rider falls headlong out of the saddle. Before he can rise he is apparently crushed by another animal, which has stumbled and fallen in. The crowd on shore gives a cry of horror, which speedily changes to one of relief, and as one of the horses breaks away and joins the flying host his owner surges after him, with the water up to his waist, and the other man remounted.
>
> By this time the swiftest ones are over and speeding up the slope of the nearest ridge. The head of the line of wagons is just emerging from the river bed. At this rate it will not be ten minutes before all are across. The racers take different directions, but most of the wagons go northwest. The glass detects dozens of men miles beyond the river. Those are boomers who have been hiding.[26]

The train, meanwhile, had moved slowly across the bridge and was now disappearing from sight to the north. Once it had crossed, some of the settlers attempted to haul their wagons across the bridge by hand. But the job was so difficult and tiresome that after two had been taken over by that mode of crossing, it was given up and the discouraged homesteaders resolved to brave the dangers of the ford instead.[27]

By two o'clock the last wagon had been pulled across the main ford, and now all across the range of view in Oklahoma could be seen the white tops of wagons. Those who had watched the spectacle returned slowly to Purcell, finding the town deserted and suddenly very, very quiet.

Those at the 7-C Ranch, who had witnessed the disappearance of many of their fellow rushees, had become concerned over the lack of any government authority to control things there. On the afternoon of April 21, a petition was circulated among the settlers, asking that troops be sent there to prevent people from crossing the line early. O. H. Hills left the 7-C campsite at about five o'clock that afternoon to deliver the petition to Colonel Wade, who was then at Oklahoma station.[28] Wade agreed to detail some troops to the 7-C point of the east line and did so.

When starting time came, however, the troops were still in the field scouring the brush along Soldier and Crutcho creeks for those who had come in early. Thus it was up to someone on the line to give the signal. One man placed himself in a visible position and, at the moment of twelve noon he hoisted a long pole with three handkerchiefs tied to the end and brought it down in race-signalling fashion.[29] This loosed the several hundred settlers at the 7-C gathering point and sent them racing to claim the rich land inside the loop of the North Canadian east of Oklahoma station. Another group entered the Oklahoma lands from the Kickapoo Flats, just north across the river from the 7-C, by way of a trail that followed the outer curve of the North Canadian loop. Some of the claims made by those who supposedly made the run from the 7-C Ranch were among the most controversial to be fought out in the courts in the aftermath of the Run of 1889.

CHAPTER XII

Guthrie and the Eight O'Clock Crowd

> "People, people everywhere and the inexhaustible subject was Oklahoma, town site, Guthrie. No one thought of anything else, no one talked of anything else." Wichita Eagle, April 26, 1889.

THERE was nothing fair to the race for land for many who lined up on the northern borders of the Oklahoma district or rode the trains in from Arkansas City hoping to obtain a homestead or townsite lot at Guthrie. They arrived flushed from the anxiety of the race only to find that hundreds of others already at the finish line had grabbed most of the land there. Their initial chagrin was turned to anger when they discovered that it was under the guise of law enforcement that they had been badly cheated in the great race for land. Though in the long run many of the lawmen and public officials who sought to capitalize on their privilege of office had their claims taken from them by the courts, the land rush into Guthrie was grossly unfair and conspiratorial.

Guthrie! The name was the magic word of the Run of 1889 to a great many people. Everywhere they talked of going to Guthrie. Not untypically, one newspaper prior to the run reported: "The big town of the territory still promises to be Guthrie. Every accession to the colony of adventurers and moneyed speculators here booms the prospect of the town."[1]

It was strange, perhaps, that a location which was nothing more than a small siding depot on the Santa Fe line through Oklahoma should become the main focal point of the Run of 1889. But to the town-schemers and the potential rushees around the country it was *the place* to go, the future capital, they said, of the promised land. Much of the attention Guthrie received was a sort of mob fascination—many wanted to go there simply because everyone else did. But there were some valid reasons for Guthrie's popularity.

First of all, it was one of the two designated land offices, a virtual guarantee that it would become a townsite location. Moreover, maps of the Indian Territory of the day projected the extension of the Atlantic and Pacific Railroad westward from Tulsa and Sapulpa through Guthrie. This significant potential as a rail crossroads plus the proximity of the site to the Cimarron River contributed to its advantage and popularity. Too, the station had been receiving good press from visiting newspaper correspondents.

Wrote a *Kansas City Gazette* reporter:

> Guthrie, the point at which one of the land offices is located, is only a station, having depot, two section houses and water tank. The Cottonwood River, a beautiful and swift flowing stream, fringed with timber, is on the west about 1,000 feet from the depot. The Cottonwood is fordable the most of the year, and the bottom lands are ample and very fertile. The country is undulating, well clothed with closely matted grass, indicating good pasturage and rich soil.[2]

Another scribe, who passed by on the train shortly before the run, gave a similar endorsement: "The Cottonwood is crossed and its beautiful valley stretches out to the west. The country is still strikingly beautiful and brought forth exclamations of surprise and pleasure from the people aboard the train."[3]

Even before Harrison's proclamation opening Oklahoma was issued and Guthrie selected as a land office site, the location had its share of squatters—enough that when the news of the opening reached there, men and women reportedly swarmed out of hiding places to learn more. Claims were already staked for miles around the station, and it was reported that three of the squatters fought over a claim, with two of them being shot fatally.[4]

On March 30 Frank Greer, a Kansas newspaperman who had enterprisingly begun a pre-run newspaper entitled *The Oklahoma Capital*—originally published at Winfield, Kansas, but slated for Guthrie—spent the night in the section house at Guthrie station in the company of boomer leader W. L. Couch. While there, Greer observed a Santa Fe crew laying off the grounds for a new depot and platform. A few days later a force of carpenters and stone masons arrived to begin construction.[5] A large group of railroad workers, many of them non-English-speaking emigrants from southern Europe, arrived to install new spurs and switches. Six of the section hands were discharged and shipped out of the Territory on the suspicion that they intended to take up claims.[6]

During the middle of April, Harry Hill opened a stage line connecting Oklahoma station, Guthrie, and Kingfisher.[7] At about the same time, the surveyors for the Seminole Town and Improvement Company arrived to lay off a townsite plat for Guthrie. Another surveying crew, this one for the Choctaw Coal and Railway Company, arrived by special car from Denison, Texas. This company looked to the building of a rail line from McAlester, Choctaw Nation, into Oklahoma.[8]

Now the transformation began. More squatters arrived, some by jumping off the trains just outside the station area to avoid detection by the troops. Others, those with official excuses for being there, arrived boldly by coach and disembarked at the station: deputy marshals, revenue collectors, and a host of others.

Colonel D. B. Dyer, former Cheyenne and Arapaho agent at Darlington, arrived on Sunday, purportedly as a representative of the Wells-Fargo Express Company. He would become Guthrie's first mayor through the support of U.S. marshal Jones and his bevy of deputy marshals stationed there. The population of Guthrie station suddenly jumped into the hundreds. "Who were and who were not officials we did not know and had no means by which we could find out," an investigator later admitted.[10]

From a freight car on the siding, workers unloaded some fifty tents which were to be erected near the depot and comprise a hotel known as the "Santa Fe House" (later renamed the "Guthrie House"), having a capacity of 200 beds with five of the tents to be used as dining rooms. The enterprise was the joint operation of three men from Springfield, Illinois.[11]

Troops under the command of Captain MacArthur made no attempt to do anything about those already at or about Guthrie but made it their assignment to prevent unauthorized persons from getting off the trains that passed through. When Nanitta Daisey came by on her way to Purcell Saturday evening, she talked with MacArthur at the depot, asking permission to ride back on an early train Monday morning and cover the run from there for her newspapers. But MacArthur bruskly refused her request. She noted then that there were already enough people at Guthrie to start a small city.[12]

A *St. Louis Republic* reporter observed Guthrie from a passing train on Easter morning and saw the infantry troops lined up for inspection. The station platform was crowded with men. On the hillside to the east he observed the unpainted, square-fronted building of the land office and nearby the tents of the post office, marshals, and others. Freight cars lined the side tracks of the station, and through the open doors of several the reporter could see people eating.[13] That evening two more carloads of men arrived at the depot, all presumably with proper credentials allowing them early entry.

Though the details and exact participants would never come completely to light, meetings were held at Guthrie station during Sunday to organize and preempt a townsite

The first Guthrie Post Office, established by Dennis T. Flynn, who later would become territorial representative to Congress (Harper's Weekly).

---

in advance of the arrival of the legal rushees. It was, in actuality, an attempt by many officials who had been allowed inside Oklahoma early to use their privileged positions to grab claims and townsite lots ahead of others. Even Captain MacArthur was approached by a part of this clandestine group, one of the deputy marshals reportedly saying to him: "Everybody here is interested except you military men."[14] Later events would reveal some of those who were "interested."

As early as eight o'clock on the morning of April 22, those already at Guthrie—eventually they became known as the "eight o'clock crowd"[15]—had begun to locate the most desirable lots at random. More tents began to appear against the hillside east of the station house. Santa Fe agent Frank Best was on hand and noted that there was considerable activity about the area. Out of curiosity he walked up the hill to where some 100 or so men were on the ground. Three or four of the men had climbed upon the back of a wagon, using it as a speaking platform to call a crowd together.

The speakers all had the same message, arguing that

there had been no need for an act of Congress to make the land available to settlement since it was already public land. No proclamation from the President was needed, they insisted, and no time needed to be set for the opening. Thus everyone had a legal right to go ahead and claim their land. There was some discussion about how wide of a frontage a town lot should have. Though this was left unresolved, the men went ahead and drove their stakes and strung rope or string to mark boundaries. It was then a matter of spreading out personal effects upon the claim and bracing for the onslaught of the rush.[16]

After listening to the talks as a curious onlooker, Best decided that perhaps the orators had a point, so he joined the others in the lot grabbing. Even then he found the pickings were slim and had to settle for a piece of land that had a bad gully through it.

Later in the morning another speaker mounted the wagon-bed platform, calling for a townsite meeting. This was H. A. Pierce of Topeka, who later claimed that he had been urged by Judge Guthrie to talk to the crowd because of concern over the staking of lots without a plat or any regards as to streets and overlapping of claims. One account, however, claimed that Pierce had insisted that "We must hurry and settle [things] and adopt a plat before the mob gets here!"[17]

Pierce was elected chairman of the meeting, and a committee was named to find and select a townsite plat for consideration. The committee, which consisted of Captain H. D. Baker, General W. H. H. Clayton, and Commissioner Galloway, had no trouble locating a plat. They returned with three, including one which General Clayton had drawn up the night before.

In less than half an hour the committee reported back, and the plat made by Clayton was accepted by the small crowd of pre-legal-time entrants. Later a news story would appear in papers around the country, saying that the crowd had rejected a plat submitted by Pierce with cries of "Down with the Topeka outfit." Pierce denied this charge, claiming the story came from the "pure cussedness of the correspondent train," which arrived afterwards.[18]

It was charged, too, that Judge Guthrie, the location's namesake, was among those who on that forenoon of April 22 "caught the fever, which he went down there to catch."[19] Securing a board from near the depot, he wrote on it: "John Guthrie claims These Two Lots." He then made a guard about them by first setting corners and then piling up bones and buffalo chips "for improvements." Other officials joined him in staking lots.

Almost as if to evidence their pride in being first at Guthrie, this group of distinguished visitors had their photo taken grouped together in front of Marshal Jones's tent, then located near Flynn's post office tent and the land office. Later this photo would serve as evidence in court cases relating to lot titles in Guthrie and help cause Judge Guthrie and others to drop their claims.[20]

Included in the group were Judge Foster; Joseph Wilson, U.S. Commissioner; William Perry, U.S. Attorney; Eugene Hagin, Assistant U.S. Attorney; George Stearratt, clerk of the U.S. District Court in Topeka; H.D. Baker of the Santa Fe Railroad claim department; Santa Fe Land Agent Frost; and others.

The plat of Guthrie established two main streets for the new city: Harrison Avenue, named for the President, and Munford Avenue, named for Dr. Munford of the *Kansas City Times*, who had done so much to promote the opening of Oklahoma to settlement.[21] This plat laid out the town on north-south, east-west lines, contrary to one of the plats which based its streets on the angle of the railroad. Quite likely this last was the Seminole Townsite Company plat.

There was no bugle sounded nor gun fired at Guthrie to indicate the magic instant of high noon. The opening of the land office doors, however, was a highly significant gesture. It was also one of much controversy later. It was charged by many that when the hour of noon arrived, two deputy marshals jumped in front of Colonel Dyer, who was first in line, and permitted Mark S. Cohn and Jehu E. Dille

The Guthrie Land Office, one of only two such designated locations in the Unassigned Lands and a major reason Guthrie initially became the largest city in the territory (Harper's Weekly).

---

to enter. Cohn was from Fort Smith, Arkansas, and a personal friend of Receiver Barnes and General Clayton. Dille was a half-brother to Register Dille.[22]

Cohn, the first to file at the Guthrie Land Office, made entry for a homestead for himself and filed three declaratory statements for others, including those for deputy marshals James H. Huckleberry and Fenton Turner. He also filed the 320-acre Clayton townsite plat.[23] Jehu Dille made application for a homestead, and he, too, filed declaratory statements for a brother and another man. The tracts thus filed by the two men virtually surrounded the Clayton townsite area even as the first legal rushees were making their anxious dash from the borders.

Meanwhile, most of the officials, who were at Guthrie ostensibly to insure fair play, were caught up in a rush of their own to grab claims and town lots. Deputy marshal A. L. Jones, brother of marshal Jones, laid claim to a choice tract west of the Cottonwood—the fifth claimant to file at the land office. Another of Jones's deputies, ex-sheriff of

Cowley, Kansas, John Patterson, had come in even earlier than most by attaching himself to the crew building the new Guthrie depot. On the morning of the twenty-second, he was busy locating lots in Guthrie townsite—"attempting to grab everything in sight," one witness said.[24]

Despite his explicit instructions not to do so, head deputy marshal Rarrick made application for the SE quarter of Section 8, T16N, R2W, a part of the Guthrie townsite. He relinquished it on November 21, 1889. Deputy marshal Ranson Payne staked the same 160-acre tract claimed by Huckleberry, then he turned a few spadesful of dirt as a token start toward digging a well. Even Commissioner Galloway laid claim to town lots for himself and his son.[25]

There were many other sooner "grabs" occurring. James W. Feagins, a section foreman for the Santa Fe at Guthrie, staked a choice claim just west of the townsite on Cottonwood Creek. The tract would be contested by the West Guthrie townsite group, who arrived there on the afternoon of April 22 and began staking off lots.[26]

Shortly after noon, at 12:10, the Winfield and Cowley County townsite colony arrived at Guthrie, coming in from the east. This was the organization which had sent surveyors to Guthrie before the run and had their own plat drawn up. The various detachments of the colony had met at Ponca agency, crossed the Salt Fork ahead of the others, and moved on down across the northern flange of the Oklahoma country to a point on the border east of their destination. They did not stop there, however, continuing on across the line and camping only one mile from Guthrie on the morning of the twenty-second. They arrived at Guthrie far ahead of others from the north only to discover, with great dismay, that they had been beaten there by hundreds more.[27]

Frank Greer, editor of the *Oklahoma Capital*, was a member of the Winfield crowd, but he had come in separately. He and two others rode on a carload of telegraph poles aboard a freight car and jumped off just past Guthrie station on Sunday evening. The three men hid out until

The first train into Guthrie, which arrived at 1:25 pm, started a mad dash for choice lots in the already crowded townsite (Harper's Weekly).

Monday morning, observing the people moving about the station area. Greer later told how one of his companions was suddenly confronted by deputy marshal Ransom Payne, who was already staking his claim as early as ten o'clock. The lawman easily won out in the confrontation. Greer cut himself a stick and put a shingle on it to claim a 160-acre tract, then went in to the townsite and located himself a lot.[28]

At 12:40 a horseman came galloping in from the east and swung to the ground on the same tract Greer had claimed just southeast of the land office, driving in his own stakes. This was Veeder B. Paine, who had come from the Turkey Track ranch in the Sac and Fox reservation. Paine attached a written statement claiming the land to his stakes, then blazed some trees on four sides and placed the same notice on them. Paine, who had changed horses with a friend on the way in, would be contested for the land by a Guthrie townsite group.

Between 12:30 and 12:45 the regularly-scheduled northbound passenger train arrived at Guthrie, having stopped at Oklahoma station at 11:00 a.m. and at Edmond station at noon. There some of its passengers had disembarked to make the run there and some to catch a freight, then sidetracked at Edmond, back to Oklahoma station. However, it still carried a number of passengers headed for Guthrie, including a *Wichita Eagle* reporter who had spent the night and morning at Oklahoma station. The reporter noted the

On April 22, 1889, competing surveying crews swept across the prairie that was Guthrie laying out town lots (Harper's Weekly).

organization of a Guthrie Settlers' Association, formed for the mutual aid and protection of a Kansas group of men.[29]

It was 1:25 p.m. when the first train from the north, loaded inside with the Arkansas City boomers and on the outside with those who had boarded at Wharton, crossed the Cimarron and pulled into Guthrie station. Long before it had come to a stop, men began throwing off their luggage, valises, tents, sacks, and whatever and jumping after them. The train shed people from its roof tops, doors, rear platform, coal car, cowcatcher, and windows. Virtually everyone had a hatchet or ax and wooden stakes with which to mark the corners of his claim. Some of the men hit the ground rolling in a cloud of dust, coming up unconcerned about the pain to gather themselves and their belongings and then follow the others in a mad rush up the hillside. It all gave the appearance of a giant Easter egg hunt.

The landseekers dashed wildly in all directions, but the majority of the first train headed up past the land office, following the stakes of the survey line as far as they went and then simply continuing on until they found a place with no stakes.[30]

Already a long line had formed at the land office, where carpenters were still at work on the roof. There was considerable grumbling and hot words among the legal-timers when they saw so many ahead of them in the line. Particularly unhappy were those men who had joined townsite groups originated in Kansas and arrived at Guthrie to find their carefully-laid schemes dashed away by the work of the eight o'clock crowd.

Eight minutes after the first train, at 1:33 p.m., the second train from the north arrived, bringing another load of approximately 1,000 settlers. Then came the third load from Arkansas City at 1:48, the fourth at 2:00, the fifth at 2:30, the sixth at 3:00, and still a seventh and an eighth thereafter. The two-engine boomer train from Purcell arrived at Guthrie at around 3:30 that afternoon. Though some of the later trains from the north carried passengers who wanted to go on farther south, it was estimated that the Santa Fe alone brought well over 6,000 people to Guthrie that day; many estimates ranged up to 10,000 or more, all of which were male save 100 or so.[31]

Just before one o'clock, the first wagons from the east side reached Guthrie, and they were followed shortly by horsemen from the north who came galloping in on spent horses. One or two riders, it was reported, had ridden their mounts to death. After them, and all through the day, more and more wagons, horsemen, and men on foot arrived to swell the Guthrie population larger and larger. Still others arrived on the trains from the south.[32]

Many of the later arrivals, who found it virtually impossible to locate a piece of ground that was not already claimed, began buying lots from those who had them. The first lot supposedly sold for the price of five dollars, but the selling price increased rapidly. By midafternoon realtors were doing a brisk business.

Also finding plenty of ready customers were the gamblers and the three-shell men who had set up operations under the shade trees and in tents along the Cottonwood. One large tent dining hall did an overflow business at fifty cents per meal, taking in about $1,500 for dinner and supper on April 22.[33] Two enterprising clerks from Washington, D.C., were sitting on the ground near the land office filling out forms for customers just as fast as it was possible for them to do so, each at five dollars a blank. Two banks were

147

American enterprise came quickly—the first bank in Guthrie, established in a tent only hours after the land run began (Harper's Weekly).

established the first day, one by a Wichita group and another by a group from California.³⁴

There was much confusion and many conflicts in staking lots. A set of men would get together and agree that a street should run in a certain direction and stake lots to face it. Men on adjoining lots would declare that the others had staked in the center of the streets. Some of the organized groups had worked out a system of protection. Whenever one of their members came into dispute with an outsider, whom he invariably accused of being a "street jumper," the member would call out "Yahoo! Yahoo!" In a short time his comrades would come swarming to his aid.³⁵

As early as four o'clock on the afternoon of April 22, an "indignation meeting" was held for the purpose of working out some of the organization. After a brief talk it was adjourned to meet again at 6:00 p.m., and criers were sent around the area to make the announcement. A large crowd attended the second meeting to hear a number of speakers denounce the premature claimants and demand their ouster. Preliminary steps were initiated to conduct a townsite survey that all could agree upon.³⁷

Despite all the confusion and disagreement and though virtually everyone carried a weapon of some sort, the huge crowd remained in surprisingly good humor with little drunkenness or displays of temper. Many had brought their own flasks, some filled with water and some with whiskey, but there were no refills available. For many the dream of Guthrie and Oklahoma had been burst. No one quite expected the magnitude of the frantic, milling, disorganized swarm of people.

The problem of drinking water, which had been intensified by the warming temperatures of the day and the lack of shade on the westerly-facing hillside, had been solved for a time by use of the railroad water tank. But when a soldier was posted at the water tank to prevent its being emptied, the only liquid left for the thirsty thousands was the muddy, red waters of the Cottonwood. Hawkers went about with buckets, selling the warm, murky liquid at five cents a glass—which customers paid gladly.[38]

Now the people who had rushed to Guthrie so headlong began to realize that they were completely without the usual comforts of life. Not only was the water muddy and hot, but there was also no coal or kerosene to burn, no toilet facilities, no candles or lamps for light in the dark of night, no stores where goods could be purchased.[39] The tent hotels and eating houses were jammed far beyond capacity. But worst of all, there simply was not enough land to go around. Some of the luckless ones headed back for the railroad depot to catch a train to Kansas, cursing the Oklahoma country and calling themselves fools for having come.

But the majority of the 10,000 to 15,000 remained. Hamilton Wicks, a New Yorker, described the scene that Guthrie presented as evening came:

> I strolled up on the eminence near the land office, and surveyed the wonder cyclorama spread out before me on all sides. Ten thousand people had 'squatted' upon a square mile of virgin prairie that first afternoon, and as the myriad of white tents suddenly appeared upon the face of the country, it was as though a vast flock of huge white-winged birds had just settled down upon the hillsides and in the valley.[40]

As dusk fell, thousands of campfires sparkled against the darkening land, and the noise of the day settled into a subdued hum. Despite the discomforts, the vast crowds, and the cheating done against them by the insiders at Guthrie, most were determined to stick it out and make a new life in Oklahoma.

CHAPTER XIII
The Grab at Oklahoma Station

"'But, of course,' he went on, 'if you people want to build a city around my farm I have no objections. I don't care for city life myself, and I am going to turn this into a vegetable garden. Maybe, though, if you want it very bad, I might sell it.'"
Harper's Weekly, *April 23, 1892.*

SHORTLY before noon on April 22, Captain D. F. Stiles, Tenth Infantry, surveyed the landscape about Oklahoma station through his telescope. The green rolling hills that stretched away from the small cluster of buildings around the depot were motionless, seemingly waiting with silent anticipation. The only persons in sight were the soldiers, the deputy U.S. marshals, and a few railroad employees. Stiles glanced at his watch. It was two minutes of twelve.

He had talked earlier with General Merritt in his private railroad car on the sidetrack. They had decided that it would take the first horseman, riding at top speed from the nearest point on the South Canadian, some fifteen miles away, at least an hour and fifteen minutes to get there. Stiles expected to spot the vanguard of the invasion from that direction in about half an hour. The minute hand of his watch closed in over the hour hand, and the officer turned to his trumpeter who stood ready. Then as the two hands overlapped, Stiles gave the signal. The bell-clear notes rang out over the otherwise silent countryside that would soon undergo the metamorphosis of civilization.[1]

151

But it took far less time than Stiles had thought for the rush to begin at Oklahoma station. Even as the settlers were crossing the South Canadian at Purcell and the long boomer train was gathering momentum to cross the railroad bridge there, even before the trumpeter's call had ceased echoing across the land, it had begun. Almost like the rush of jack rabbits from cover, men suddenly appeared out of the long grass around the depot area, bounding here and there. They dropped from the leafy branches of trees; they crawled out of and from under freight cars; they sprang from gullies and bushes; they poured from the few buildings at the station; and they suddenly came galloping up on horseback from nowhere. A. H. Dunham later wrote:

> On that memorable day, April 22nd, in order to get a better view, I stood on a box car along side the depot at the zero hour of 12 o'clock noon. My astonishment was complete—people seemed to spring up as if by magic as far as the eye could reach. I could see them racing in every direction, some on horses, some in vehicles, and a greater number on foot. They were carrying all sort of impedimentia—some had spades, some stakes, some clothing, some hand-bags, some had pots and pans, or other cooking utensils. My words are not adequate to describe the scene.[2]

What had one moment been vacant meadow along the bank of the North Canadian had now become alive with men, and some women, dashing about in the wake of a crew of surveyors who were dragging their steel chains along at a run, their red and white barber poles and transits visible against the green of the land, leaving behind neat rows of wooden stakes which marked the lines of streets and city blocks. These men had arrived on the regular north-bound train from Purcell at 11 a.m., and even before noon came they had been put to work by head surveyor Charles Chamberlain, who had supervised the original platting of a townsite immediately to the west of the depot. By 12:20 there were already some forty tents erected inside the rectangle of pegs which marked individual lots.[3]

The full truth of what took place at Oklahoma station between high noon and the arrival of the first legitimate settlers will never be known. Some of the Run of 1889's most famous sooner cases, replete with charges and counter-charges and perjurious testimony, have obscured many aspects of what happened. Still, it is possible to trace the actions of many of the first claimants of land in the vicinity of Oklahoma station.

A reporter for the *Wichita Eagle* arrived at Oklahoma station on the evening of April 21 and filed a story the following morning, reporting the presence of General Merritt and his staff, four companies of the Tenth Infantry under Lt. Col. Snyder, Beidler, and some fifty deputy U.S. marshals under Marshal Jones. Surveying crews for both the Choctaw Coal & Railway Company and the Cherokee Coal and Iron Railroad were running their lines through the station area and laying off depot grounds.

A number of females—likely the Radebaugh girls and two domestic girls working for Sommers—were busy locating side saddles and preparing sign boards with which to stake claims. The north-bound passenger arrived at about 11 a.m., the reporter noted. It was loaded with boomers, but the soldiers would not permit them to leave the train. On the night before, a passenger had jumped a train just before reaching the station to evade the soldiers and had broken several ribs.

Just before noontime, Quartermaster C. F. Sommers, accompanied by another man and two women, rode from his house on the military reservation to the cavalry camp just to the northwest. He had made plans well ahead of time, even to having a house built on rollers so that it could be easily transported to the claim site. At the camp Sommers requested that Captain W. C. Forbush, Fifth Cavalry, give them a starting signal at the proper time. He said that he had intended to claim the tract immediately to the north of the reservation, but heard that someone else was aiming for it so he was going farther south.[4]

153

Forbush provided the signal at noon, and Sommers and his party left the reservation at a gallop, shovels and stakes in hand. Sommers rode to a location which bordered the rail line three tracts north of the reservation (NW ¼, Section 27, T12N, R3W) where he dismounted and did some digging with his shovel, staked the claim, and rode back to his house. Later he asked a soldier to go with him to the place to witness his claim.

At the same time Sommers was making his claim, another government official, Postmaster George Beidler, was laying claim to a 160-acre homestead on a soldiers' declaratory just to the west of Sommers's, the railroad between the two tracts.[5]

U.S. marshal W. C. Jones had arrived at Oklahoma station on Sunday in company with J. E. Frost, manager of the Seminole Town and Improvement Company, and Sidney Clarke. Though Jones did not claim a 160-acre homestead, evidence indicates that at the hour of the run he was less busy with minding the peace and order than he was in rushing about to stake one of the most valuable lots in the Seminole plat of Oklahoma City at the corner of Main and Broadway.[6]

The deputy marshals at Oklahoma station, likewise, showed less concern about their official duties than in grabbing land for themselves. Deputy Ewers White rode his horse along the railroad right-of-way, carrying a board on which was attached a crosspiece bearing his name. As he went he warned the other sooners to be certain to keep off the adjoining land until after twelve o'clock. When the moment of noon came, he rode east off the right-of-way to a tract just to the south of the Sommers claim (SW ¼, Section 27, T12N, R3W).[7]

Deputy marshal Asa Jones also made the pretense of remaining on the right-of-way until noon, then he dashed off to stake a claim just to the northwest of the townsite area (NW ¼, Section 33, T12N, R3W).[8] The tract immediately to the northeast of the townsite, the one which Sommers had heard was already taken (NW ¼, Section 34, T12N, R3W), was claimed by another deputy marshal, J. B. Koonce.[9]

Further evidence of a conspiracy of privilege among the lawmen lies in the fact that, though they were at Oklahoma station on April 22, Ewers White and Asa Jones were sixth and eighth, respectively, to file at Guthrie—well ahead of hundreds of others already in the land office line on April 23.[10]

George Thornton, the deputy marshal who had resided at Oklahoma station since 1888 and had a small house and some other improvements there, asserted a homestead claim at the residence by driving stakes and posting notices of his action. This key tract (NE ¼, Section 4, T12N, R3W) lay directly south of the proposed townsite.[11]

The Couch family and their old boomer friends—Samuel Crocker, T. W. Eckelberger, Daniel Odell, Rachel Haines, and some others—also made their runs for land from the railroad line at Oklahoma station. Thomas A. Couch, who acted as contractor for the Couch grading crew, and his father, Meshack H. Couch, who did chores around Camp Couch in addition to some blacksmithing when it was needed, left the railroad at about twenty minutes of noon and met William L. Couch just to the south of the depot shortly before twelve.

W. L. Couch moved to the claim he had long since selected, the 160-acre tract immediately west of the Santa Fe depot (SW ¼, Section 33, T11N, R3W). Other homesteads were claimed south of the river by John M. Couch and Charles B. Couch. Edward DeTar, a long-time boomer and brother-in-law to W. L. Couch, laid claim to the same tract as filed upon by deputy Thornton.[13]

Samuel Crocker staked the 160-acre tract immediately north of the townsite, and Daniel Odell the one just north of Crocker (NE ¼, Section 33, T12N, R3W, and SE ¼, Section 28, T12N, R3W, respectively). T. W. Eckelberger's claim was to the immediate south of the military reservation (NW ¼, Section 3, T11N, R3W) and that of Mrs. Haines was just south of Eckelberger (SW ¼, Section 3, T11N, R3W), straddling the North Canadian.[14] All of these claims would face strong court challenges.

There were still others present at Oklahoma station at noon who were busy making claims to land. Carley Blanchard, a farmer from Cowley County, Kansas, was a former boomer who had been at the station in February and again in March 1889 to work as a carpenter. The last time he brought his family and their household goods with him and set up residence in a tent. On April 19 he went to work for the railroad as a laborer, cutting off his beard and dying his moustache black to avoid detection and arrest by the troops.

At two seconds after twelve o'clock noon he ran from the railroad north of the depot and drove his stake into the ground on the same tract as claimed by deputy Ewers White. Another man picked up his tent, rushed it to Blanchard, and helped him pitch it. Then Mrs. Blanchard came running up with their child and took a place in the tent.[15]

Another sooner was government freighter Thomas Wright. Wright, who later claimed that he was held at the station because of military impressment of his teams and wagons for wood hauling, was on the Fort Reno road leading westward from the depot before noon on April 22. He had just fixed an iron tire on his wagon—"Wedged it, knocked it, and put it on"—when a man came running up, calling Wright's attention to where his trunk had just been unloaded from a hack and where he had driven a stake. Wright laughed and said, "Pretty early, are you not?" The man looked about nervously and saw the soldiers standing on the track and at the depot, then darted off to look for another piece of land.

It was about this time that Wright's son called out, "Dad, there they come! Look, yonder they are coming!" Wright looked toward the river and saw people scattered out over the river bottom, whipping their horses toward the station area. Wright himself hurried about and drove his claim stake, then, in doubt that he had placed it correctly, looked up the corner stone and reset the stake. Once this was done he instructed his son to take his wagon, go to the stockade at the depot and pick up their bedding, cooking utensils, horse feed, and other items, and come on down.[16]

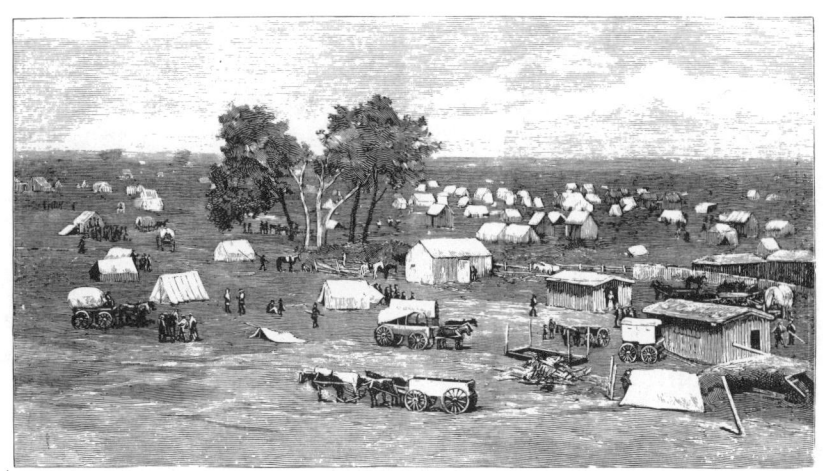
Oklahoma City, only days after the land run, looked like a "handful of white dice thrown out across the prairie." (Harper's Weekly).

Among the noontime crowd which poured forth upon the townsite area were two boys from Kansas who had sneaked aboard an unlocked freight car at Arkansas City on the previous Saturday night and ridden to Oklahoma station, jumping out on the outskirts to hide out until Monday. At noon on the twenty-second the boys joined the crowd in rushing from their hiding places and grabbing some lots in the townsite. When three of their friends arrived at 5:00 p.m. Monday on the third boomer train out of Arkansas City, the two boys had five lots on Main Street marked off with ropes. They had put up a large sign which read "Oklahoma Mercantile Co.," causing other rushees to dash on past.[17]

Many of the town lots had already been claimed by principals in the Seminole Company: Clarke, Couch, Weaver, Marshal Jones, and others. According to the affidavit filed at the Guthrie Land Office by Louis O. Dick for the Seminole Company at 3:15 on April 22, the group claimed the equivalent of two quarter sections—the maximum claimable for townsite use—west of the Santa Fe line.[18]

Even as the footracers were posting their claims, horsemen were dashing in from the south and east. These were sooners who had waited only long enough to make their appearance look legitimate. Some were those who had crossed the South Canadian the night before, and some had hidden out in the brush along Soldier, Crutcho, and Lightning creeks. Of special interest were several horseback riders who arrived within the first hour after noontime. William J. McClure, owner of the 7-C Ranch, and three companions had come over the Shawnee Town Road by way of a horse relay which McClure had established. The ranchman claimed the quarter section immediately north of the military reservation (NW ¼, Section 34,T12N, R3W). Two of his companions also staked tracts in key positions.[19]

Another early arrival was Frank Gault, nephew of McClure, who had led a party of cowboys, he claimed, on a route from the 7-C Ranch directly across country to Oklahoma station. He located on the same tract which Samuel Crocker had claimed, directly north of the townsite area.[20] Another rushee who claimed to having ridden in from the east line was Katie Woodruff, a young woman of twenty-one, who staked a tract of land due east of McClure (SE ¼, Section 27, T12N, R3W). Her father and uncle located on nearby tracts.[21]

Recognized by many as being among the very first legitimate rushees to arrive at Oklahoma station from the South Canadian, the closest point on the border, were Reverend Murray and Kincaid of the "Colony crowd." These men arrived at the station at 1:15 p.m. in a buggy, their foam-lathered horse giving testimony to their having come the fifteen miles at a furious gallop. Directly behind them came a wave of others in buggies, wagons, and on horseback, pouring over the landscape wildly, driving in stakes, having doubts about their choice and dashing to another location to hammer their markers into the unbroken sod.[22]

The Colony crowd, which had organized itself as the "Oklahoma Town Company," found that the Seminole Company had the area west of the depot already locked up, and they made the mistake of trying to settle on the military reservation tract. When they learned of their error, they moved back to the west of the railroad and initiated a townsite south of the Seminole townsite, renaming it "South Oklahoma City." Later in the afternoon the Oklahoma Town Company held an election, choosing mild-mannered Reverend Murray as president. Some 304 persons signed the company's poll book as electors. They would later file a townsite plat overlapping that of the Seminole Company plat (E ½, Section 33, T12N, R3W).[23]

At 2:10 p.m. the double-engined, twenty-four-car boomer train from Purcell arrived. As a woman already at the station described it, the train looked like a huge centipede with hundreds of arms and legs and heads sticking out everywhere.[24] Though it had shed some of the landseekers at Norman and Verbeck along the line, the train still carried an estimated 2,500 people. In many respects the scene emulated that at Guthrie, with people rushing madly hither and yon at break-neck risk and falling over one another in great confusion and disorder; but others seemed almost stunned by the enormity of the crowd that was already there ahead of them. Almost mechanically they walked calmly over to the townsite, took what was left for them, and then kept on staking lots some two or more miles out onto the prairie from the station.[25]

Most of this extension was onto the claim of W. L. Couch, and it was necessary that afternoon for troops to come out and remove settlers. The military, its operations limited by the order to act only in conjunction with the U.S. marshals, did what little they could to maintain the peace and lawful order. On the morning of the twenty-second, Captain Stiles had established a guard at the depot. He contacted Marshal Jones who gave him a list of some half dozen deputies who were to keep the peace and with whom Stiles could work. But as the day progressed and the swarms of people fell in upon the station area, with arguments and disputes erupting, none of the deputies could be found. Jones himself, Stiles learned, had caught the boomer train on to Guthrie to tend to his own land claims, and most of the deputies were busy with their own land grabbing.[26]

159

Among those arriving on the boomer train was T. M. Richardson and his father. They had spent a week in Purcell and managed to get good seats on the east side of the train. Richardson's father was one of the lucky ones, locating lots on Grand Avenue at Harvey where he later started a lumber yard, the lumber having already been shipped in and waiting on a sidetrack. It had also been arranged for the family tents and camping outfit to be brought in by wagons from the South Canadian, and these arrived at around four o'clock that afternoon.[27]

Thirty-year old Frank Harrah came from Sedalia, Missouri, to Purcell to make the run. Studying a map of Oklahoma, he picked Norman station as his choice of destinations, but when the boomer train reached that point he decided that it was too barren and rode on to Oklahoma station. There he tossed his suitcases under the depot platform and ran east. When told that he was on the military reservation, he ran back to the west of the tracks and staked a lot on California Avenue.[28]

Walter E. Larsh, who had been selling tickets for the Santa Fe at Purcell, decided to make the run himself. He did not attempt to locate a town lot at Oklahoma station; he just stood and watched the excitement. J. A. Ryan jumped off the train to land in the middle of a coal pile but dashed on down California to locate a lot. Father J. A. Burt, who made the run to escape the cold winters of Wisconsin, was on the first coach of the boomer train. After a mad scramble he located a lot at the corner of Robinson and Third.[29]

One female rushee was in such a hurry to get off the train that she departed unladylike through a car window and almost immediately upon hitting the ground drove her stake right there. This happened to be on the east side of the tracks, and when soldiers told her that she was on the military reservation, she suspiciously refused to listen and would not budge. Another woman, it was later told, drove her stakes between the ties of the railroad track, declaring that it would take a locomotive and an entire train of cars to move her.[30]

An eyewitness told the story of a very large man who wore a heavy beard and looked very much the villain. When an argument erupted between him and some others over a piece of land, the man threw down his bedding roll and pulled out of it a shotgun which he snapped together expertly. In no polite terms he told the others to clear out. The contestants hung in bravely until a woman came dashing up and threw her arms around the neck of the man with the shotgun, crying out, "Please don't kill anyone else! We've had enough trouble already!" This convinced the other claimants, who departed in a hurry.[31]

Charles F. Ashinger arrived on the boomer train from Purcell and hit the ground running to the east, sprinting as fast as he could to post a claim to the tract just northeast of the military reservation (NE ¼, Section 32, T12N, R3W). Later the claim would be challenged in court by Katie Woodruff. The woman's attorney scorned the idea that Ashinger could run nearly three-fourths of a mile in the three and a half minutes as he claimed he had done. To prove the point, and with a side wager of ten dollars with the attorney, Ashinger repaired to the depot along with the attorney, judge, contestants, court officials and about 100 witnesses. At a signal, Ashinger repeated his feat of the run, dashing the distance in three minutes and twenty seconds. He won the case.[32]

The day of April 22 sped on in confusion and near-chaos. More and more people flooded into the Oklahoma station area, the number estimated at more than 10,000. Tents were erected, and even on the first day the sound of hammer and saw told of the beginnings of enterprise. Men talked and debated and argued, making deals on lots, gathering crowds to hear speeches and hold elections and others to protest the elections.[33]

As at Guthrie, water quickly became a problem, and the Santa Fe water tank was the only oasis for the milling horde of men and animals. An enterprising gambler took over the site, seating himself there with a revolver and a tin basin and holding out for five cents a pint of the precious fluid. He was soon deposed by the soldiers.[34]

161

Oklahoma City, four weeks after the opening, appeared to be a town "born grown" (Harper's Weekly).

There were only the two "hotels" at Oklahoma station, and while both served food they could hardly begin to handle the crowd. Some of the newcomers had brought the equivalent of picnic lunches, but for many it was simply a matter of tightening their belts until tents and lunch counters could get under way. Edibles of any kind were in brisk demand. Lemonade and poor sandwiches were dispensed to the hungry multitude.[35]

Finally the day came to its conclusion, dusk settling over the place which for a brief period had been known as "Oklahoma station." A temporary hush quieted the din of the unusual day, and men and women looked to their night's lodging in tents or under the stars, building their camp fires for companionship through the night. They had come to Oklahoma, and while none knew what claims were valid, which township would win out, or what the morrow would bring, they had all participated in an exciting and historic event. As dark closed in on Oklahoma station that night of April 22, 1889, there was a certain feeling of brotherhood among all who had shared the adventure of the run. Befittingly, perhaps, once again the old call of comradeship among those encamped on the distant prairie of the Indian Territory sounded through the night—"Oh, Joe! Here's your mule!"[36]

CHAPTER XIV
New Empire

These pilgrims do not drop on one knee to give thanks decourously, as did Columbus according to the twenty-dollar bills, but fall on both knees and hammer stakes into the ground and pull them up again, and drive them down somewhere else at a place they hope will eventually become a corner lot facing the post-office, and drag up the next man's stake, and threaten him with a Winchester because he is on their land, which they have owned for the last three minutes. Harper's Weekly, *April 23, 1892.*

WHILE Guthrie and Oklahoma City caught the main force of the immigration onslaught, other smaller dramas were being played out in the development of towns and communities throughout Oklahoma. Each of these settlements sprang into being with great hope and expectation on the part of those who settled there, all desirous that theirs would possess the magic of becoming a future metropolis. Every site drew its own set of merchants, realtors, doctors, lawyers, newspapermen, and other professional and trade segments of society which normally comprised American towns.

Some of these new settlements failed quickly and some struggled along for a time, dying slowly; but most became residential communities serving the surrounding agriculture as Oklahoma gradually made the transition from frontierland to civilized state.

There was never any doubt that Kingfisher station would become a townsite; the only questions concerned the particular tract location and ownership of the townsite land. The northliners under Hubbard had preselected the north half of Section 15, T16N, R7W, which encompassed the old relay station and stable as well as the land office building. A serious controversy would erupt over both the northeast and northwest quarters of the section.

John Wood, the government teamster who had been hauling wood a mile from the land office on the morning of April 22, was the first to arrive upon the land. Within eight minutes after noon he had laid claim to the northeast quarter as his homestead, staking it and beginning immediately to dig a well as an improvement.[1]

William D. Fossett, a former Kansas lawman who had lined up legally with others on the line west of Kingfisher station, owned one of the fastest horses there. When the signal was given he quickly outdistanced others and raced to the northwest quarter of Section 15. Jack Admire, the Receiver at the land office, watched from the door of the office as Fossett jumped off his horse some 250 yards west, jerked his saddle to the ground, and waved his blanket as a sign of conquest. Fossett immediately began digging a dugout, and later he did some plowing.[2]

The race from the west line was made in four minutes by the leaders, with the mass of settlers trailing behind. Within half an hour the run from that direction was over, but it was an hour later before the hard-riding advance guard from the north line arrived at Kingfisher. Within that time, Kingfisher station had become a village of 200 tents, and men were staking lots in the townsite which had been surveyed off on the south half of Section 15. Streets were laid out and named, lawyers and real estate men were hanging out their signs, and men were scurrying about in mass confusion. The prairie around had suddenly become dotted with white tents—1,200 of them, a reporter estimated.[3]

A meeting had been held on the west line on Sunday night in an effort by that group to organize a townsite south of the land office. But attempts to elect a mayor and common council had failed, the majority of those present objecting to having things pushed through too quickly. There were some hot words and heavy swearing, but the matter ended peacefully, if inconclusively.[4] It was estimated that some

2,500 westliners swarmed into Kingfisher within a few minutes after noon, many of them cowboys and other speculators who were out to grab as many claims as possible and then sell them. At first lots sold for as high as $350 at Kingfisher, but the price soon came down to $50 or even $25 when it became evident that the legality of ownership was often much in question.[5]

When the northsiders reached Kingfisher station at around one o'clock, the townsite group which had organized at Buffalo Springs immediately surveyed off the north half of Section 15, the same two quarter sections as claimed by Wood and Fossett. Even as the surveyors were marking off lots, blocks, streets, and alleys for townsite use, other men were practically on their heels staking claims. The westliners had chosen the name of "Lisbon" (as the post office had been named when established there on April 20, 1889) for their townsite, and the northliners now took up the name of "Kingfisher" for theirs.[6]

As at Guthrie and Oklahoma City, there were many who had hidden out in the brush and gullies around Kingfisher station and made the run from there. It was later told that one man who did this soaped his horse so that it would appear lathered when he arrived. With the westliners arriving so early, it was more difficult at Kingfisher to identify illegal entrants.[7]

The land office at Kingfisher found it impossible to open for business on the day of the run. The building was not yet completed, there were no shelves or fixtures installed, and the wagon carrying the General Land Office forms did not arrive until the morning of April 22. Thus the crowd of men which gathered in front of the land office that afternoon was forced to go into camp there and wait through the day and night for the office to open on the twenty-third.[8]

A meeting was held on the evening of April 22, largely among the old soldiers and members of the Odd Fellows. Again an effort was made to nominate and elect city officials, but the meeting was broken up when someone shouted out: "We want to see what the men look like whom it is proposed to make our officials. Let's wait for daylight." A yell of approval followed, and the meeting ended.[9]

Another mass meeting was held on the morning of the twenty-third, and it was agreed that John D. Miles, a former agent for the Cheyenne and Arapaho Indians like Dyer at Guthrie, would present a plat of the town of Lisbon to the land office officials. Miles was also elected mayor of the new settlement.[10]

On the following day still another meeting was held among the northliners. The townsite of Kingfisher was organized, and George Hubbard was named as its mayor. But even a second townsite did not satisfy everyone, and a third was platted to the north on the south half of Section 10. This was at first called "Perkins," and later it was known as "Coletown" after its developer, E. C. Cole.[11] However, this plat was never submitted to the land office.

By the time that Wood and Fossett made their entries of claim at the late-opening land office (entries 3 and 5, respectively), there were already some 500 settlers and numerous places of business on their tracts. Eventually the courts would rule that the Buffalo Springs group had no special prior rights on the land. Wood was declared to have had unjust advantage and was disqualified as a claimant, but Fossett's entry was held to have been made in good faith.[12]

There were three organized groups which sought to be the founding force at Edmond station: the Seminole Town and Improvement Company, which had presurveyed a townsite surrounding the depot and had a plat prepared before the run; the Chicago Colony, enroute on April 22 by train with seventy-two people from Illinois and Michigan; and a group of forty-eight persons from Springfield, Missouri, who also came in by train. The Springfield group arrived from the north during the afternoon of the twenty-second, but it was 8:30 that evening before the coach cars of the Chicago Colony were sidetracked at Edmond.[13]

There were also three local contenders for the prime property around the station, principally two Santa Fe section hands named John R. Smith and Alexander B. Smith (no known relation) and Eddy B. Townsend, a partner in the IOA cattle spread on the nearby Iowa reservation. Townsend had shipped cattle from Edmond station before the run.

At the time of the run, Edmond station sat on the flat, treeless dividing line between the wooded hills to the east and the rolling plains to the west. The only other regular residents besides the John Steen family were the telegrapher and a coal-heaver who resided in the railroad section house.[14] Alexander Smith, who had come to the station as a section hand on January 30, lived in a tent on the right-of-way with his family, refusing to leave despite the notice on the section house that employees of the railroad would not be eligible to make the run if they remained.[15]

The morning of April 22 at Edmond station was serenely at peace, the sun gradually warming the springtime air as the workers at the station went about their duties. It remained that way until shortly before noon when a freight train from the north, loaded with coal, arrived and pulled onto a siding. Aboard the caboose of the freight were four men who had bribed the conductor to be allowed on in Arkansas City. One of them, A. F. Jackson of Minnesota, had hired the others to help him establish a lumberyard at Oklahoma station.[16]

The freight had been sidetracked in favor of a passenger train (the first regular passenger which had passed through Purcell and Oklahoma station ahead of the boomer train from the south). This train arrived at Edmond a few minutes after twelve, discharging among others the surveyors for the Seminole Company, who now rushed about to resurvey the townsite and drive in their wooden pegs for streets and lots.[17]

Also aboard this train, having boarded it the night before when it was made up at Fort Worth, Texas, were Captain Joseph Anderson and his two daughters, O. N. Jaynes and his wife, and a number of others who were coming from Texas to make the run. Anderson and his daughters had tried to disembark at Oklahoma station when the train made its stop just before 11:00 a.m., but the soldiers there would not allow them to do so. Thus their plan was to continue on to Guthrie and catch the train back after the legal hour had passed. As the passenger train pulled into Edmond, the occupants could see people running about staking claims.[18]

At high noon, Alexander Smith moved his tent, possessions, and family from the right-of-way onto the quarter section that lay on both sides of the railroad line just south of the depot and staked it as his claim. John R. Smith made the run from the right-of-way at the same time, making a Soldier's Declaratory claim to the quarter section just north of Alexander Smith. This was the same land where the Seminole surveyors were busy staking out their townsite.[19]

What other sooners may have been at Edmond will never be known for certain. Eddy B. Townsend, who arrived to stake the same prime quarter section as claimed by Alexander Smith, insisted that he left the Iowa line at noon after helping start the group there by his watch. Though some witnesses testified to having seen him inside Oklahoma before the run, other testimony tells of Townsend, Hardy C. Anglea, and J. Wheeler Turner galloping into Edmond station on foam-lathered horses at about 1:20 p.m.[20]

T. F. Cole, later an Edmond grocer and considered by sooner investigator W. F. Harn to be a notorious sooner, claimed that he had started Townsend and the others from Sections 36 and 25, T14N, R1W, by firing his Winchester three times. Coal-heaver John Adams claimed that he had eaten dinner with Townsend at the station house on the day before the run, while S. K. Van Voorhees testified that he had watched the run from the top of a box car at Edmond and saw Townsend, Turner, and Anglea ride in about 1:00 or 1:05 p.m.[21]

Perhaps the most damaging evidence against these men would simply be the fact that they secured some of the closest and choicest claims around Edmond station when it was known that a large crowd of land seekers was there at high noon staking claims.

The long, two-engined boomer train out of Purcell reached Edmond shortly before three that afternoon. Though most of its original occupants had left the train at Oklahoma station, there were a number who had continued on with Edmond or Guthrie as their destination. Aboard were some of the Oklahoma station boomers and deputy marshals on their way to the Guthrie Land Office to file their claims.

Another passenger on this train was Nanitta Daisey, the *Dallas Morning News* reporter who had caught the train at Purcell. At Edmond station she persuaded the engineer to let her ride on the cowcatcher as the train pulled out, going very slowly, toward Guthrie. The colorful, petite Kentucky woman, wearing a six-shooter around her waist, clung to the platform until two miles north of Edmond. There she jumped from the cowcatcher and scrambled across the bar ditch east of the tracks.

Passengers cheered from the train windows as she planted her stakes in the ground, threw her duster cloak over them, then sank to her knees and fired her pistol into the air and claimed the land. She then ran back across the bar ditch and was pulled aboard the rear platform of the train by her fellow reporter from the *Dallas Morning News*. This feat of the female eighty-niner was published in papers around the country, often embellished beyond the truth but winning her somewhat of a national reputation as a fearless female of her day.[22]

The next train to arrive was from the north, reaching Edmond at around 3:30 p.m., the first of the Arkansas City boomer trains to come on south from Guthrie. Aboard this train was Thomas G. Miller of Illinois, who said there were only about forty people at Edmond when he got there. He did not locate on a quarter section but "took lots, put up posts and nailed boards on the posts and notices on the boards that the lots had been taken by me and then procured a tent; others pitched tents and opened up eating establishments, cigar stands and other kinds of trades that evening . . ."[23]

It may well have been this train on which the Springfield,

Missouri, colony arrived, headed by W. E. Drum, John Allman, and John W. Hardesty. The competition of the Seminole Company caused the Springfield and Chicago groups to consolidate on the evening of the twenty-third in a meeting around a rousing camp fire. Town officials were elected, Drum being named mayor and James Martin of the Chicago group treasurer. On the twenty-fourth the Springfield-Chicago crowd conducted its own survey of a townsite, celebrating the event that night by baking bread in an oven built from sandstone.[24]

The Seminole Company had filed an affidavit for the townsite of Edmond at the Guthrie Land Office on the day of the run. But on April 24 W. E. Drum filed a declaratory statement for the townsite. It originally carried the name of "Birge City" after the leader of the Chicago group, but this was scratched out and "Edmund" written in.[25] John R. Smith, who claimed the tract of the townsite, relinquished his claim to 120 acres to the city of Edmond for $550.[26]

The Seminole survey had been based upon the line of the Santa Fe tracks, while the Springfield-Chicago survey had been made according to the four points of the compass. This situation caused a considerable amount of conflict and hard feelings among those who had purchased lots from the two townsite groups. This was resolved on May 8 when Inspector J. A. Pickler arrived at Edmond to work out a compromise which accepted both surveys in part and called for a new election of city officers.[27]

The land dispute between Alexander Smith and Eddy Townsend would be fought in court for several years until finally the U.S. Supreme Court would rule against Smith and in favor of Townsend. The case became a landmark decision establishing the illegality of making the run of 1889 from the railroad right-of-way.[28] As such it would serve as a precedent in deciding the ultimate fate of many others who made the run from the Santa Fe rail line.

Norman station, created when the Santa Fe established it as a potential depot in 1887, took its name from Abner Norman, a member of the Barrett survey party of 1873. The surveyors camped at a spring there and left behind burned into a large elm tree a sign reading, "Norman's Camp." Another identification of the site as "Dugout" came from the cattle-driving days on the Arbuckle Trail, which passed the point. Some black cowboys working for Chickasaw rancher Montford Johnson had once lived in dugouts here to kill wolves that were plaguing cattle. When the railroad built through in 1886 and 1887, it first used the name of Dugout but later identified its station as Norman.[29]

For a time Norman station had existed as a single boxcar equipped with a telegraph, but a section house was soon erected and a telegrapher assigned permanently. Early in 1889 the Santa Fe constructed a house on its right-of-way at Norman for use by Agent Andrew Kingkade, his wife, and their four-year-old son. Another family, that of J. L. Hefley with his wife and eight children, took up residence in the section house for a time.[30]

Norman station was one of the principal targets of the Seminole Town and Improvement Company, and a pre-run survey and plat had been made for a townsite there. Also interested in the site was the Santa Fe agent at Purcell, D. L. Larsh. A short time before the run, Larsh called a meeting of a small group of local acquaintances in the freight office of the Purcell depot. They included some Chickasaw Nation cattlemen and others, among them attorney Albert Rennie. At Larsh's request, Rennie undertook the preparation of a townsite plat for Norman and a townsite agreement for the Norman Townsite Company.

On the day of the run Larsh boarded the twenty-car boomer train and rode to Norman station, arriving to find that the Seminole surveyors had already staked off the townsite. Larsh had little choice but to stick his townsite plat back into his pocket and go along with the Seminole scheme. A townsite affidavit was filed for Norman at the Guthrie Land Office at 3:00 p.m. on the day of the run by Frank E. Clark, who was thought to be a member of the Seminole group.[31]

Santa Fe agent Andrew Kingkade did not attempt to

claim land in the run of 1889, though later he did purchase a homestead with his mother. Hefley, however, did attempt to claim a tract of land. With the border of Oklahoma running along the South Canadian River only three miles distant, Hefley waited until he saw the people coming up from the river bottom before he stepped onto the northwest quarter of Section 32, T9N, R2W. He would later be declared a sooner and lose his claim.[32]

Some 500 persons, chiefly from the south, descended upon Norman during the afternoon of April 22 and claimed lots staked off by the Seminole surveyors as well as agricultural homesteads in the surrounding area. Larsh and Kingkade were among the board of councilmen who were elected on May 4, 1889, along with Mayor T. R. Waggoner. On July 14, 1890, Norman was legally organized as a village.[33]

The site of present downtown El Reno (the west half of Section 9, T12N, R7W) had been targeted by at least two groups of Kansas-based townsite speculators who recognized the value of the location as a potential railroad crossroad and center for the fertile farming lands surrounding it. One of the townsite groups, composed of men from Wichita, Wellington, Caldwell, and some other Kansas towns, made arrangements with two men from Fort Reno to enter upon the two quarter sections and hold the land until the townsite group came. The president of the company, E. G. Smith, was to make the run from north of Kingfisher and file upon the land while other members were advancing through the Cheyenne-Arapaho reservation.

The secretary of the company, B. J. Dreeson, arrived at the location and began surveying only to learn that Smith had not been able to place a filing. But now a second townsite development company moved in behind the other and settled on the two quarter sections. This group, the El Reno Townsite Company with ex-governor Crittenden of Missouri as president and ex-governor Glick of Kansas as vice-president, had hired two old soldiers to make homestead claims on the land. The company then leased the land for a period of 99 years, the two claimants agreeing that when the government issued them a patent to the land they would deed it to the townsite company.³⁴

However, one of the claimants, John A. Foreman, was challenged in court by a man named Anson A. Davis. Davis charged that Foreman was a sooner who had not made entry upon the land for agricultural purposes and that he had committed fraud in an unlawful collusion with the townsite organization.³⁵ Davis's affidavit was supported by William T. Darlington of the Darlington Indian agency.

Foreman testified in rebuttal that he was a victim of the townsite lot-jumpers who invaded his land and began surveying, building a boarding house, grading roads, and making other improvements against his wishes. He stated that he had planned originally to make the run at the ninety-eighth meridian but found a large crowd there and moved one mile south on the west line. On the day of the run he traveled a half mile and settled on the NW quarter of Section 9, filing a declaratory statement on the tract. Two days later he went on a four-day trip and returned to find a town located on his place.³⁶

Both the U.S. marshal and the military authorities had refused to run the men off, Foreman claimed, and finally he felt intimidated and gave in and signed the lease agreement. The General Land Office, which took Foreman's statement and heard no one in opposition, approved Foreman's entry on the disputed land. However, an appeal to Secretary of the Interior John Noble produced different results. Basing his opinion primarily on a letter to Senator Perkins which was published in the *Congressional Record* and was signed by Foreman along with El Reno city officials asking that contracts between the Oklahoma Homestead and Town Company and the homesteaders be legalized, Noble ruled that Foreman had, indeed, acted in collusion with the town company. Approval of Foreman's right of entry was overturned.³⁷

When this decision, made on February 6, 1892, reached El Reno, declaring Foreman's claim to be public domain, a second land rush was made by lot-jumpers. In less than an hour every lot on Foreman's tract was occupied: "All night long the deafening sound of the hammer was heard in every portion of the city and when dawn broke upon the scene, El Reno presented an appearance never before witnessed in this section. Shingles, pieces of scantling foundation, dugouts, and skeleton frames loomed up from two thousand places which gave the city the appearance of having been visited by a cyclone."[38]

Other tracts within the El Reno townsite area were filed upon initially by Thomas Jensen, Napoleon B. Wass, James Thompson, and Julius A. Penn. Thompson was Post Saddler at Fort Reno, while Penn was in charge of troops monitoring the run on the west line at Fort Reno. Penn, too, succumbed to the mania of the day, staking a claim to the northeast quarter of Section 9, T12N, R7W. However, he eventually found he was not an eligible claimant and relinquished the tract on July 18, 1889.[39]

Albert Rennie, who had studied some law in Toronto and whose brother James was the principal merchant at the Chickasaw Nation settlement of White Bead Hill, had been inside Oklahoma on numerous occasions prior to the run. In addition to his Norman station interest, Rennie had become taken with a particular site where the railroad line ran very near a high bluff of the Canadian River. Rennie visualized a trading center there which would serve the ranching and agricultural area across the river in the Chickasaw country.[40]

Accordingly, Rennie interested J. W. Klinglesmith of Pauls Valley and others in the financial potential of such a settlement and proceeded to organize the Pauls Valley Townsite Company for a future town to be named after Secretary of the Interior John W. Noble.

On April 22 Rennie, who could not swim, rode his horse across the swollen South Canadian and laid claim to the east half of Section 27, T8N, R2W, in the name of the townsite company and to a quarter section for himself at the townsite's southeast corner (which he ultimately lost). The remainder of the townsite company, including Klinglesmith, caught the train to Purcell on the night of April 21—

"a jolly party with lunchbaskets"[41]—some making the run from there while the women of the party went to Red Hill at Purcell and observed the great rush from there.

On April 24 Rennie went to Guthrie and filed a declaratory statement for the "Inhabitants of Noble." On May 20 the site was surveyed and lots distributed. The town was slow to develop, however, because the Santa Fe had no depot there, the closest being Walker station. However, by August 1889 a depot had been secured, along with shipping pens, a post office had been established there with Rennie as the first postmaster, and the town had begun a modest growth.[42]

The location of the settlement of "Stillwater" made by W. L. Couch and the Payne Oklahoma Colony in December 1884 held a central position in the eastern "panhandle" of the Oklahoma country. Thus it was a logical site for a new town following the run. Settled in part by men who had come down with the Arkansas City exodus and in part by men believed to be sooners, the area soon drew the attention of a town company, which was organized in Winfield, Kansas, in May 1889. Another company was formed among a few of the settlers on Stillwater Creek. The former company was incorporated under the laws of Kansas, but there is no evidence that the latter had a charter of any sort.[43]

On May 24 a locating committee of the Winfield company voted to accept an irregular area of 240 acres in Sections 14 and 23 of T19N, R2E. Robert Lowry, a leader in the settler townsite group, led a move to merge with the Winfield town company and took part in laying out the town. After a meeting of the Stillwater Town Company on June 1, a corps of surveyors was put to work platting the site. About 800 lots were staked and recorded. A drawing was held among those who had paid their five-dollar assessments, after which the remaining lots were thrown open to the public.[44]

The 240 acres of the original Stillwater townsite came from relinquishments of 40 acres each by David Husband, who had been with the Payne Oklahoma Colony at Stillwater in 1884, and Sandford Duncan; an 80-acre relinquishment by Robert Lowry, who had made the run on horseback from the head of Cow Creek after coming down from Arkansas City in a wagon; and a controversial 80 acres, which was claimed by Garnett Burks, a member of the townsite locating committee who had staked the previously-unclaimed land as a member of the committee. Burks filed a personal claim to the land. But on March 14, 1891, Secretary Noble ruled that Burks had not made his claim in good faith, and it was cancelled.

At noon on April 22, Charles W. Blakeslee, agent for the Santa Fe at Alfred station, and C. E. Minor, night telegraph operator, climbed atop the water tank at Alfred and waited for the great race to begin seven miles to the north. From their perch they could see the boxcar station house, a small station house where section boss Al Seeley lived, the stockyards, and a small section house where owner Jim Bryant and his wife operated Hotel Alfred. Section hands and passers-through were fed meals there by Mrs. Bryant.[45]

Soon after the noon hour the men on the water tank began to discern a cloud of dust to the north. Presently they could make out the moving forms of horsemen and white-topped wagons. At about 12:30 they spotted five horsemen riding at a full gallop ahead of the others. In the lead was Zack Mulhall, frontier personality who had taken advantage of his position as Assistant Live Stock Agent for the Santa Fe to build up a sizeable cattle operation for himself at Alfred before the opening.

Mulhall filed on a quarter section close to the Santa Fe depot where he had already constructed a headquarters dugout. Another cattleman named Sam Matthews, who had a herd of Texas longhorns at the stockyards, also filed nearby. Not far behind these five men were Jim Bryant and Al Seeley, who also drove their stakes on tracts of their choosing. Presently Mulhall's chuck wagon rattled up loaded with tents, supplies, and equipment for the new settlers.

On the heels of the horseback riders came the first train from Arkansas City, bulging with humanity. After a brief stop it moved on southward, followed by the frantic wagons, riders, and pedestrians. During the afternoon at Alfred, men came to open tent stores and build shanties.

177

On May 8, 1889, a townsite was organized under the name of Alfred, and a mayor and city council were chosen. The original townsite encompassed 240 acres along Beaver Creek, but when the plan was contested a compromise was made to accept two 40-acre relinquishments from C. P. Lannon and Sam Matthews. The name of the town was changed from Alfred to Mulhall in June 1890.[46]

The town of Perkins came into existence in 1890, but settlement efforts were made as early as May 8, 1889. Located on the north bank of the Cimarron River at Section 4, T18N, R3E, it was originally filed as a forty-acre townsite application under the name of "Cimarron" (not to be confused with another townsite by the name of "Cimarron City" six miles to the east or with the present Cimarron City) and again in December 1889 under the name of "Italy." Its first town election was held on August 20, 1889.[47]

Situated southeast of Fort Reno between the North Canadian and South Canadian, the townsite of Union City developed out of settlement of the area by well-to-do farmers from the Caddo and Chickasaw country, men who had previously leased their farming lands from the Indian owners. The townsite comprised 160 acres, and its development potential was enhanced considerably when the Rock Island Railroad surveyed a line through the new settlement.[48]

The townsite of Orlando, the closest rail station to the north line of Oklahoma, was originally developed on land belonging to claimant J. M. Syke, who gave his consent to the use of eighty acres (east half of SE ¼, Section 2, T19N, R2W). The area was platted, lots were sold, and a lumberyard and lodging house were begun. Application was made for a post office permit, and the Santa Fe put in a switch there. Townsite leaders petitioned for a depot.

Syke, however, had a change of heart after consulting with an attorney, deciding that the townsite would look speculative and might well damage his homesteading rights. He tried to back out of the offer he had made, but his consent had been given in front of witnesses.[49]

The town of Crescent, located west of Guthrie, was founded by a group of men who were mostly from Iowa and who had formed the Crescent Townsite Company. Prior to the opening, the promoters had had a representative at work on each train for a few miles prior to reaching Arkansas City, attempting to interest rushees in their town venture. A meeting was held in the interest of the townsite at Arkansas City; speeches were made in the public square, but nothing tangible was accomplished.[50]

The townsite was settled as planned during the run, and in early July the mayor of Crescent City was in Guthrie saying that city authorities were making good progress. Bridges and culverts were being put in, and the road running from Guthrie to Kingfisher through Crescent was being improved. He reported, too, that one of its streets was named "Kicking Bird" in honor of Milt Reynolds.[51]

In June 1889 a townsite group led by Kansas Senator F. E. Gillett of Kingman, Kansas, met at the site of the Hennessey Massacre on the Caldwell-Fort Reno Trail and held a town organization meeting. Gillett was elected temporary chairman while J. H. Bross was chosen as the first mayor of the new town of Hennessey (Section 34, T19N, R7W).[52]

With depot grounds of the Rock Island having been laid out and the telegraph line already completed, the new officials and "several business men from eastern points" made speeches regarding the beauty of the location and its promising future.[53] Construction of the city's first hotel was soon under way.

CHAPTER XV
The "Bubble Towns"

> *While the Run of 1889 saw many successful city foundings, there were those destined to fail—the "bubble towns" of Oklahoma, one newspaperman termed them.* Kingfisher New World, *May 25, 1889.*

ALMOST without exception, the life or death of a new community was related to the presence of a railroad line. In a frontier world where horseback and wagon transportation were the only alternatives to serve commerce and travel, the railroad was a vital element to the life and advancement of any new community, a virtual requirement for the recruitment of new citizenry.

Locations along the already established Santa Fe line offered the best chances for city success, but for other sites it was purely speculative as to whether or not a rail line would eventually come their way. The Rock Island, already extended into the Cherokee Outlet as far as Pond Creek and having made its survey southward across the Oklahoma country, loomed as a potential life-giver to new towns along its course. But this was far from certain, as one foundling city discovered when it refused to put up the incentive capital demanded by the railroad.

Reno City had been founded with great hopes and expectation. Located on the north bank of the North Canadian two miles east of Darlington, it had been organized, it was said, by the consolidation of at least ten powerful town companies.¹ The resulting townsite merger produced a 130-man town company, which surveyed off some 1,200 lots on a 160-acre tract; and on May 6, 1889, a drawing was held for the lots. The first four men to pitch a tent on the grounds of the new city were from Wellington, Kansas.

That same afternoon of May 6, an election of city officials was held, with Colonel J. DuBois, a former locating engineer for the Frisco Railroad, being chosen as mayor. The councilmen who were chosen reflected the origins of various town companies: Wichita, Wellington, Caldwell, Anthony, Kiowa, and Harper, all in Kansas.³ Efforts had been made to interest some of the Fort Reno army officers as well as traders and others from Darlington. Frontiersman and deputy U.S. marshal Jack Stilwell was appointed as city marshal.⁴

One of the principal reasons that the site for Reno City had been chosen was the fact that the Rock Island Railroad survey ran through it. The city fathers, thinking that the railroad would not deviate from its survey, refused to donate the sum requested by the road. As a result, the Rock Island changed the course of its line and went to El Reno instead. This move brought about the ultimate failure of Reno City and boosted the progress of El Reno.⁵

The old soldiers colony of Wichita headed by Dr. Minick reached the preselected site on the north bank of the North Canadian (west half of Section 6, T12N, R5W) and promptly began the development of a townsite, which was first named "Veteran City" but later renamed "Frisco."⁶ Some 200 to 300 colony settlers took up claims on farms surrounding the townsite and began breaking the soil and building homes.

The town was organized on May 1, 1889, with J. T. Godfrey being elected mayor. In July 1889, the town made its mark in Oklahoma history by serving as the site for the "Frisco Convention," called as a countermove to the early effort by Guthrie to become the capital and dominant political force in the new country. However, when the Choctaw Railroad built up the south side of the North Canadian rather than along the north side, Frisco was finished as a townsite.⁷

A short time after the run a small settlement called Harrison was established four miles east of Frisco in the North Canadian valley (NW ¼, Section 4, T12N, R7W). A hotel building was erected there, but the Frisco site dominated, and the hotel was eventually moved to Frisco.⁸

Another "bubble town" of this area was that of Rock Island, which was located about equidistant between Reno City and Kingfisher (Section 10 and west half Section 11, T14N, R7W). Perhaps more as a pitch to lure settlers and investors, it was reported in early June that several buildings were up at the townsite and wells had been dug. However, the settlement project, initiated by N. Campbell, D. C. Bothel, M. Licee, and W. M. Spice, gained little support and soon faded away, remaining for a time only as a country store.⁹

William M. Mathewson, the original "Buffalo Bill" who had years before helped Jesse Chisholm blaze the Chisholm Cattle Trail and who was now president of a Wichita bank, headed a Kansas combine to found a settlement at the center point between Guthrie-Fort Reno and Kingfisher-Oklahoma City (NE ¼, Section 25, T14N, R6W). Situated at the headwaters of Cottonwood and Deer creeks where the old Abilene Cattle Trail crossed, "Mathewson" looked to the potential of being a junction of railroads connecting the four cities—the Choctaw Railroad having already surveyed its route from Oklahoma City to Kingfisher and the Santa Fe Railroad having a line from Guthrie to Reno City in planning stage.¹⁰ Neither of these roads came into being, however, and neither did Mathewson City as a community.

A town company formed by a group of Guthrie business men founded Cimarron City on the north bank of the Cimarron River twenty miles northeast of Guthrie (Section 1, T17N, R1E). They billed the location as the site of "Payne's Paradise Prairie," which Payne had supposedly chosen as his ideal city, though there is no evidence that Payne ever even camped near there. The Guthrie men saw

The terrain near the Cimarron River, located in the western reaches of the Unassigned Lands, was reached by legal land seekers only minutes after the opening signal (Harper's Weekly).

---

the location as a potential wholesale distributing hub for satellite cities of the area. The site, however, failed to fulfill its destiny and soon disappeared, though the name of "Cimarron City" would reappear in other places.[11]

The town of Sheridan was established by settlers who were mostly from Kansas and Missouri and it was named in honor of General Phil Sheridan—reflecting the Civil War service of some of its founders. Located on a quarter section of land eleven miles east and a half mile north of Hennessey (the quarter section was at the junction of Sections 14, 25, 22 and 23, T19N, R5W), the small community eventually succumbed to the dominance of nearby Marshall when the latter became a railroad stop. George Rainey, an early Oklahoma writer and historian, was postmaster and a merchant at Sheridan for a time.[12]

When Harry Hill opened his stage line from Guthrie to

Kingfisher, it became necessary to establish a midway relay station. Located two miles south of the Cimarron (Section 1, T15N, R5W), the site for a time promised to benefit from the projected line of the Frisco Railroad westward from Sapulpa. The Santa Fe took over the route, breeding renewed hope for a rail line that would make the location prosper.

Accordingly, a townsite was organized by the Downs Townsite Company, and a small business community sprang into existence. At one time Downs could boast two grocery stores, two blacksmith shops, a drugstore, a hotel, a saloon, a hardware store, and a harness shop in addition to two churches and a school. But again, the railroad did not come, and Downs was doomed for extinction.[13]

During the year 1879 a large number of blacks had migrated from the southern states to the north and west, many settling in Topeka where they found little opportunity for work or livelihood. Kansas blacks had long been interested in the Oklahoma movement, hopeful that it would offer new opportunity but overwhelmed and intimidated to a degree by the intense activism of the white boomers.

During the run of April 22 some black families secured claims north of the Cimarron above Kingfisher, east of Red Fork (later Dover). Two black towns eventually resulted from this, one at Red Fork, called Red Wing (Section 2, T17N, R7W), and another ten miles east on the north side of the Cimarron (NE ¼, Section 13, T17N, R6W). Still another group of blacks located in the vicinity of the bubble town of Wanamaker north of Lincoln (Section 25, T18N, R6W).[14]

Marion Blair, formerly of Caldwell and active in the founding of Hennessey, saw the potential of developing what was billed as "the first African town ever started in a civilized country" and began recruiting a colony of black people at Topeka. He was assisted in his enterprise by Reverend Swartz and Reverend H. H. Martin, who looked to building an academy at one of the locations with $3,000 from the American Freedmen's Fund.[15]

The land along the Cimarron was sandy black-jack country and not the most desirable for farming. It was hoped the homesteaders would be able to survive by selling wild game (deer, turkey, and wild hogs which had been abandoned in the area earlier by ranchers), fence posts, and fire wood. The colony at Lincoln was subdivided into small farms, many not exceeding forty acres, and soon an industrious program of church, school, and civic development was underway.[16] On July 13, D. B. Garrett and John Goring represented the Lincoln and Red Wing communities at the Frisco Convention called to counteract Guthrie's influence in forming a territorial government.[17]

The white population of Kingfisher looked with disdain on the growing community of blacks and petitioned a man named Lewis to circulate a letter among the black community of Topeka to discourage them from investing money or joining the Lincoln enterprise. But Blair guaranteed purchasers a good title to their own land, and a colony of 200 was soon reported to be 1,000 or more.[18]

But by August 1889 the influx of black population into Kingfisher indicated that the black settlers, as with a great many whites, found the growing much too far advanced and the land much too difficult to subsist upon that first year.[19]

Dr. Minick had not remained with his colony on the North Canadian for long, having other ambitions at heart. Soon after the run he platted a townsite a few miles north of Edmond on the Santa Fe line (Section 36, T16N, R3W). It also was to be called "Harrison." The townsite contained an ambitious ninety-six blocks and covered an entire section at what Minick believed would be the junction of the Santa Fe and Frisco railroads.[20] The townsite, however, was on a section of land reserved for school use, which Minick attempted to contend was the very place for towns to be located. The government strongly disagreed, and Inspector J. A. Pickler visited the site in early May.

Pickler found the section staked off into lots, a tent standing, and a large signboard facing the railroad with the townsite name in large letters. Minick offered Pickler a choice lot if he would put in a store. Pickler declined.[21]

It was these few communities which "bubbled up" from the Run of 1889 but failed to survive. By 1895 there were nearly fifty others which had come into existence but which since faded away to become ghost towns or forgotten cemetery plots. Some of these lost communities were Ball, Berry, Beulah, Bowman, Buckhead, Canadian (or Virginia), Case, Cedar, Chaddick, Clarkson, Clayton, Columbia, Conception, Council Grove, Denver, Dodsworth, Eda, Franklin, Hall, Hartsell, Herron, Hico, Ingalls, Lakeview, Lawrie, Liberty, Lima, Miller, Morena, Myrtle, Omer, Paradise, Quincy, Ralston, Silver, Snyder, Springvale, Standard, Thurston, Tobee, Walker, Wandel, Waterloo, Whisler, Yates, and Zion.[22]

CHAPTER XVI
The Sooner Cases

Innocent men were sworn into the penitentiary or sworn out of their lands or lots. Sturm's Oklahoma Magazine, *April 1929.*

CHALLENGES over who had entered Oklahoma legally and who had done so illegally, as well as government-initiated cases of perjury against those believed to have given false testimony under oath in the sooner cases, were destined to fill the courts for years to come. There were thousands of such cases, the majority of them being decided by the Register of Deeds and the Receiver of Moneys in the local land office at Guthrie, Kingfisher, and, after a land office was established there in 1890, at Oklahoma City. From the local land office, there was appeal to the General Land Office in Washington, D.C., and then to the Secretary of the Interior, whose decision was final. Some cases were heard by the U.S. district courts, the Oklahoma Supreme Court, and the U.S. Supreme Court. Quite often a case would drag on for several years in appeal, sometimes being reversed and counterreversed while the contestants continued to reside on a given tract with bitter animosity toward one another, both or all continuing to make improvements.

Many an honest homesteader had waited until noon on April 22 to enter, rode his horse or drove his wagon furiously to reach a claim of his choice, and then found that another, who was afoot or whose horse showed no signs of exertion, was already there.[1] Often the homesteader, either to avoid conflict or fearing to risk the chances of losing out altogether, would hurry on to another piece of land. But many chose to stick it out, hold out for their rights, and trust that the law would ultimately reward their honest efforts over the connivance of the other.[2] This was especially true where the tract was of high value, such as at Oklahoma City where some quarter sections had as many as ten or a dozen claimants.

Further complicating the situation was the fact that the initial legislation and the President's proclamation were both untested and uninterpreted in court. This meant that each individual had to make his own private interpretation of what was legal and what was not legal and could only guess as to what the courts would ultimately rule. It was very easy to let aspiration temper judgment, and many people made hopeful interpretations of the letter of the law.

It was not altogether certain whether twelve o'clock high noon meant standard time or sun time, whether the Santa Fe Railroad right-of-way through Oklahoma constituted a point exclusive to the Oklahoma country or whether the run proclamation meant only that a man could not lay claim to the land before noon but that he could legally be near or upon it before noon. The words "enter upon and occupy" in the settlement act were subject to the contention that a visit to or even entry upon the land before noon did not disqualify the settler.[3]

There were hundreds of cases where several people stopped on the same quarter of land, all being separated by trees or hills, and no one knew who was there first. Contests could be made on four grounds: (1) when the other claimant or claimants were sooners; (2) when a previous settlement had been made under the Homestead Act by a contestant; (3) when the homestead entry had been made for pure speculation and not in "good faith" as a homesteader; and (4) when the entryman had fraudulently transferred his land to his wife and children in order to claim another 160 acres of land.[4]

When a notice of contest had been filed at the land office, witnesses were called before the Register and the Receiver, sworn in, and cross-examined with a recorder taking down the testimony. The land office officials would examine the evidence and render a decision. Dissatisfied parties would then appeal to the Land Office in Washington. This procedure caused a great demand for legal services. Since few settlers had much money, the legal fees were often paid for with a portion of the land in question. As a result, lawyers ended up with much of the land rewards of the Run of 1889. The lawyer for Frank Gault, for instance, was said to have received half of the contested claim in present downtown Oklahoma City.[5]

The greatest trouble by far came from those rushees who surreptitiously or blatantly cheated in the run and then lied under oath concerning the matter. These men, and some women, were often supported by others who either joined in with them by formal pact or whose testimony was given for friendship, kinship, fear, money, or other reward. The committing of perjury by witnesses in the land cases on a wholesale level was caused in part by the incorrect belief, as was encouraged by some lawyers, that lying to an official of the local land offices under oath did not constitute perjury.[6]

> A few, and it is a very few at that, regarded their oaths too solemn for them to swear falsely for a paltry quarter section of land, but chose to stand or fall on their legal rights, if they had any. The great majority, however, determined to swear themselves from the line at any cost, and the audacity with which they sought to carry out their plans is such as to make a professional stand aghast.[7]

W. F. Harn, who was assigned as special prosecutor of the sooner cases in the fall of 1890 and arrived at Oklahoma City in January 1891, later listed several secret organizations which were conceived after the run for the express purpose of banding illegal settlers together to protect their claims against challenge. These groups held secret meetings, took blood oaths, arranged for testimony in given cases, and even trained and drilled witnesses for courtroom appearances. Often a legal claimant was overwhelmed by an array of witnesses which the organization introduced, or on other occasions the legal occupant was intimidated and frightened away.[8]

Prosecutor Harn pointed to the fact that prior to the run the Indian Territory had been a haven for outlaws and hard men—some thirty-eight U.S. marshals had been killed in the Chickasaw Nation in two years, he said—and many of these adventurers and criminals were among those who entered Oklahoma illegally. Not a few of these desperate men, Harn claimed, later served prison terms on other counts or "died with their boots on" in gun shootouts.[9] Credit must be given to most of the old Couch boomers, however, who simply stood on their contention of prior rights and refused to perjure themselves in protection of their claims to valuable homesteads.

Harn claimed further that at one time during the sooner trials, most of which were fought with great desperation and passion, a conspiracy to dynamite the courthouse was uncovered, the purpose being to kill Judge John G. Clark, U.S. Attorney Horace Speed, and Harn. Later a bomb was thrown under Harn's house, but the fuse was put out when the bomb struck some bushes. On another occasion, a marshal grabbed the hand of a relative of a perjurer as he was about to stab Harn in the back as he was leaving the courtroom.[10]

One of the more active of the secret sooner groups was the Crutcho Organization, composed of members who lived along the rich-soiled Crutcho Creek. A prominent organizer and president of the group was W. A. Arnold, the old Union soldier with whom Lieutenant Carson had scuffled while removing him during the preceding March.[11] This organization's charter declared it to be for the protection of members against claim jumpers, but in reality it was an instrument to support their own illegal sooner claims. One section of the Crutcho Organization by-laws stated on implied threat that "Any person found guilty of violating any of the rules of this organization or of carrying news to the enemy shall be dealt with according to a two-thirds vote of the members present."[12]

It was proven that many members of the group had hidden out in the brush along Soldier and Crutcho creeks prior to the run, and some like Arnold were known to have been inside Oklahoma long before April 22.

Another such conclave was the Lightning Creek Combination, a group comprised of men who had settled along that North Canadian tributary below Oklahoma City. On Sunday evening preceding the opening, a group of men entered the Oklahoma lands from Downing's Ford on the South Canadian. They traveled northward until they reached the watershed divide between the North and the South Canadian rivers, some stopping there and others traveling on to the North Canadian near Oklahoma station. At about noon the latter group returned south to the claims they had picked out much earlier along Lightning Creek.[13]

After the run, these men met to form an organization for the purpose of swearing for one another in the land cases. Altogether they held three such meetings at homes of members and agreed to testify for one another that they had entered at noon on April 22 from Barrow's Crossing. This they did in several sooner cases. However, a number of witnesses told of having seen the men inside the Oklahoma lands on Sunday evening and Monday morning.

John M. Murphy and George W. Fisher of the Lightning Creek Combination were arrested and placed on trial for perjury. During the trial, Perry Fuller, another member who with four others of his family had been among the group that came in early from Downing's Ford, testified for the government and gave a complete description of the group's movements. Murphy and Fisher were both found guilty of perjury and sentenced to four years at hard labor.[14]

Still another band of men who came in on Sunday evening from the South Canadian included former Oklahoma station hotel keeper George W. Gibson. He was accompanied by J. C. Adams, who among others would contest the claim of W. L. Couch. Gibson drove his mule team and wagon across the river a little before sundown on the twenty-first. After eating supper, Gibson and the others started on toward the divide, some walking and some riding in Gibson's wagon. At the divide the party separated, Gibson and Adams heading for Oklahoma station and the others going west to the mouth of Mustang Creek with Mrs. Gibson and the wagon. Gibson later became a government witness and testified in cases involving the Lightning Creek perjurers and the Adams-Couch contest.[15]

Another important sooner group was the Bohemian outfit which had crossed early on the morning of the twenty-second at the Long-O Crossing. These were members of a dozen or so Bohemian families from Omaha, Nebraska. They had laid their plans so that one group would visit Oklahoma well ahead of time and select a claim for each member. The other half would enter from the South Canadian above Purcell so they could prove they had made the run legitimately. Some of those of the first group had been arrested and removed by Fort Reno troops sweeping the North Canadian before the run.[16]

The second group, led by Captain Anton Caha, had taken their position on the sandbar at the Long-O Crossing on Saturday preceding the opening. Witnesses would later testify how early on the morning of April 22, the Bohemians had helped to pull a wagon from the south bank to the sandbar with a long rope and how soon after, at around eight, the Bohemians had crossed to the north bank and proceeded inland. Other witnesses told of watching the group as they drove across the open country at the divide between the North and South Canadians.[17]

Still others told of hearing Caha make his speech saying how he understood the settlement law from reading the proclamation and the newspapers and that he had been advised by General Weaver and by the governor of Nebraska that the law intended only that a settler not go onto his claim until noon. It was perfectly legal, he argued, to enter Oklahoma and be near the claim prior to the twelve o'clock deadline. Later Caha and the others would insist in unison that they had not crossed the river early but had instead moved upriver on the sandbar that morning.[18]

The Bohemians were among the first to be arrested for soonerism. As early as June 9, 1889, they were jailed and tried before U.S. Commissioner E. V. Sumner at Oklahoma City. General Weaver represented the defendants.[19]

In this hearing and in others at Kingfisher and Guthrie, the Bohemians were found to be sooners and were disqualified from their homestead claims along Mustang Creek. The group was charged with perjury in July 1891, the case being tried in Wichita, Kansas, before a Kansas jury. Verdicts of guilty were rendered for terms of a year and a day to four years. Anton Caha's case was eventually heard by the U.S. Supreme Court which upheld the decision of the U.S. district court at Wichita.[20]

While the Crutcho, Lightning Creek, and Bohemian groups were the most notorious of the sooner conclaves, other such combinations existed. Harn listed one on the South Canadian, another between Yukon and El Reno, numerous small groups in choice rich valleys inside Oklahoma, and a number of exclusive sets surrounding Oklahoma City.[21]

While the term "sooner" had rapidly become accepted to describe those who had entered Oklahoma early, it was not until October 1, 1890, that Secretary of the Interior John W. Noble handed down a decision in the *Townsite of Kingfisher vs. John H. Wood and William Fossett* case that "soonerism" was legally defined. Arguing that the entry law was intended as a strong obstacle to the principle of forcible intrusion as attempted by the boomers, the Secretary contended that it sought to prohibit *anyone* from entering the Oklahoma lands, whether with permit or without it, prior to the legal time. Such advantage, he argued, destroyed the claim of those attempting to gain it.[22]

With the ruling in this landmark case, many of those who had been openly admitting their prior entry now began to say differently and seek out others to testify in their behalf. The "legal sooners" now attempted to work out compromises with other claimants, but in most cases their claims were demolished.

Another precedent-setting decision was rendered in the *Alexander Smith vs. Eddy B. Townsend* case, centering on the issue of Smith's making the run from the railroad right-of-way. Initially the land officers Dille and Barnes ruled on July 29, 1890, that Smith was a legally qualified homesteader and was entitled to the Edmond claim. But on October 30, the assistant commissioner of the General Land Office reversed the Guthrie decision and disqualified Smith. This action was sustained on February 29, 1891, by Secretary of the Interior Noble.[23]

The ruling was a bombshell against the Couch group of old boomers and others who had, particularly at Oklahoma station, made the run from the Santa Fe right-of-way. It virtually wiped out their last contention of legal claim to the homesteads they were contesting with others. Thus the two cases—*Kingfisher vs. Wood-Fossett* and the *Smith-Townsend*—settled a great body of controversy in two vital areas, leading to victory for the legal-time rushee in the majority of cases.

Still, there were those contests in which the soonerism of occupants could not be proven in court, and the history of the Run of 1889 must record the probability that a good number of people entered early and got away with it. Further, there were some questionable decisions rendered which seem to defy justice and leave us to wonder whether or not the law was administered fairly in all instances. This was particularly true at Oklahoma City where a long series of court battles revealed much about the land claims and how they had been made.

CHAPTER XVII
The Land Fights at Oklahoma City

> *In most cases the rightful claimant in the end prevailed, notwithstanding repeated defeats in civil suits. And yet there are instances where valuable claims were held by "sooners," and all efforts to dislodge them proved to no avail. The suspected persons were smart enough to keep their matters to themselves but as one or more would part with his interest he would often confide the true facts to a friend.* Luther B. Hill, History of Oklahoma.

THE old boomers led by W. L. Couch had chosen Oklahoma station as their place of destiny, their choice of locations in the promised lands of Oklahoma. It was they who had first surveyed and staked homesteads there in defiance of the government, who had secured the pretense of employment with the railroad inside Oklahoma, and who had been among the very first upon the land on April 22. Further, through connections with the marshals and land office officials, the Couch boomers were placed at the head òf the line at Guthrie on April 23. But the old boomers were by no means the only ones who had their eye on the great potential of the Oklahoma station land, nor were they the only early ones there.

As titular head of the boomers and as a director of the Seminole Town and Improvement Company, W. L. Couch had first choice, and he claimed the tract due west of the Seminole Company townsite area. Since the quarter due east of the depot had been set off as a military reservation, Couch's tract had enormous potential for future townsite expansion. But not even the boomer leader would escape

195

Oklahoma City, within days after the opening, was racked with charges of "soonerism" and alleged lot jumping (Harper's Weekly).

---

challenge. At the fore of that challenge was the man who had entered early with Gibson, J. C. Adams.

Adams had been one of the men hanging around Oklahoma station before the run, and evidence indicates that he had already built a dugout on the tract before he made the token gesture of going to the South Canadian line shortly before April 22. From Gibson's testimony and that of others who saw him a few minutes before noon on the claim, it is apparent that Adams simply hid out during the forenoon of the day. One man testified that he saw Adams come out of his dugout at about eleven o'clock on the morning of April 22, waving a flag and motioning for a woman sooner to keep off his quarter section.[1]

There were still others challenging for the claim. Dr. Robert W. Higgins, who had made the mistake of driving into Oklahoma for a short ways before making the run from the east line with a wagon and team, would later file an affidavit of contest against Couch and Adams. This was followed by a similar action against all three by John M. Dawson. The tract was also sought by a townsite group who wished to establish West Oklahoma City on it. In fact, Adams was at one time known as the mayor of West Oklahoma City, even as Couch was mayor of Oklahoma City proper.[2]

A bitter feud erupted between Couch and Adams, and both men became involved in the violent quarrels of the new settlement on the North Canadian. Finally in April 1890, Adams shot Couch in the knee, the wound resulting in gangrene and the death of the boomer head. Adams was arrested and sent to prison, but the land case dragged on in the courts until August 1892 when the Oklahoma Land Office awarded the homestead to Dawson, finding the other three guilty of soonerism in one form or another. This decision was upheld by the Commissioner of the General Land Office in April 1893.[3]

Another key tract was that just north of the military reservation, and its principal claimant was William J. McClure. As owner and operator of the 7-C Ranch on the east line of Oklahoma, McClure knew the country well. His cattle grazed into the area known as the 7-C Flats just west of the east line, and he had on many occasions visited Oklahoma station during its two years of prior existence. As a rancher he appreciated horses and loved a good race. Thus it was not out of character for him to conceive the idea of establishing a horse relay inside Oklahoma for the purpose of capturing the valuable land around Oklahoma station ahead of others.

McClure was joined in his plan by three other men: Frank Cook, Vestal Cook, and C. H. Kingsbury, each of the four men putting up fifty dollars to pay two of McClure's cowboys to set up relay stations inside Oklahoma. The stations were to be on the Shawneetown Road, one of them five miles from the east border and the other ten miles along the fifteen mile road which swung northwestward with the sweeping bend of the North Canadian River, crossing it at the north and continuing southwesterly along the river to Oklahoma station.[4]

By his testimony, McClure left the line at noon riding at top speed and changing horses twice. He arrived on his claim at Oklahoma station shortly before one o'clock, followed closely by the other riders.[5] McClure's quarter section (NW ¼, Section 34, T12N, R3W) was the same as that already staked by deputy U.S. marshal J. B. Koonce, who did not file.

The tract was also claimed by John A. Meyers, who was later convicted of perjury in connection with his entry and was sentenced to five years in the penitentiary.[6] Though McClure was upheld at the local land office, his entry was eventually cancelled through contest in the General Land Office on February 28, 1891, and the tract was entered upon the same day by George W. Massey.[7]

Another crucial quarter section was that due north of the Santa Fe depot quarter, the one upon which Samuel Crocker had settled. The south half of this tract would be filed upon by Louis O. Dick for the Townsite of Oklahoma City. Eugene and Randall Fuller, both sooners, also staked the quarter section; but the principal contestee was Frank M. Gault. Gault, a nephew of William McClure, had been invited to join McClure's horse relay venture but did not. Instead, according to his testimony, he and several cowboy friends lined up with the rest of the crowd at the east line near the 7-C Ranch. They started, Gault claimed, at noon time by his own watch with the rest of the crowd.

Gault said that he rode a dark bay horse and that the route he and his companions took was directly southwestward toward Oklahoma station. His friend, J. W. Brusha, was about 400 yards behind him and the others behind Brusha.[8]

Gault swore that soon after arriving upon his tract, he borrowed a spade and a flag from a man, dug a hole for the beginning of a well, and raised the flag to mark his claim. Though a number of other witnesses testified to having

Oklahoma City and the intersection of Main and Broadway three years after the land run. Many claim disputes still were still being fought bitterly in the courts at that time (Harper's Weekly).

---

seen Gault, Brusha, and the others on Soldier Creek on the forenoon of April 22, the land office officials ruled that this testimony was not enough to outweigh the testimony of the large group of witnesses supplied by Gault.

Yet historians are forced to consider the affidavits of Pleasant Gilbert and Charles F. Johnson, members of Gault's party who later recanted their testimony and supported the stories of Thomas Moss and John W. Booth, all of whom claimed that Gault and his group were indeed at a McClure relay post on Soldier Creek prior to noon, that they were scattered by a posse of soldiers early on the morning of April 22, but later regrouped at Soldier Creek and made their run from there.[9]

Both Gault and Brusha were upheld by the courts, while Crocker and the Fullers were declared to have no legitimate claim. Gault, however, was awarded only the north eighty acres of the tract, the south half being entered upon as a townsite, Gault relinquishing his claim to it for a consideration of $5,000.[10] It can only be hoped that justice was served in the cases of Gault and Brusha. Gault went on to become an early mayor of Oklahoma City, a member of the school board, and a representative to the Territorial Legislature.

Brusha was a claimant on the quarter immediately west of the Gault claim, the one upon which deputy marshal Asa Jones had settled (NW ¼, Section 33, T12N, R3W). Brusha had arrived on the heels of Gault, dug a hole a couple of feet wide and two or three feet deep, piled up the dirt, and planted a flag on the top of the pile. His story of having left the east line was corroborated by Gault and several others of the party. But, as with Gault, there were those who swore otherwise. T. C. Reynolds said he saw Brusha on Sunday, April 21, at 2 p.m. on Soldier Creek seven or eight miles inside Oklahoma. G. Turner testified that he was at Crutcho Flat on the morning of April 22 and saw Brusha on Soldier Creek about a quarter of a mile from its mouth. Gault was with him.[11]

Other contestants for the tract were W. F. Lamb, Huger Wilkinson, Peter Ismet, and M. L. Lockwood. All of these men were judged to be sooners by the courts. Lockwood had been a member of the surveying crew of the Choctaw Coal & Railway Company and made his settlement immediately after noon near where he was working. Wilkinson's watch, the court held, had been fast, and he had run from the right-of-way. Though the Department of the Interior awarded the tract to Brusha in November 1893, deputy marshal Jones—who in July 1889 was shot in the face by Wilkinson during an argument over the claim—kept the case in court on appeal until 1895 when his entry was cancelled and Brusha was awarded the land.[12]

Directly at noon on April 22 at least two men stepped off the Santa Fe right-of-way to the west onto a tract a mile north of the station (SE ¼, Section 28, T12N, R3W). One of these was Daniel J. Odell, an old boomer who had once hand-fought with troops on this spot in 1884; the other was a Santa Fe section hand named Willis Kesler. Within the hour these men were joined by several others, one of them being Frank Cook, who had ridden with McClure's horse relay.

It was Odell who was in line at the Guthrie Land Office on April 23 to file Entry No. 12 for the tract, evidently with the assistance of the deputy marshals there. Other contestants for the tract were J. L. Brown, M. J. Bixler, and E. W. Bourn. On May 21 Kesler initiated a contest against Odell, charging that Odell and Crocker had pretended to be deputy U.S. marshals in an attempt to scare him off but that he had made a settlement prior to Odell's.

This complicated case was referred by the Guthrie Land Office to the General Land Office for a ruling. Commissioner Lewis A. Greff replied with a recommendation for continuance. It took until July 1894 before the issue was finally decided in favor of Bourn. Odell took the matter to the Supreme Court of Oklahoma Territory, only to lose there also.[13]

Vestal Cook, also a horse-relay member and a brother of Frank Cook, had settled on the tract just across the railroad tracks to the east, the quarter section which Carley Blanchard and deputy marshal Ewers White had staked (SW ¼, Section 27, T12N, R3W). White filed Entry No. 6 at the Guthrie Land Office on the quarter section on the morning of April 23.

Though Cook had been seen at the 7-C point on the line a short time before the start, no one could say they had seen him at the time of the start itself. The Guthrie Land Office ruled in favor of White and rejected the challenges of Blanchard and Cook. The claims of all three men were denied on appeal in July 1891. Strangely, though it ruled favorably in regards to relayist McClure, the local officials decided that Cook "by his servants, agents and stock entered and occupied the said land unlawfully."[14] Regarding White, the decision noted: "White was in the territory on special duty, as he had a right to be, but it is held to be bad policy to allow him to take advantage of his position to gain a preference over those who did not possess such opportunities. Not only this, but he was given preference in the line at the land office which was unjust to the others and contrary to the spirit of the law."[15] White relinquished the land on November 29, 1890, in favor of Samuel Murphy.

The Oklahoma City Post Office, July 4, 1890. While land seekers fought court battles over claims, the future state capital quickly developed into a town of brick and stone structures (Harper's Weekly).

    Almira C. Robb (nee Wilkerson) and Conradina Sorenson, a twenty-three-year-old girl who knew little English, worked as domestic servants in the home of quartermaster agent Sommers at Oklahoma station. At twelve o'clock noon on April 22 the two women left the Sommers residence and located upon tracts of their choosing. Robb staked the quarter section due east of the Blanchard-Cook-White claim (SE ¼, Section 27, T12N, R3W), while Sorenson chose one just to the southeast of Robb (NW ¼, Section 35, T12N, R3W). A man named Clay Peters also staked the one chosen by Sorenson.
    Robb's quarter section also was staked by Frank H.

Woodruff, John Burton, and Henry Howe. It was Howe who made the homestead entry at Guthrie on April 25. When his application was challenged and testimony taken, it was revealed that Howe had entered into a plan with his son, a photographer, who came to Oklahoma before the legal time, settled on the land, and held it for the father who had arrived on the two o'clock train from Purcell on the day of the run.

Woodruff claimed to have come in from the east line at the 7-C Ranch with his daughter Katie, his brother Luman C., and others at the legal time. But a host of witnesses proved that he was lying, that in fact he had left the 7-C early on the morning of the twenty-second and was, indeed, a sooner. Howe charged that John Burton, a lawyer, had violated privileged conversation in filing his own claim application. After hearing testimony, the court upheld Howe's charge and disqualified Burton.[16]

On June 19, 1891, the Oklahoma City Land Office ruled in favor of Howe and held for dismissal on the contests of Robb, Woodruff, and Burton. Woodruff appealed, but Robb did not. The General Land Office reviewed the case and overturned the Howe ruling, disqualifying him also. But in February 1894 Secretary of the Interior Hoke Smith reversed the General Land Office decision and gave the homestead tract back to Howe.[11]

Sorenson, likewise, lost out, being declared a sooner. Contestant Clay Peters was eventually found guilty of perjury and sentenced to the penitentiary, and Andrew J. Brown was awarded the land.

It seems strange, indeed, that while Robb and Sorenson were declared to be sooners for making the run from the Sommers home, C. F. Sommers himself was ruled by the Oklahoma City Land Office to be a legitimate settler on the tract he had pre-selected (NW ¼, Section 27, T12N, R3W). The decision caused widespread comment among settlers, being the first decision following the Secretary of the Interior's ruling on advantage that was in favor of someone who had been within the territory at the time of the run. Most people did not think it would stand.

But in July 1891, Assistant Commissioner of the General Land Office W. M. Stone concluded that Sommers had been at his post at the military reservation on April 22 and had been obliged to remain there, that it had not been the intent of Congress to require him to go to the border to make the run, and "that he did not seek to take advantage of that fact and the date of his settlement, April 23, 1889, shows conclusively that he did not gain any advantage, for the territory is small and was mostly settled, or filed upon within two or three days, and the land in controversy is only about 15 miles distant from the eastern boundary of Oklahoma."[18]

In this decision favoring Sommers, who was a U.S. commissioner at Oklahoma City for a short time after the run, Stone was not only reversing the argument of advantage made in other instances but he was ignoring the vital distinction between the time of filing on a claim in the land office and that of actual settlement. And the fifteen miles distance to the border which Stone minimized could be translated into at least a forty-five-minute head start.

The claims of contestants Lucian H. Barlow and W. H. Belcher were dismissed on grounds of soonerism. The ruling was further difficult to understand in that Sommers was no more tied to his assigned duties than were the deputy marshals or Oklahoma City postmaster George A. Beidler. Not surprisingly, Sommers's entry was eventually cancelled by the General Land Office on February 4, 1897.[19]

Postmaster George A. Beidler's claim to the tract due west of Sommers (NE ¼, Section 28, T12N, R3W) was challenged in August 1889 by J. F. Winans on the grounds that Beidler was a sooner. The Guthrie Land Office upheld Winans's challenge, concluding that Beidler was not a qualified entryman. Beidler appealed his case to the General Land Office, arguing that he had not previously planned to take up land but had done so when the opportunity presented itself. The postmaster, who had once been an agent for David L. Payne's Oklahoma Colony in Pennsylvania, further contended that Winans was disqualified for having taken a job following the run as a copyist in the Recorder's

Division of the Oklahoma City Land Office. On August 6, 1891, the General Land Office reversed the ruling of the local land office against Beidler, cancelling Winans's entry. The matter went to the Secretary of the Interior, who reversed the General Land Office decision, now cancelling Beidler's entry and reinstating Winans as the legal owner of the tract.[20]

The case of deputy U.S. marshal George Thornton and Edward DeTar, both of whom had been on the premises of Oklahoma station prior to noon on April 22, in contest with the South Oklahoma City townsite group was first heard by the Guthrie Land Office in July 1890. At that time the Guthrie decision in favor of Wood over the townsite of Kingfisher still stood, and using this precedent Dille and Barnes ruled in favor of Thornton. But in September of that year a new hearing was granted, and the case was transferred to the Oklahoma City Land Office for the consideration of Register John H. Burford and Receiver Carroll Delaney.

Now having the decision of Secretary Noble in the *Kingfisher vs. Wood and Fossett* case to use as a guide, the Oklahoma City official concluded that Thornton and DeTar were both disqualified as sooners and ruled in favor of South Oklahoma City.[21]

Calvin A. Calhoun, an ex-Union soldier from St. Joseph, Missouri, had worked as a carpenter for the Santa Fe Railroad in 1888 at Oklahoma station. He and his son returned to the station on April 20, 1889, and remained all night before returning to Arkansas City. Though he said during his hearing at the land office that his trip had no relationship to his claim, he did admit that he had made a map of the exact location of the claim prior to coming to Guthrie on April 22. At Guthrie he filed for 148 acres along the north bank of the North Canadian just east of the railroad tracks—the same tract claimed by T. W. Eckelberger (NW ¼, Section 3, T11N, R3W).

But while Calhoun was at Guthrie, his son reappeared at the Oklahoma station claim, erected a tent, and established residence. On May 27, 1890, James McCormack filed a contest against both Calhoun and Eckelberger, charging both with being sooners. The Oklahoma City Land Office heard the case, and in June 1891 it declared Calhoun and Eckelberger both to be sooners, the old Payne boomer Eckelberger having openly admitted to entering at noon from the railroad right-of-way. The land was awarded to McCormack, and the decision was upheld by the General Land Office.[22]

The quarter section claimed by Meshack H. Couch and by freighter Thomas Wright had still another claimant in Edward Orme. Orme had left his home in Arkansas on April 17 and arrived at Oklahoma station at 2:15 on the afternoon of April 22 to stake his claim. All three men established homes on this select site just southwest of the Santa Fe depot (SW ¼, T11N, R3W), and the townsite of South Oklahoma City attempted to include the land in its application. Other contests for the tract were filed by Frank S. Phelps, Anson Wall, Nathan N. Miller, and Kate E. May. In July 1891 the Oklahoma City Land Office decided that Orme was the only qualified non-sooner in the group and awarded the homestead to him. The General Land Office affirmed that decision in 1892, as did Secretary of the Interior Noble in 1893.[23]

Meshack Q. "Quint" Couch, brother to W. L., was contested for his claim to a prime north bank quarter section (SE ¼, T11N, R3W) by Robert J. Lee, and they were both contested in turn by H. George Kuhlman. Couch was able to convince the court that he had made the run from the east line, though Lee had filed an affidavit alleging that he was on the land before Couch. Lee, who had testified in another case that he had not been inside Oklahoma during the probationary period, was later convicted of perjury. On May 25, 1893, Quint Couch lost the land by a ruling of the General Land Office, the tract being awarded to Kuhlman.[24]

As the common-law wife of David L. Payne, Rachel Anna Haines had contributed much to the cause of the Oklahoma boomer movement. After Payne's death she had become a favorite among the old boomers, who knew her as "Ma Haines." Most of them felt that she justly deserved the homestead she claimed. Located just east of the railroad tracks south of the Oklahoma station depot, it was split by the North Canadian River with 19 acres on the west bank of the winding river and the remaining 144 acres on the east or south bank. After the run she erected a small house on the east part. In August 1889 the citizens of Oklahoma City held a picnic and dance at "Haines Park."[25]

But Mrs. Haines's claim to the land was not to go unchallenged. On July 26, 1889, Belle Caldwell filed an affidavit of contest alleging that Mrs. Haines had entered Oklahoma before noon on April 22 and was thereby a sooner. The local land office ruled against Mrs. Haines, and that decision was upheld by the Secretary of the Interior Hoke Smith in April 1894 and again on review in October 1895. An appeal to the Supreme Court of Oklahoma Territory also failed, being denied in February 1897.[26] Mrs. Haines ultimately left Oklahoma with deeply bitter resentment and returned in poverty to Oregon, from where she had migrated to Kansas before joining Payne at Wichita in 1879 to begin the Oklahoma boomer crusade.

Ambrose F. Jackson, a native of Minnesota, knowing there would be a great demand for lumber in Oklahoma after the opening, had come to Oklahoma station about March 15, 1889, to look into the matter of opening a lumberyard there. Also, he looked about for a claim. Arrested by Lieutenant Carson and told to leave, Jackson returned to Minnesota and ordered a large load of lumber sent to Oklahoma station. Arriving at Arkansas City a few days before the opening, he hired a man to go to Guthrie and file a soldiers' declaratory statement for him on some land near Oklahoma station, saying that just any tract in Sections 27 or 28 would do.

On the evening of April 21, Jackson and three other men in his employ caught a freight train out of Arkansas City thinking that they would reach Purcell just in time to catch the north-bound train back to Oklahoma station, or so Jackson claimed. However, delays on the busy rail line caused the train not to reach the north border of Oklahoma until four o'clock in the morning, and it was noon when the freight reached Edmond station and sidetracked for the north-bound passenger. Jackson and the others continued on with the freight when it departed Edmond at 12:30 p.m. However, when the train came to a prearranged halt at the Deep Fork trestle bridge, Jackson got off along with other passengers, going southwestward along the west side of the Deep Fork exploring for land. Eventually he staked a claim northwest of Oklahoma station (NW ¼, Section 28, T12N, R3W).[27]

In his hearing before the local land office, Jackson blamed the railroad delays for his being inside Oklahoma earlier than noon. However, the land office officials ruled that his presence on the train was voluntary and that he had boarded at his own risk. His application for a homestead was denied, and that decision was upheld by the General Land Office.[28]

Another land decision that seems curious involves a tract of land claimed by a host of claimants, including Thomas Couch, Mary Radebaugh, John Fowler, Virgil Radcliff, and Colonel Parker (he used no first name or initials). Couch had made the run from the Couch camp on the right-of-way, and Mary Radebaugh from her father's hotel, where she had formerly served as a clerk in the post office while her father was postmaster. Colonel Parker had come to Oklahoma station with the Santa Fe Railroad for the purpose of overseeing construction of a freight house and platform at the depot prior to the run. At noon he, too, left the railroad right-of-way and rode north and then west some distance, eventually returning to the station and going on the tract of land immediately west of the W. L. Couch, Adams claim (SE ¼, Section 32, T12N, R3W).

Parker staked the claim at around 2:30 in the afternoon. Fowler and Radcliff, both legitimate settlers, arrived after Parker had made his claim. In ruling on the case at the Oklahoma City Land Office, Register Burford and Receiver Delaney disqualified Couch and Radebaugh as sooners. But, strangely, they ruled that Parker, having reached the land later than the arrival of the first train at Oklahoma station, had not taken advantage of his privilege of being inside Oklahoma. The railroader was awarded the land over Radcliff and Fowler.[29]

An exciting and interesting contest took place over the claim of Otto C. Durland and twenty-one-year-old Katie Woodruff. When Katie's filing was challenged by Durland, she swore that she had entered the Oklahoma lands at noon with her father and uncle and several others. She was supported by a number of witnesses, including Curt Blackburn, who swore he saw Katie ride from the 7-C Ranch at noon.

But in the court hearing, and in the Curt Blackburn perjury hearing that followed, Durland and the state produced an array of witnesses who said otherwise. One man told of seeing the Woodruff group leave the 7-C Ranch at two o'clock on the morning of April 22 and head west. Another testified that he saw them on the Shawneetown Road later that morning, and several people said they saw Katie ride onto the claim in contest (NE ¼, Section 34, T12N, R3W) just after noon.[30]

The U.S. Land Office at Oklahoma City ruled that Durland had presented a preponderance of evidence that Katie had entered early and was on the land long before the time when she or anyone else could have reached it from the east line after twelve noon. Durland won at Oklahoma City and later before the Commissioner of the General Land Office. While an appeal to this decision was pending, a compromise was finally worked out whereby Katie sold her entry to Durland and relinquished her claim.[31]

Blackburn was tried on perjury counts and found guilty. Katie Woodruff's lawyer, Grant Stanley, was also placed on trial for dictating an affidavit to a witness in the case. He was also found guilty, but the verdict was eventually reversed by the Supreme Court of Oklahoma Territory.[32]

Lum Woodruff suffered much the same fate as his brother and niece. His claim to the 160-acre tract due east of the military reservation was challenged by Willie A. Wallace.

When witnesses testified that Woodruff had been inside Oklahoma before March 2 and had made his run on the morning of April 22 well before noon, the quarter section (SE ¼, Section 34, T12N, R3W) was awarded to Wallace.[33]

CHAPTER XVIII
Other Sooner Cases

A fellow over in the west bottoms at Guthrie put up his tent on his claim and went to sleep under it the other night; when he woke up in the morning the tent was gone and he was gazing up at a brilliant sun in a beautiful sky. He swears the ways of the transgressor will be damned hard if he gets his hands on him. The Oklahoma Capital, *May 4, 1889.*

OKLAHOMA City was by no means the only location where the Run of 1889 spawned court contests which laid bare sooner activity that otherwise might never have come to light. Virtually every section of the Oklahoma country had key cases involving important claims or townsites, and it often took years of hearings and appeal before the legal claimant could be determined, if indeed it was. Sometimes the fine lines of legal determination became so entangled that the final result rested solely upon individual interpretation rather than upon a solid precept of law. There seemed to be an endless number of extenuating circumstances which gave shading to the definition of the word "sooner."

One such case involved John G. Chapin, a former Union soldier during the Civil War, who had come to the Oklahoma country in 1882, first as an employee of an Indian trader and later to operate the Red Fork Ranch trading post on the Fort Reno-Caldwell road. In 1888 Chapin received a license to trade with the Cheyenne and Arapaho Indians, and he continued to reside on a tract of land at Red Fork, later Dover, which he laid claim to at the opening in 1889.

On July 2, 1890, Frank A. Taft filed contest against Chapin's entry, but the Kingfisher Land Office supported Chapin and issued him a final certificate for the tract (NE ¼, Section 2, T17N, R7W). Taft appealed to the General Land Office, which rejected Chapin's proof and cancelled his certificate. Chapin in turn appealed to the Secretary of the Interior, who held that Chapin's occupation of the land prior to the run was lawful and that it was no bar to his entry of the land. His ownership was reinstated.[1]

John B. Taylor and his family came from Missouri in 1888 to operate the stage relay station near present Yukon. Taylor was contracted by the stage company to mind the station as well as furnish meals for employees and passengers. On April 22 he went upon a 152-acre tract of land along the North Canadian (NE ¼, Section 4, T12N, R5W) and claimed it. He was challenged in court by Solomon S. Riddle, who charged that Taylor had selected and settled upon the land before the legal time. Assistant Secretary of the Interior George Chandler eventually held that Taylor had been in the Oklahoma district legally and had selected the land after the legal hour. Also, Riddle's challenge had been instituted some months later. Chandler thus upheld Taylor's entry.[2]

Another man named Taylor, John D., filed Entry No. 77 at the Guthrie Land Office for 160 acres of land on Mustang Creek (NE ¼, Section 35, T12N, R3W). William Monroe filed contest charging Taylor with being a sooner, and Francis M. Jordan, a physician for the Santa Fe Railroad, filed contest against them both. The Guthrie Land Office found Taylor disqualified and recommended the cancellation of his entry; but the General Land office reversed that decision when it concluded that a preponderance of testimony showed him to be a qualified entryman. Frank Johnson filed an appeal to the General Land Office decision, alleging it had erred in upholding Taylor. Monroe filed a similar appeal in his own behalf.

Between the time of the action by the General Land Office and consideration of the case by the Secretary of the Interior, Taylor relinquished all rights to the tract. This left Dr.

Jordan as the earliest entryman remaining. Jordan had made visits from his office in Purcell to Oklahoma station on three occasions to tend sick patients, but he was never more than a few steps away from the railroad right-of-way at any time. On April 22 he rode the boomer train to Oklahoma station and from there walked westward the ten miles to the disputed claim. The Secretary of the Interior concluded that Jordan held no special advantage over others and awarded him right of entry to the claim.[3]

Edgar Turner had worked for the Star Mail and Stage Company before going to work as a teamster for C. B. Bickford inside Oklahoma prior to the run. On April 22 he was on the North Canadian some four to six miles east of Fort Reno. At around five o'clock that afternoon he settled on a tract (NE ¼, Section 17, T12N, R3W) and made acts of settlement. He was contested for the land by John P. Cartwright, the case going to the General Land Office. There it was held that Turner was a sooner, the decision later being upheld by the Secretary of the Interior.[4]

Oliver N. Ratts entered the Oklahoma lands from a sandbar along the South Canadian near the upper Barrow's Crossing on April 22. The exact time of his entry was much in question. A number of the crowd at the crossing, estimated at 25-30 by some and 75-100 by others, crossed over to a sandbar in the river, some wading and some by horseback. There was some general talk about the correct time, and nearly everyone's watch differed. One man got up in a wagon and made a talk, suggesting that they use the watch of a man who had just arrived from Purcell and who claimed that his watch had the correct meridian time.

Ratts claimed later that he set his watch by the man and waited on the sandbar until someone fired a gun at noon. Riding one horse and leading another he crossed the channel to the north bank and headed west of due north to the North Canadian, some ten miles distant. There he hitched his horses, disrobed except for his underclothing from the waist down, his hat, and his boots, and crossed the swollen stream by means of fallen trees. As he undressed he glanced at his watch, and it read 12:34 p.m.

Once across the North Canadian he ran about a half a mile to a tract of land (NW ¼, Section 3, T11N, R4W), which he claimed. He remained there about half an hour, then returned to where his clothes were, put them on, and went back to his claim.

Other witnesses testified that it was before noon, probably around 11:20, when Ratts crossed the river. However, Ratts's claim to the disputed land was denied by the General Land Office on the grounds of his having made the run from the South Canadian sandbar. But the Secretary of the Interior reversed this decision, arguing that the sandbar was, indeed, a legal point of entry.[5]

Mrs. Poisal, an Arapaho half-blood whose tribal name was Snake Woman, had been located on a ranch inside Oklahoma ten miles east of Fort Reno and just south of the North Canadian since 1872. The government had built her a house and fenced in some ground for her where she cared for a small garden. At 76 years of age she was decrepit and almost blind, and she failed to respond to a notice sent her before the run saying that she must have her tract reserved in order to keep it. The courts later were not at all certain that the notice reached her or, if it did, was read to the Indian woman who did not speak or read English.

Thirteen months prior to the opening, Thomas Fitzgerald went to work for Mrs. Poisal. On April 22 at noon Fitzgerald staked his claim to the tract on which Mrs. Poisal lived (NE ¼, Section 17, T12N, R6W), and afterward he drove the old lady off the land and appropriated her improvements. When soldiers brought her back to her home, Fitzgerald resisted them.

The case reached the Secretary of the Interior, who concluded that the rights of Mrs. Poisal were not affected by the act of March 2, 1889, opening the Oklahoma lands to settlement, even though she had not responded to the notice to have her tract reserved. By then, however, she had died, and the property fell to her heirs.[6]

Another example of how the long delays in deciding ownership to land could affect its use or value involved a tract contested by the Frisco Township in a suit against James W. Call (SW ¼, Section 6, T12N, R5W). This fight over what was apparently valuable townsite land took place at the Kingfisher Land Office during February and March 1890. The local land officers decided in favor of the townsite, but some time later—November 1893—the Secretary of the Interior reversed the decision, awarding the land to Call. By then the railroad from Oklahoma City to El Reno had by-passed the townsite, and there was little left of the town when Call finally won out, his property having far less value.[7]

William S. Hurt made the run from the west line to a tract of land some three miles east of Kingfisher station (SW ¼, Section 14, T16N, R7W). He immediately put up a stake with a card tacked on it reading: "This claim taken by W. S. Hurt, 10 minutes past 12 o'clock, April 22." A surveyor, who testified to seeing the stake, suggested to Hurt at the time that he mark the tract more plainly. Hurt put up another stake four feet high with a sign reading: "This claim taken by W. S. Hurt, Co. K, 106 Ills. Vols., 1 o'clock and 25 minutes." He then hurried off to the Kingfisher Land Office to file a Soldier's Declaratory Statement, but he found the office was not yet open.

Returning to his tract, Hurt now found three other stakes on it, placed there by men named Busher, Jarrett, and Northup. Hurt remained on the land, sleeping there that night, though he was up very early and in line at the land office before 4 a.m. He waited in line most of the morning, reaching the Receiver at about 11 a.m. He was told then that entry for the land had already been made, and his entry fees were refused.

Hurt returned to the land, secured a team and plow, and tried to do some plowing. But the soil was too hard to break, and after scratching a few furrows he gave it up. He slept on the land on the twenty-third and twenty-fourth, later digging a foundation for the start of a house.

His principal contestant for the land was Abiel W. Giffin, who claimed that he had reached the tract at 12:12 on April

22, set up a piece of shingle four by five inches wide and a foot long, and placed two clods of dirt against it. He claimed he had written on the shingle: "I hereby claim the SW ¼ of Section 14 as my homestead." Giffin said that he then rode to the land office and found a notice on the door saying that it would not be open until the next morning. He stayed in Kingfisher that night, but he was sixth in the line with his papers prepared on the morning of April 23.

By then he had changed his mind, he said, and decided to file on the northwest quarter of Section 22. There was a man named Erwin in front of Giffin. Having some intimation that Erwin was going to file on the northwest quarter of Section 22, Giffin offered him $500 to exchange places with him in the line. Erwin refused, saying that he had settled on the tract and intended to keep it. As a result Giffin sent for a pen and some ink and changed the description in his application to cover the southwest quarter of Section 34.

When the case reached the Secretary of the Interior, it was decided that Hurt had made a valid settlement of the land and that Giffin was lying when he told of putting up a stake with a card. Thus Hurt was awarded the land.[8]

The case of *East Guthrie vs. Veeder B. Paine* revealed some unique circumstances. Paine, who had claimed a key tract at Guthrie (SW ¼, Section 9, T16N, R2W), was a man with an interesting background. A former Michigan lumberman, he had once written a scholarly article for *Harper's New Monthly Magazine* entitled "Our Public Land Policy." He later came to the Indian Territory to work on the Turkey Track Ranch on the Sac and Fox reservation. On April 20 he left the ranch with the three owners of the Turkey Track: Arthur Hill, James Jerome, and Leslie Combs. Combs and Hill were in a buckboard on their way to catch the train at Guthrie for Fort Worth. Jerome and Paine were on horseback, and Jerome planned to catch a train for Michigan. There was a sizeable crowd gathered at the Iowa reservation line some nine miles east of Guthrie.

The buckboard driven by Combs and Hill carried camping and cooking equipment as well as Paine's coat and camping gear. The buckboard started west from the Iowa line between 8 and 9 o'clock on the morning of April 22. Jerome at first thought he would stay and watch the run, but before noon he decided to go in ahead of the crowd. Paine left at noon mounted on a strong horse, but in crossing some rough ground the horse stumbled and fell to the ground, bursting the saddle girth. Paine continued on, however, and within two miles of Guthrie he overtook Jerome, trading horses with him to finish the run. He arrived on the tract at 12:40 p.m., finding no one on the tract under contest.

Paine immediately drove in some stakes with a written statement on them saying that he had claimed the land. He then went to a nearby tree and blazed it on four sides and wrote the same notice on it. He was undisturbed for about three-fourths of an hour when the first train arrived from the north, and the newcomers flocked to his land and commenced staking off lots. Paine went among them giving notice of his claim, but it did little good.

When the case of *East Guthrie vs. Paine* reached the General Land Office, it was ruled that Paine had made his entry in good faith. But Secretary of the Interior Noble held that Paine had connived with the others in his entry and had an advantage over others making the race from the line. Accordingly, Paine's entry was rejected.[9]

Another critical land contest at Guthrie involved the tract of land filed upon by deputy marshals Ransom Payne and James H. Huckleberry as well as Xenophon Fitzgerald (NW ¼, Section 9, T16N, R2W). Fitzgerald had been a cowboy in the Indian Territory for twelve years. He had herded stock in the vicinity of the Oklahoma district but had not been at Guthrie since July 1888. Unmarried, he made the run on horseback with a friend from the Iowa line at noon on April 22, reaching Guthrie at about 12:55 p.m. He rode first to the land staked by Veeder B. Paine, who directed him to the northwest quarter of Section 9. Fitzgerald rode about the area and finding no one there dismounted and drove a stake into the ground with his name on it. Then, being hungry, he went to the nearest tent where he could find food. When he returned to his claim he found townsite claimants staking off lots. He warned them that he had made prior claim, but they paid no attention to him and kept on with their staking.

Secretary of the Interior Noble disqualified deputy Huckleberry on the ground that he was a sooner, just as Payne had likewise been ruled by the General Land Office. Payne took his case to the Supreme Court of Oklahoma Territory where he was again found to be disqualified, and even to the U.S. Supreme Court, which ruled against him in 1898. In the meantime, William W. Stone, Commissioner of the General Land Office, held that Fitzgerald was a legal claimant, and on January 13, 1891, the land was awarded to him.[10]

Indian Territory cowboy George S. McPeek was not so fortunate, however. After guarding cattle within the Oklahoma lands from March 1 to March 15, 1889, he left and went east to the Cherokee Nation and remained there until April 15. He then returned with some other men and went into camp on the north line of the Oklahoma country not far from where he had herded cattle.

Though there was conflicting testimony regarding the matter, McPeek claimed that he and his brother left the line at twelve noon on April 22 and rode directly to a tract of land eight miles west of Mulhall (NE ¼, Section 6, T18N, R3W) and claimed it. Early entry was in question but by no means established in the case.

In reviewing an appeal on certain lots within this tract, the office of the Secretary of the Interior concluded that McPeek and his brother had acted in collusion, that even if McPeek had not preselected the tract of land then his brother had done so for him. Accordingly, it was determined that McPeek was not a qualified entryman, and the General Land Office decision to deny his entry was upheld.[11]

Still another important Guthrie case was that involving a tract claimed by James Feagins (SW ¼, Section 8, T16N, R2W). Feagins, a section foreman for the Santa Fe Railroad at Guthrie, made settlement along Cottonwood Creek just south of the railway station, filing for homestead entry on April 23, though the tract had been included in the filing made by Mark S. Cohn for the townsite group on the day previous.

On May 8, 1889, Ezra Maples filed a contest for the Feagins claim, alleging that the railroader was a sooner. This was followed by another challenge by Henry H. Bockfinger on May 24, and on June 15 a townsite application was filed for West Guthrie at the land office. Officials Dille and Barnes ruled that Feagins was disqualified but recommended that a hearing by the General Land Office be conducted to determine the rights of other homestead claimants on the tract. Secretary Noble found Cohn, Feagins, and deputy marshal Thomas J. Taylor to be disqualified as homesteaders because of their early presence in Oklahoma and that Bockfinger arrived too late to acquire any interest in the land. All of the individual contestants acquiesced except Bockfinger, but on review Secretary Noble upheld his earlier opinion and again denied Bockfinger's entry.[12]

Another shading of soonerism, that of unwitting mistake, was brought up in the *T. M. Golden vs. Charles Cole* case. Cole had left Arkansas City with a group of six in two wagons about April 17, traveling by way of Willow Springs, Ponca agency, Otoe Springs, and across the northern panhandle of the Oklahoma country to the Iowa reservation. The party was guided by I. N. Terrill (later a Territorial representative from Stillwater who killed a man and was sent to prison), who, it was claimed, became confused by the various trails and led the group into the Oklahoma country by mistake. Terrill insisted that he did not tell the others that they were inside Oklahoma, and the party did not look for land while there.

From all testimony, Cole remained south of the Cimarron outside of Oklahoma until noon on the twenty-second. He then crossed the river and reached a claim only to find that it was already taken. He went to a second tract and likewise found it claimed. Then he went to a third which was unclaimed a mile or so east of the junction of Stillwater Creek and the Cimarron River (NW ¼, Section 5, T17N, R2E).

Cole's claim was challenged by T. M. Golden on May 28, 1889, but before the case came to court Cole died. Ultimately it was decided in favor of Cole's heirs, and the decision was upheld by the Secretary of the Interior, who held that Cole had received no advantage from having inadvertently been inside Oklahoma prior to the legal hour.[13]

A case similar in some respects involved the entry of Samuel D. Martin, who traveled with his father, brother, and others in two wagons from the north and crossed the panhandle of the Oklahoma lands on April 21 in order to reach the east line. Before arriving at the line, Martin claimed, a soldier had told them they would be halted by an officer and, not meeting one, they had crossed the line in ignorance of its location and continued on. However, others indicated that the Martin party encountered a large number of people encamped at the line but chose to believe that they did not know any more about where the line was than did he, nor did he bother to make inquiry of them.

Martin made the run from the east line, supposedly at the legal time, and claimed a tract of land just north of present Langston (NW ¼, Section 11, T17N, R1W). His entry was challenged by M. M. Laughlin, who had been a cattle herder on the Iowa reservation and in the Oklahoma country for nearly seven years. Though Laughlin was well acquainted with the area and had camped near the land in question, he argued that he had held no special advantage. The Secretary of the Interior held otherwise. Both Martin and Laughlin were disqualified to hold title to the land.[14]

Because of a peculiar overlapping of original land claims at the present site of Stillwater, Oklahoma, an eighty-acre tract ended up unoccupied on the north half of the northeast quarter of Section 23, T19N, R2E. Robert Lowry had staked the northeast quarter of Section 23; John H. Barnes, the southeast quarter; and Robert Copper, the southwest quarter. However, the only claim at first for any of the northwest quarter was made by Sanford Duncan, who erroneously claimed 160 acres which was divided half on Copper's southwest quarter and half on the northwest quarter. Thus the north half of the northwest quarter was unclaimed.

The locating committee for the Stillwater Town Company left Winfield, Kansas, for Guthrie on May 20. With the group was 47-year-old Garnett Burks. Though the committee originally intended to locate at the old Payne Oklahoma Colony townsite, it instead became interested in an area a few miles upriver. On the night of May 21 the committee encamped near the present site of Stillwater, and on May 22 rode about looking over the countryside.

It appears that Robert Copper was the only one who knew of the vacant eighty acres, and that he divulged the information to the committee, recommending it for a townsite. Copper escorted Burks to the land, and Burks drove two stakes there. While others of the committee later claimed that Burks was supposed to have done this in the interest of the townsite company, he instead filed on it under his own name at the Guthrie Land Office.

The Stillwater Town Company contested the filing. On June 16, 1890, the Register and Receiver at Guthrie began hearings in the Burks case, and on August 11 they decided in favor of the town group. Burks appealed the case to the Commissioner of the General Land Office, who upheld the local land office decision. Secretary of the Interior Noble likewise agreed on March 14, 1891, that Burks had not made his entry in good faith and cancelled his entry.[15]

An interesting case of soonerism involved O. H. Hills, the man who had ridden to Oklahoma station from the 7-C Ranch on the night of April 21 to petition the military command for troops to monitor the east line and keep people from crossing early. After delivering the petition to Colonel Wade, it was late and Hills remained overnight at Oklahoma station, leaving at 8:00 a.m. on April 22 and supposedly returning to the line. Though he claimed that he arrived back at the 7-C Ranch at 11:45 and made the run at 12:15, there later could be found no one who could verify his return or had even seen him enroute, not even the troops he had caused to be sent out. Hills filed on a tract of land near present Spencer (SW ¼, Section 3, T12N, R2W). Finding his story unsupported by any witnesses and difficult to believe, the Oklahoma City Land Office cancelled Hills's homestead application.[16]

The complexities of the sooner cases following the Run of 1889 were virtually endless, giving little reason to wonder, perhaps, why the courts took so long to determine valid ownerships of land claims and often rendered contradictory opinions. There still remain those decisions which appear to defy the ends of justice, as well as many acts of soonerism which were never revealed and properly adjudicated. But, though there would be other land runs to follow, the sooner cases would eventually reveal that this was an unfair and inadequate way of distributing lands of the public domain.

CHAPTER XIX
The Eighty-Niners—I

After the run a story surfaced about a tramp who had passed out from booze in a boxcar in Kansas. When he awoke and staggered out of the car door, he found himself in strange surroundings. A rider came dashing up and excitedly offered him $500 for his claim. Much confused, the hobo rejected the offer. But by the time his head had cleared, he had signed a quit-claim relinquishment, and $800 had been thrust into his hand. He was then told to vamoose, which he did. Wichita Eagle, *July 26, 1889, citing* Reno City Eagle.

WHILE the sooner cases revealed much about the participants during the Run of 1889, there is yet another body of material which lends even deeper insight into the human experiences of the settlers. That is the reminiscences and accounts written or narrated by the people who made the run, secured land, and built homes in the new country. For most of them, the Run of 1889 was a thrilling, memorable experience which bonded them together as "Eighty-Niners." It would remain with them as a matter of special pride for the rest of their lives.

M. O. Stetler came from Minneapolis, Kansas, with his two brothers, a brother-in-law, and his son, Eugene Stetler, to make the run into Oklahoma. High water and muddy roads delayed them on their way to Caldwell, and they did not reach the Kansas border until after the main body of settlers had departed.[1]

While waiting their turn to cross the Salt Fork the men killed time by playing their fiddles and accordians, but all were soon across and on their way to Buffalo Springs, where the immense crowd took turns dipping water out of the springs to drink and cook with.

Stetler was on the front line when the signal was given. He took a southeasterly course and outran all but a heavy rig with a team of mules, though he got ahead of even it when the feed box on the wagon came loose and required a stop for repairs. Stetler found a claim at the site of the Hennessey Massacre near the old Chisholm Trail. After staking his claim, he took a wagon wheel, measured its circumference, and tied a red hankerchief around the rim to mark each round. After using the wheel to measure off his property lines and locate his corners, Stetler then plowed a furrow around the quarter section.

At Kingfisher he had to remain in line for two and a half days in order to file his claim. As much as $50 was being offered by men to buy a place in line.

Robert Galbreath, who would ultimately become one of the most famous oil wildcatters in Oklahoma by making the Glenn Pool discovery near Tulsa, was among those who came south with the Caldwell crowd. He was just another young adventurer seeking his fortune in the first great land rush, and on the morning of April 22 he and his brother were at the line on horseback.

The boys got off to a good start, racing down the route of the Chisholm Trail until they reached the Hennessey Massacre site, there cutting off southwestward to Turkey Creek. Finding a piece of ground that he liked, Galbreath jumped off his horse and began driving in his stakes. He had no sooner done so than a man stuck his head up from the bank of a creek and told him to move on. The man had a gun in his hand, and another man stepped out from behind a tree with a Winchester rifle, repeating the suggestion to "Move on!"

"If there are two of you," Galbreath agreed good-naturedly, "I guess I had better move on, alright."[2]

As he started off, one of the men pointed up the valley to where two men and a woman were riding up. They were coming to take the claim next to his, the man said, but Galbreath could claim it if he would hurry. Galbreath moved quickly and staked the tract. He then pitched a wagon sheet over some poles and made a tent of it, staying until late afternoon when he and his brother, who was too young to take a claim, went in to Red Fork Station to get something to eat. When he returned he found a man with his wife, family, and a team of ponies occupying his claim.

Galbreath had no trouble convincing the man that he was the first claimant, but as the man was departing he made an emotional appeal.

"I have a wife and three children, ponies, covered wagon and four or five chickens and a little money. What will you take for this claim?"

"Friend," Galbreath said, "I have 160 acres here that I want."

"I know," he replied, "but you are a young man and can get around. I will give you fifty dollars for it."

Galbreath studied the matter for a while. He had been traveling around a good deal lately and was hard-pressed for cash. Deciding the other could use the land better than himself, he accepted the fifty dollars and sold out, going to Kingfisher, where he helped organize the first city government for the town.

Much of Endsley Jones's boyhood had been spent at Red Fork Ranch, which his father operated as a cattle spread, commissary, and stagecoach station during Indian Territory days. Prior to the run his father took the family to Caldwell, but he returned on the morning of April 22 and made the run from the line west of the ranch. He was already located when the crowd from the north passed by.

During the afternoon of the twenty-second a man named Halstead with five children arrived driving a team of oxen, staking the claim next to that of Jones. That night Halstead came over to Jones's tent and asked if he could get something to eat. He said that his wife had died recently in No-Man's Land and that he had no money with which to support his five children, the youngest of which was only one year old. Jones offered the man two dollars to plow a fire guard around the tent with his oxen. Halstead did the chore, then took the two dollars to the Red Fork commissary and bought some food.

On the following morning Halstead came over and said that there were six men on his place who demanded twenty-five dollars or they would jump his claim. Jones got on his horse and rode to get some friends together. They then went to Halstead's homestead and told the men that if they were still there that night they would be hanged. The men left and never came back, and Halstead eventually became a prosperous farmer of the Kingfisher area.[3]

William Kenworthy had been a compositor for the *Kansas City Times*, a strong supporter of Oklahoma settlement. Kenworthy's growing interest in Oklahoma was brought to a head when he met George Cooper, the colony leader from Emporia who was visiting in Kansas City, Missouri, before the run. Kenworthy became a member of Cooper's colony, and on the Thursday preceding the run he traveled to Arkansas City.

In outfitting himself for the run, Kenworthy loaded up with crackers, cheese, bologna, bacon, dried peaches, and coffee. He equipped himself with two pie pans, a tin cup, spoon, knife, fork, a change of underwear and shirt, and three handkerchiefs. He packed these items into a grip and carried, in addition, a blanket, hammock, oil cloth, ax, shovel, and a canteen of water.

Kenworthy was on the first train which pulled out from the Arkansas City station amid the cheers and hurrahs of the throng there. The Emporia colony had decided upon Guthrie as its destination, but the place was so crowded that Cooper told them it was best to go on to the next stop, which was Seward some six miles south of Guthrie. The Colony disembarked there, Cooper driving his stakes near the flag station and telling others to scatter out.

Kenworthy hurried off to the east of the tracks, finding a good claim along a creek. After tying his oil cloth fast over a bush and attaching a notice of his claim to it, he began digging a small plot to plant a few hills of corn. Early on the morning of April 23 he set out with some friends to search for markers, soon finding a witness tree which was blazed with the inscription "N. 7, Tp. 15—T2W." Stepping off 880 steps to the south, the men found the half-section stone and from there other corner markers. Walking through heavy brush and over rough countryside for most of the day, losing the course and having to go back and start over again, was very fatiguing. By sundown Kenworthy was too weary to continue. Asking the others to bring him something to eat from his grip in the morning, he swung his hammock between two sapling trees and flopped into it.

Soon after two men came along carrying a suitcase. They were George and Sidney Williamson from Ohio. Kenworthy asked if they happened to have any food with them, and they willingly obliged him and invited him to join them at their campfire not far away.[4]

Two weeks before the run, Lincoln Grant Shoop received an invitation from his cousin Billy Speer at Winfield to come and see the excitement. Shoop did so, meeting Frank Greer who was publishing the first issues of the *Oklahoma State Capital* newspaper at Winfield. Greer hired Shoop to set type for the sheet.

On the day before the run, Shoop went to Arkansas City, meeting two other young men from Colorado who were there to try their luck. The boys were at the depot very early on the morning of the twenty-second, purchased tickets, and debated between two trains that were made up and preparing to leave. His friends boarded one by climbing to the top of its caboose. Shoop himself held up, waiting until one of the trains made the first move. When one finally did, he ran alongside trying to board each coach in turn. But the men aboard struck and kicked at him, refusing to allow him to climb aboard. Finally at the last car, a big, red-faced man yelled: "Boy, throw me your bundle." He then reached down a big hand and helped Shoop aboard to join his friends.

The conductor eventually came crawling up atop the car to take tickets, finding that a group of Chicago toughs were there without any. He ordered the brakeman to kick the abusive toughs off the train, but the brakeman only smiled. As the train sped toward Oklahoma, Shoop passed out some cigars that he had with him. Presently the brakeman took

Shoop's bundle down into the caboose and later invited the boy to join the group of railroad officials and dignitaries who were riding there. The speeding train offered a grand view of the racing horses and wagons as it crossed the border and sped toward Guthrie. Shoop had purchased a ticket to Laurie, a flag station a few miles above Guthrie, but the train did not stop there. But on the conductor's advice, Shoop waited for the train to slow at the approach to the Cimarron River bridge where he tossed off his bundle and jumped after it.

Shoop landed safely and soon arrived at a fine quarter section of rich valley land at the junction of the Cimarron and Cottonwood. Though he was certain that he had been the only one to leave the train where he did, Shoop found six men had beaten him to the claim. Four of the men, two of them armed, were quarreling over the claim. Deciding he had not come this far merely to commit either homicide or suicide, Shoop went on into Guthrie where he found his two friends and secured a town lot adjoining theirs. Eventually he erected his home on the lot.[5]

Winifred Morton, who had moved with her family from Wisconsin to Missouri to Arkansas City, was thrilled that she would be permitted to go with her father to make the run. Her father, a Civil War veteran, was secretary of an old soldiers' colony which had chartered two railroad cars on the first train to leave Arkansas City. At 4:00 a.m. on the morning of April 22, Winifred and her father left their house with some food, a spade, two flags and a canteen of water. Walking through the morning darkness her father decided the whole thing was just too much of an undertaking, but Winifred was determined to see Oklahoma, insisting that she was going to be one of the lucky ones who got a homestead.

At eight o'clock the train whistled, and the shout "All aboard" sounded. Then they were off for Oklahoma, their destination being Seward station between Guthrie and Edmond. At Guthrie their car was sidetracked for three hours, during which time many of the old soldiers decided to get off. Winifred's father wanted to do the same, but she insisted that they remain on the train. Finally they moved on to Seward where sixty of the colony members disembarked.

Evidently by prearrangement of the colony, a man met them at Seward and led them across a purplish prairie spotted with the white of indigo plants and blooming dogwood. Prairie chickens and deer flushed before Winifred as she headed west from the railroad tracks. Though her father and some other men threw branches across Cottonwood Creek, she slipped and fell in the water to her knees. Stockings and skirt wet, her shoes sloshing heavily, Winifred continued on. After several miles, and at about 3:00 p.m., two men riding mules came up and offered her a lift. She took them up on the offer, riding about two miles before resuming her journey afoot.

Near Deer Creek they were met by I. N. Donald, a teamster for the government and a member of the colony. Another female rushee, Ada Baskins, was there to help Winifred dry her wet clothes and insist she drink a cup of hot coffee—her first ever. Donald hitched up his mules to a wagon and drove Winifred and her father out to locate a claim. Within a mile and a half they came to Deer Creek and a stand of timber. Winifred walked to where no one could be seen occupying the land, found a cornerstone, and staked her claim to the land. She planted her flag and did some spading on the following morning.

On May 1 Winifred and her father found a man with a team and wagon to take them to Kingfisher to file on their claims. The town was crowded and the land office surrounded by soldiers. A U.S. deputy marshal standing at the door saw Winifred and took her around to the back door to let her in ahead of the regular line.[6]

The young woman who had helped Winifred dry out her clothes, Ada Baskins, had previously lived near Bluff City, Kansas. She had been visiting friends in Linden, Kansas, when she, being old enough to claim land, was called home to accompany her father to Oklahoma. She and Mr. Baskins were on the third train out of Arkansas City. At Guthrie they changed cars and continued on to Edmond station, where they also were met by Donald. The teamster drove them to a place nine miles northwest of Edmond, where Ada found a claim, put up her American flag there, and erected a tent. Her father took a claim nearby.

One of her neighbors was Henry Jorgenson, a Danish immigrant who had come to Oklahoma with a colony from Iowa. He brought his team and plowed her land. Eventually Ada married Henry Jorgenson, and the two lived on their homesteads for thirty-seven years before he died and she moved into Edmond.[7]

Another young woman who decided to make the Run of 1889 was Edna Helm. Having read much about the new country of Oklahoma when she resided in Logan County, Kentucky, she became "all pepped up" about making the run and getting her own land. So she caught a train by herself and headed for Arkansas City. It did not occur to her until she got off the train at the busy border town on April 21 that she would have to find her own way to make the run, having neither horse nor wagon.

Gathering up her heavy suitcases she began walking in search of a hotel or a boarding house where she could stay. But the town was overflowing with people, and every place was taken. Edna soon became very tired and sat down beneath a shade tree to rest. While she was sitting there a man came up to her and offered his help.

He said his name was Martin Ahrens and that he was a widower with three children and badly needed a housekeeper. He said he, too, was planning to make the run into Oklahoma. Then he made a suggestion. She could take care of his children while he did so. Then, if he were successful in getting a homestead and if she were willing, they could get married. She said she was agreeable, so Ahrens took her to a friend's house to stay. He made the run, secured a claim near Kingfisher, and returned for her and the children. They were married by a justice of the peace and started for their new claim in a covered wagon.[8]

As an eighteen-year-old, Andrew Dave Robertson accompanied his father and family from Abilene, Kansas, to Fort

Reno to make the run. Robertson rode his spotted pony beside the family's torn and dingy covered wagon, which was pulled by horses whose ribs stood out like those of a skeleton. His father and mother rode on the wagon seat, while five children were crammed onto a makeshift bed in the wagon. A big iron washpot swung beneath the wagon, while a water bucket and other odds and ends were strapped to the sides. On the back of the wagon was a chicken coop containing his mother's prize Rhode Island hens. Their large shepherd dog trotted along in the shade of the wagon, his tongue lolling out.

Other families joined them on the way, some with "Oklahomy or Bust!" painted crudely on their canvas. The Robertson family arrived on the Fort Reno reserve nearly a week before the opening and went into camp on a small creek east of the fort. Their entire worldly goods were right there with them in the wagon, including several items his mother had slipped in without his father knowing about it—a jar of soft soap, a sack of carpet rags, a gunny sack of potatoes, and an extra heavy iron skillet.

Andrew, who was too young to claim land, had many requests from men who wanted to ride his pony in the big race; but he refused all, hobbling the horse close to camp for fear he would be stolen. Shortly before the run, his father decided he would ride the pony himself. Andrew admonished him to take good care of his pony.

Andrew accompanied his father to the line on the morning of the run, reaching a point just west of present El Reno at ten o'clock. At ten minutes of twelve noon the soldiers ordered everybody who was going to make the race to move up on the line. Spectators were told to remain back a distance. When the post cannon at Fort Reno was fired, the soldiers on the line shot off their guns and the race began.

The horseback riders immediately sprang forward to take the lead. Buckboards and light spring wagons followed close behind at first, though some of the drivers smashed their axles or splintered shafts in their anxiety. There were many spills and runaways in the mad dash for land. The heavier wagons were soon lagging far behind, but before long they, too, had disappeared into the distant woods or over a far rise.

The women and others on the line settled down to their wait as young boys in faded overalls hawked drinking water for five cents a cup. Women in long, faded skirts strolled about with a flock of youngsters at their heels while both young and old mothers and wives waited hopefully for their entrant in the once-in-a-lifetime race to return with good news. Andrew's mother was one of the fortunate ones, for Andrew's father was successful in staking a claim six miles southeast of where El Reno would rise.[9]

Another Kansas wagon-immigration was that made by Mina Wade Patterson, who in 1888 at the age of sixteen had married twenty-year-old Lee Patterson. In the spring of 1889 the young couple decided to seek a home in the Indian Territory, as he had just turned twenty-one and was of legal age to file a claim. It was the middle of March when they loaded up their covered wagon with a few farming and living necessities—breaking plow, axes, saws, carpenter tools, bedding, and a few pieces of furniture. Hitching their two oxen to their wagon, they bade friends and relatives farewell and headed off to start their new life in the Territory.

The oxen soon became footsore, causing the Pattersons to move slowly, stopping once to have the oxen shod by a blacksmith. They reached Fort Reno some ten days before the opening, camping on the fort reserve. During the wait, it became a habit each night that an old army and frontier call would sound through the camp: "Oh, Joe! Here's your mule!" It would sound through the camp until sleep finally overtook all.

Not owning a horse, Lee Patterson became discouraged, particularly when he saw all of those who did have fine animals. Still he was determined to have his try on foot. On the morning of the run everyone was up before dawn had broken, getting breakfast, harnessing teams, rubbing down their horses, and saddling them. Mina and Lee ate a quick breakfast of pancakes and bacon, then hitched up their oxen and rode to the line. Even as early as they were, they found the line was crowded with people for as far as they could see south of the North Canadian. They decided to cross to the north bank, but there, too, the countryside was covered with people.

Mina was concerned that Lee would not be able to get a claim. On an impulse just before the run she tore some strips from her red calico apron and tied them around his arms, ankles, and head. Everyone along the line noticed him, of course, and were amused. A story began circulating that Patterson was a famous runner who had won ribbons at various races. At high noon the cannon roared, and the racers were off. Among them was Lee Patterson with his red calico ribbons flying in the air. Other racers would veer away from him for fear that he was too much competition for them, giving him a freer field.

It was late that evening when Lee Patterson came back to the wagon to tell Mina that he had, indeed, located a claim! They drove their wagon to the tract of land and lived in their wagon for about a week before Patterson made a small hut of cottonwood bark, poles, brush, and prairie grass for their first home in Oklahoma.[10]

Also making the run at Fort Reno was German-born Karl Reichert who had migrated to St. Louis and then to western Kansas. He had been working on a ranch in No-Man's Land when he and others decided to leave the drought-stricken area and make the run into Oklahoma. Packing all of their possessions into their wagon, they headed east, passing through Gage and Woodward and heading down the North Canadian trail. The Reicherts arrived at Fort Reno with a group of other settlers on April 10. People were pouring into the area from every direction in wagons, buggies, on horseback, and by foot. While waiting for time to make the run, the people in camp gathered in large groups and talked about their forthcoming venture to find free land.

Reichert made the run on horseback. But for two days he searched over hills, valleys, creeks, and rivers without finding a homestead claim. It seemed almost that people had dropped out of the sky, and every tract appeared to be staked. He returned to his camp at Fort Reno finally, weary and very discouraged. His wife Anna was very disappointed, also, but she avowed her intentions of finding a claim herself. Karl tried to tell her it was impossible, but she left her baby with her mother, crawled onto a two-year-old colt, and rode off into Oklahoma. She came back that night to announce that she had found a tract of land that was not staked and had claimed it. It was located seven miles northeast of where Reno City would be founded.[11]

De'Leslaine R. Davis was one of the few black men to make the run of April 22, 1889. Born in South Carolina, he had arrived in Wichita in 1887 and worked at odd jobs there. He met another black man, Peter Oliver Flinn, whose mother encouraged Davis to go with them to Oklahoma and make the run for free land.

Davis and Flinn made the race on horseback from the line north of the North Canadian River, the only two black men to make the run in Canadian County. Both succeeded in locating claims four miles northeast of present El Reno. Davis's claim was very heavy with timber, and it took him four years to clear out even small patches. He cut wood and hauled it to Reno City where he sold it for fifty to seventy-five cents per load. He also raised corn and sold it for fifteen cents a bushel.

Davis's first house was a small log shanty, eight to ten feet square, with one window and one door. He cooked on an open fire the first year and baked bread by patting it out on green cottonwood slabs and holding it close to the fire until it baked.

Davis never married, living on the farm for forty-eight years alone. He never saw any of his relatives until the summer of 1936 when a sister from Florida paid him a visit. Peter Flinn and his mother lived on their claim until they died, both being buried on their own land.[12]

Karl Bornemann had come to the United States from Germany as a young man and migrated from Michigan to Montana, where he took up the life of a cowboy. Eventually he went south to Texas where he hired on with the O. K. Cattle Company to drive cattle across the Indian Territory. He helped drive herds up the Chisholm Trail in 1887 and 1888. During 1888 he hired on at Bull Foot Ranch, located on the Chisholm Trail.

When the Oklahoma fever heated up, Bornemann decided to give up the hapless life of a cowboy and make the run to obtain some land. He and nine other men began making plans. At first they intended to run from the north side, but as people began pouring in they decided they could do better from Fort Reno. However, they feared to risk driving their wagons and goods overland from Kansas across the Oklahoma country lest they be considered illegal entrants. So instead the men chartered a Santa Fe freight car and loaded onto it their two wagons, teams, bedding and farming implements, all of which they had shipped to Purcell.

At Purcell they hitched up their wagons and drove northwest along the South Canadian to Darlington, arriving on April 16. Throngs of settlers were pouring into the Fort Reno-Darlington area, and in later life Bornemann could still picture vividly in his mind the big covered wagons with their assortment of items lashed to their sides, the worn-out, lame horses in front, and three or four limping, half-starved dogs trailing behind. In sharp contrast were those who had some of the finest race horses in the country, each carefully groomed for the great race.

Bornemann made the race, found himself a 160-acre homestead, and gave up forever the roving life of a cowboy.[13]

CHAPTER XX
The Eighty-Niners—II

William Fry and his friend Pat McGinty made the run together to Rock Creek near Orlando. The grass had been burned off and was green; but there were no roads, no buildings, and the land looked pretty dismal to the men. "Are you going to stay?" McGinty asked in disgust. "I've got to stay," Fry answered. "I haven't any place else to go." Indian-Pioneer Papers.

MRS. Welling Haynes was a child living with her family in Kansas when her father died. Her mother, Mary Wiley, sold the crops, tools, and stock to pay the doctor and funeral costs. She kept their team, wagon, furniture, and chickens, and moved in with her parents. But the grandmother did not like having the three young children about and made it known. Thus when Mary Wiley heard the talk of free land in Oklahoma, she decided to make the run herself.

Selling the furniture, the frontier woman purchased a tent; then she wired the chicken coop to the back of the wagon, hitched up the team, loaded the children in the back, and headed for Oklahoma. They crossed the Cherokee Outlet in four or five days, reaching the Oklahoma line on Easter Sunday. Early on the morning of the twenty-second, Mrs. Wiley pulled the wagon into line. When the signal was given, she let the horses run free until they came to some land where only a few people were.

The stalwart widow jumped from the wagon and drove her stakes into the ground. The claim held a wide rock canyon and a good spring of water. That first night someone stole their chickens, creating a severe loss to the fatherless family. On the next day, Mary Wiley went in to Guthrie and filed on her claim. The family lived in the tent for a year before a small house was finally erected.[1]

Charles C. Alling came from Crowley County, Kansas, at the age of twenty-one to make the run. He drove a mule-drawn spring wagon which carried groceries, blankets, and other camping items. After being held up with the others at Arkansas City until April 18, Alling felt that the trails were too jammed with horses and wagons traveling across the rain-softened ground for him to be able to make the starting line by April 22. So he pulled his wagon out of the line of march and headed southwestward across the prairie. He found the prairie uncrowded and the grassy land firm for traveling.

However, when he reached the Chikaskia he discovered the river was running bank full, with driftwood and uprooted trees floating downstream in the red water. As he was trying to figure out a way to cross, several other wagons pulled up. Alling discussed the problem of crossing the river with the new arrivals, and they decided they would pitch in together and build a raft to take the wagons across on. It was also decided not to waste time by waiting for morning.

Big bonfires were built on both sides of the river to provide light as logs were cut and lashed together to create a raft. The wagons were unhitched and taken across one by one on the rope-controlled raft. The livestock was made to swim across. By morning the last wagon had been taken across to the south bank, the teams rehitched, and all were headed south again.

Alling and the others reached the flooded Salt Fork at what was then known as Yellow Bull Crossing (now inside the city limits of Tonkawa, Oklahoma). The flood stage of the river had crested, and the men decided upon another method of crossing. One man swam the swollen river on his horse, trailing a long rope made by tying lariats together. The rope was then used to pull the wagons across. It was sunrise Easter Sunday morning when the caravan left Yellow Bull Crossing.

At Red Rock the brush was so thick that the men had to chop a path through it for their teams and wagons. The creek itself was a deep ravine, and the wagons had to be lowered by rope into and pulled out of the gulch. It began to appear that they would not make the line in time for the start of the run, but they did arrive just before noon. Alling had not eaten since Saturday night and had had only two hours of rest since leaving Arkansas City.

Still, when the gun sounded, Alling plunged his weary horse across the line just north of Orlando and rode hard for a time. Presently he came to a beautiful glade just north of present Crescent, Oklahoma. There he unsaddled his sweating mount and began cutting his initials into a post oak tree. While he was doing so a big, red-whiskered man appeared. He carried a Winchester, and around his waist were two cartridge belts, each holding a sixgun.

"Thinking of staying here?" the man asked.

"Well, it's a pretty place," Alling said, "but I'm just letting my horse rest a while."

"That would be all right," red-whiskers said, "but I wouldn't stay long if I were you. Sixteen of us in here have an oath to stick together. It's really quite an unhealthy place. There is lots of malaria, and some people even die of lead poisoning."

Alling had no trouble deciding whether or not to move on. He saddled up and rode on south, soon locating another claim just south of the Cimarron. It was four o'clock that afternoon before he had his first meal in two days.[2]

James K. Hastings was another twenty-one year old, ready for adventure when he left home at Lake Erie, Ohio, on April 8, 1889, and headed for Oklahoma. He took the train to Springfield, Missouri, where he purchased a saddle pony and, with a friend named George Fairbanks, rode from there to Arkansas City. On the way the boys stayed at farm houses at little or no costs as farmers enjoyed their company. Hastings and his friend found Arkansas City to be a bedlam of land-seekers from every state in the Union who were frantically making last minute preparations and purchasing supplies.

Hastings and Fairbanks rode their cow ponies out of Arkansas City on April 19, following along behind the big crowd of wagons and horseback travelers. The boys did not have much food, but Fairbanks had once worked at a ranch on the Chikaskia, and they headed for it across the trackless prairie, reaching the place after dark. A new owner now operated the ranch, however, and while the boys obtained some food, they could not get grain for their ponies.

The pair made the same discovery that Alling had made concerning the flooded river, and they witnessed the settlers rafting their wagons across the river by huge bonfires. The boys slept close by their horses that night, and on the following morning they followed the Chikaskia's north bank to where the river joined the Salt Fork, then moved on down that flooded stream to where the Arkansas City crowd was crossing the Santa Fe railroad bridge with the help of troops. The boys crossed by the bridge, also, and rode on to Red Rock Creek. There an Indian policeman, who wore a big .45 on his hip, guarded the bridge to keep settlers from overloading and breaking down the structure.

The two young men camped along the Santa Fe Railroad line on the night of April 20, spending a comfortable day of rest under leafy cottonwoods beside a creek all of Sunday. During the day wagons would pull in to rest, unhitch their teams and feed them; but when others would pass by, they would become fearful of being left behind and would hitch up their still-hungry teams and hurry on.

Hastings and Fairbanks saddled up early Monday morning and rode on. As the sun rose higher in the sky, the two decided to leave the main body of immigrants and turned off to the southeast. Shortly they came to a line camp of the Z. V. Cattle Ranch at the Oklahoma border where a group of men stood about discussing the matter of just when they should enter. Since there were no U.S. troops there to sound the time of entry, the crowd was started at around noon when one man strolled down to a corner stone at the border and claimed a tract of land as his.

Hastings and Fairbanks started south with the rush, but

239

not at a hard gallop for their horses were tired. It was 1:25 p.m. when Hastings dismounted at a creek bottom claim six miles east of Alfred station and drove his stakes. One man came up to contest the claim, but Hastings had clearly beat him to the site.

Hastings went to sleep that memorable night under the open sky with stars sparkling and camp fire burning. His cow pony was his only company in the still-untamed country of Oklahoma. Whenever Hastings would smell the smoke of a camp fire in years to follow he would always remember that first night of the Run of 1889.[3]

M. T. Hoover and his cousin, who also came down from Arkansas City, did not reach the line until midmorning before the run. The soldiers guarding the line showed them clearly where it was, but the two men still went inside the line some thirty yards to make camp, remaining there until the starting gun was fired. They then went some thirty yards farther in just to be certain they were across the line, erected their tent, and laid claim to two tracts of land very close to the railroad flag station at Orlando. Hoover built a dugout and planted cane and watermelon, and his cousin erected a sod house.[4]

Not everyone who made the Run of 1889 secured a claim, of course, and one was Matilda Pontious. She was a young widow with two daughters at the time of the run and had been keeping house for her father and brothers at Oxford, Kansas. Her father was fairly well-to-do and owned plenty of horses and buggies. He gathered a company of twenty people together to make the run, furnishing them with transportation. He took charge of the cortege of two spring wagons, one big wagon, two buggies and one large six-passenger phaeton in which Matilda rode with her two children.

One man tried to persuade her father to enter from the east line where it was not nearly so far to Guthrie, but he would not change his plans and took a position on the north line. As leader of the group, he kept the others from plunging forward when the run began, saying that those ahead would soon tire their stock, wreck their wagons, or injure their horses. He and his outfit would soon pass them, her father predicted. However, the Oxford group passed many good farms on the way to Guthrie only to find them all claimed already.[5]

Alfretta Jennings's family left Barnard, Kansas, on April 8 in two covered wagons, one drawn by a team of grey horses and the other by mules. They led two other horses and two cows. Her mother drove the greys, and her father the more difficult mule team. Her mother's wagon was loaded with two trunks of valuables, a Singer sewing machine, a box of dishes, cooking utensils, laundry materials, and other household paraphernalia. The wagon driven by her father carried their plow, rake, scythe, hoe, grubbing hoe, four straight-back chairs, rocking chair, iron cook stove, iron heating stove, seeds and seed potatoes, tubs, buckets, grub box, and a big stone jar full of California plums.

The family was very excited over making the run. They traveled to Wichita and on to Winfield, where on the night of April 13 a very severe rain and lightning storm struck. The children held the tent poles to keep them from blowing down, and it was necessary to pile bedding on chairs to prevent them from getting soaked by water flooding the tent.

The Jenningses were among the great exodus of settlers and wagons which departed Arkansas City on April 18 and moved down the Ponca Trail. They were at the Salt Fork when the railroad bridge was planked to permit the settlers to cross, and they reached the Oklahoma line just north of present Orlando and made the run from there when the signal was given at noon. Alfretta's father left the family in camp at the border and made the run on horseback. He filed on a claim that later became involved in a sooner contest. It took him seven years and all of his money to fight the contest, eventually settling with the other man. He paid for buildings, fences, and other improvements, and the two divided the land.[6]

Mrs. E. A. Barnum (nee Brown) came with her family from Kansas at the age of sixteen. They drove two covered wagons and trailed a buggy. Her father chose to make the run from west of Kingfisher. Laura and her older sister Nellie, who was twenty-one, were to drive the mule-drawn buggy across the line and take the first claim they came to while Mr. Brown made the run on horseback. The girls did so. Nellie jumped to the ground and drove her stakes. Then she dug up some weeds and grass and spread her wagon sheet on the ground and sat down on it.

A soldier nearby observed her action. He laughed and pointed to where some men were doing the same thing on the same tract.

"Stay with it," the soldier advised the girls. "They won't contest a woman."

The girls stayed and won the claim.[7]

Byron Dick Webb, whose father was a frontier freighter, came from Iowa to Dodge City as a youngster. Though only seventeen at the time of the run, he joined his father and older brother on the line. They had a covered wagon and four head of horses. The wagon was loaded with a few pieces of furniture, a sod plow, a few chickens and pigs in crates, and other items wired to the outside of the wagon.

Webb rode a saddle horse. The plan was for him to ride ahead and stake out claims for the others. Even though he was not old enough to take a claim, he was to bluff his way through if he could.

When the signal was given, pandemonium broke loose. There was a great cloud of dust, and chickens which had been shaken out of the wagons fluttered everywhere. Webb rode to Guthrie, but found no land on the first day. He slept that night under a wagon, and on the following morning he rode out to the southwest of Guthrie where he found some unclaimed land and staked claims for the others. His father and brother arrived on the evening of April 23 and took possession of the land, later building a sod house there.[8]

William Rogers lived between Fort Gibson and Tahlequah. On April 11 he started for the Oklahoma country with two covered wagons, one of them pulled by a yoke of oxen.

The Rogers family brought all of their household goods, with the exception of a heavy cooking stove for which there was not enough room in the wagons. Arriving on the Iowa reservation-Oklahoma line on April 20, they went into camp on a creek bank until time for the run. Rogers, his father, and sister all made the run, taking claims three miles north of Edmond station.

The Rogers family lived in a shelter made from the canvas of the wagons for a good while. Having no stove to cook on, they used an open fire with skillets and long-legged kettles over hot coals. The two oxen were sold to pay expenses until a crop could be harvested. Later they cut logs and built a cabin on two of the claims and bought a cow to have their own milk and butter.[9]

James McKee Owen left Arkansas City on April 11 with an ox team, farm wagon, spring wagon, a team of horses, one tent, and a camping outfit. Upon reaching the flooded Salt Fork, Owen and his party built a raft upon which to ferry their feed, chuck, bedding, and utensils across the river. The stock was made to swim. The Cimarron River was also up, and Owen's ox team became stuck at midstream, requiring the men to unload the wagon and carry the supplies over on their heads and shoulders.

The Owen party reached the Oklahoma border on the Kickapoo reservation between the Deep Fork and the North Canadian on the evening of April 19. It was a fine moonlit night, and camp fires gleamed around their camp. Not far away was a Kickapoo village, and the beating of tom-toms and chanting over a death in the tribe could be heard through the night.

Owen made the run, reaching what later became the Oak Park addition of Oklahoma City, going into camp there. Early the next morning he hitched up his wagon and drove into the center of Oklahoma City, laying claim to two lots in the South Oklahoma City area. Possessing the cash assets of $100, Owen pitched his tent and started a real estate business. He later liked to point to the fact that he made the run into Oklahoma without the benefit of rifle or revolver.[10]

A. M. DeBolt, on the other hand, came well armed with a

rifle and two pistols. He had first arrived at Oklahoma station on April 3 and was told to leave. He then went to Purcell, but decided to make the run from the east line at the 7-C Ranch. It took DeBolt an hour and fifteen minutes on horseback to reach his claim two miles east of Oklahoma station on what is now Reno Street.

He pitched his tent as soon as he had staked his claim. Presently three or four men came up and tried to make him leave. DeBolt noted that they had no saddle horses or teams, which meant they had likely been hiding out in the brush. He held his ground and set about building a dugout in which to live.[11]

L. F. Carroll entered Oklahoma from near the Kickapoo village. He had come down from Kansas through Coffeyville and Tulsa, crossing through the Sac and Fox and Iowa country to Wells's store and then on to the North Canadian. He went into camp with some 100 wagons already there. That night the men of the camp held a stag dance for their entertainment.

On April 21 the North Canadian was too high to be forded. Though it had ebbed some by the time the run began on Monday, Carroll took a course up the river's north bank, crossing over the divide to the Deep Fork, where he found all the best land already taken. He camped that night on the north bank of the North Canadian and searched all the next day without success. Eventually he struck the tracks of the Santa Fe line and followed them to Oklahoma station, camping just outside the location. He continued his search for land south of the North Canadian but without luck, finally becoming discouraged and starting the long journey back "with plenty of company" up the Red Fork Trail past the Sac and Fox agency and back home to Kansas with nothing to show for his efforts except the adventure of having made the great rush for land in 1889.[12]

Joseph W. Bouse, who claimed that he had been on vacation in Florida from his home in Pennsylvania and made the run aboard the boomer train out of Purcell, tells a fanciful story of staking a choice tract between Moore and Oklahoma City. Interviewed late in life, Bouse told of being run off his claim by four outlaws. The story is hard to accept, however, for the records of the Run of 1889 show that a Joseph W. Bouse was the first claimant to a tract near present Yukon and that he relinquished the claim on November 7, 1889.[13]

There are many falacious notions which still abound in regards to the Run of 1889. But as time heals many wounds, it also dissolves many of life's conflicts. Virtually forgotten today is the bitter rancor against the sooners. The term "sooner" has lost its negative identification and has instead become a term of recognition and pride for Oklahoma, emphasizing determination and achievement rather than the negative aspect of breaking the rules.

A story told by Oklahoma historians Joseph B. Thoburn and Muriel H. Wright in *Oklahoma, a History of the State and Its People* illustrates, perhaps, the attitude of many sooners of 1889. Emil Bracht was asked in court, point-blank, just where he was at noon on April 22, 1889. The crowded courtroom became hushed with anticipation while Bracht prepared his answer.

"I was lying in a little clump of brush about one hundred yards east of the Santa Fe Railway on the northeast quarter of Section 22, Township 12 North, Range 3 West, Indian Meridian."

Everyone seemed to heave a sigh of relief as Bracht was excused from the stand. As he was leaving the courtroom, another known sooner came up to him and whispered, "You damn fool, what did you do that for?" Bracht's reply was that he was a Kentuckian who would not forsake his personal honor for the best quarter section of land in Oklahoma Territory.[14]

While the story illustrates that Bracht was too proud to lie in court for personal gain, it overlooks his act in hiding out in the bushes before the run in the first place. But then it has never been easy to hold American enterprise within the rules of the game. An editorial writer for the *St. Louis Post-Dispatch* penned an apt analysis on the eve of the Run of 1889 when he wrote: "The spirit which animates these people, evil and good, is the spirit which has made this continent a garden. Within an incredible time what was a barren waste and wilderness will be turned into thriving cities, farms and homes ... The inspiration of human progress is in the spectacle."[15]

Notes

CHAPTER I
This Coveted Land

[1] *Congressional Record*, Vol. XIX, July 26, 1888, p. 6870.
[2] Cited by *Winfield Courier*, September 2, 1886. The railroad survey into the Oklahoma country had been preceded by a private survey out of Arkansas City for a wagon road through the Otoe Agency at Red Rock to Council Grove in October 1885. *Arkansas City Traveler*, October 28, 1885.
[3] August 18, 1886.
[4] *Ibid.*, December 16, 23, 1887.
[5] *Wichita Eagle*, February 3, 1888.
[6] *Ibid.*
[7] *Kansas City Gazette*, February 3, 1888.
[8] *Ibid.*, February 9, 1888.
[9] *Ibid.*
[10] *Ibid.*
[11] Dan W. Peery, "The First Two Years," *The Chronicles of Oklahoma*, Vol. VII, No. 3 (September, 1929), p. 281.
[12] *Ibid.*
[13] *Congressional Record*, 50th Cong., 1st sess., 1887-1888, Vol. XIX, p. 1564.
[14] *Kansas City Gazette*, February 1, 1888.
[15] *Ibid.*, February 2, 1888.
[16] *Congressional Record*, Vol. XIX, p. 6870.
[17] *Ibid.*, p. 6875.
[18] *Kansas City Gazette*, July 28, 1888.
[19] *Ibid.*
[20] *Congressional Record*, Vol. XIX, pp. 8051-8058.
[21] *Ibid.*, pp. 8082-8087; *Kansas City Gazette*, April 29, 1888.
[22] *Congressional Record*, Vol. XIX, pp. 8116-8120; *Kansas City Gazette*, August 30, 1888.
[23] *Wichita Eagle*, November 23, 1888.
[24] *Kansas City Gazette*, November 21, 1888.

25 *Ibid.*
26 *Ibid.*
27 *Ibid.*, October 22, 1888.
28 Joseph B. Thoburn and Muriel H. Wright, *Oklahoma, a History of the State and Its People*, Vol. II, pp. 529, 533.
29 *Congressional Record*, 50th Cong., 2nd sess., 1888-1889, Vol. XX, pp. 1400-1402.
30 *Kansas City Gazette*, February 2, 1889.
31 *Ibid.*, February 6, 1889.
32 *Ibid.*, February 13, 1889.
33 *Ibid.*, February 16, 1889.
34 *Ibid.*, February 21, 1889.
35 *Ibid.*, March 4, 1889.
36 Dan W. Peery, "Colonel Crocker and the Boomer Movement," *The Chronicles of Oklahoma*, Vol. XIII, No. 3 (Fall, 1935), pp. 286-287.

CHAPTER II
Getting Set

1 *St. Louis Republic*, April 22, 1889.
2 *Guthrie Daily Capital*, May 18, 1889.
3 Woodson to Adjutant, Fort Reno, January 31, 1889; Woodson to Adjutant, Camp Price, February 26, 1889. National Archives, Record Group 393, Letters Received. Fort Reno, I.T., 1888-1889 (hereafter cited as NA, RG 393).
4 Lillie was described by a reporter of the day as a "long-haired young man with an effeminate face and mild and gentle manners." *New York Herald*, April 20, 1889.
5 Glenn Shirley, *Pawnee Bill* (Albuquerque: University of New Mexico Press, 1958), p. 124.
6 *Arkansas City Republican-Traveler*, January 17, 1889.
7 *Ibid.*, January 3, 31, 1889.
8 *Ibid.*; *Emporia News*, January 24, 1889.
9 *Arkansas City Republican-Traveler*, January 17, 1889.
10 Shirley, *Pawnee Bill*, p. 130; *Wichita Eagle*, February 8, 1889.
11 *Arkansas City Republican-Traveler*, February 14, 1889. On February 4, 1889, a *Wichita Beacon* correspondent wrote from Caldwell: "Pawnee Bill sits on the hotel steps at Hunnewell and scans the clear outlines of the 'divide' which mark the horizon in the desolate promised land, and Harry Hill is again in Wichita, waiting, like Micawber [sic], for something to turn up . . . Harry Hill came to the line Saturday, determined to stop the invasion. He knew it must be done, or the success of the bill might be jeopardized in the Senate. Pawnee Bill had been at Arkansas City. Wagons were strung along the line and camps had been formed awaiting the opportunity to make the entry. The boomers were notified that it was best to concentrate at Caldwell, and camp-breaking commenced. It is impossible to estimate the number of men waiting to go into Oklahoma. In the border towns are a large number of people who have recently moved in. They have rented houses and would leave for the territory, if any prospects of success were offered them. No one wants to go alone, and everyone is waiting for someone to make the move. Pawnee Bill is much disturbed over the change in events."

In one sense Lillie was certainly the equal of Dave Payne—he could manipulate information to his own advantage. He later claimed that the mounted Indian police had been sent by Cherokee chiefs Mayes and Bushyhead with orders to shoot him down if he set foot inside the Territory. "We had succeeded in our mission," he concluded, "as we had woke up those fellows in Washington." "Life Story of Pawnee Bill," p. 17, Barde Collection, OHS.
12 *Kansas City Gazette*, March 6, 1889.

[13] *Ibid.*, March 9, 1889.
[14] *Ibid.*, March 7, 1889.
[15] *Wichita Eagle*, March 22, 1889.
[16] *Ibid.*
[17] *Ibid.*
[18] *Ibid.*
[19] The first to establish trade in Purcell was C. F. Wantland, who opened a tent store three miles south of Purcell on January 1, 1887. He completed his first building in August, 1887, and his son John M. Wantland became the town's first postmaster when the post office was established on April 21, 1887. *Purcell Register*, December 3, 1887.
[20] *Wichita Eagle*, March 22, 1889.
[21] *Kansas City Gazette*, March 4, 1889.
[22] Copy of Warning by Oklahoma Legion, Harn Collection, OHS.
[23] *Kansas City Gazette*, March 15, 1889.

CHAPTER III
Boomer Bastion

[1] *Wichita Eagle*, March 22, 1889.
[2] Letter, December 11, 1886, Item 3548, Vol. LII, Letters Received, Department of the Missouri, NA; Letter, April 14, 1887, Item 1095, Vol. LIII., *ibid.*; *Muskogee Indian Journal*, January 19, 1887.
[3] J. P. Sanger, Inspector General, to AAG, Department of the Missouri, September 27, 1889, *Senate Executive Document 72*, 51st Cong., 1st sess., pp. 15-17.
[4] *Purcell Register*, March 3, 1888.
[5] April 29, 1887.
[6] *Arkansas City Republican-Traveler*, October 21, 1887.
[7] After the run, the body of a young Texan who had been murdered was discovered at the crossing. He was identified as John W. William by his saddle. *Oklahoma Gazette*, June 4, 1889.
[8] *Winfield Courier*, May 19, 1887.
[9] *Arkansas City Republican-Traveler*, February 28, 1889.
[10] Letter, May 12, 1888, Item 1361, Letters Received, Vol. LIV, Department of the Missouri, NA; Letter, April 25, 1888, Item 1146, *ibid*.
[11] *Wichita Eagle*, February 22, 1889.
[12] A. W. Dunham, "A Pioneer Railroad Agent," *The Chronicles of Oklahoma*, Vol. II, No. 1 (March, 1924), p. 50; A. W. Durham (Dunham), "Oklahoma City Before the Run of 1889," *The Chronicles of Oklahoma*, Vol. XXXVI, No. 1 (Spring, 1958), p. 72.
[13] Alvin Rucker, "Postmaster and Population Before the Run," *Daily Oklahoman*, April 16, 1933.
[14] Joseph C. Chrisney, "The Promised Land," *Oklahoma, The Beautiful Land*, pp. 39-55.
[15] Rucker, "Postmaster."
[16] August 25, 1888.
[17] Eckelberger had been president of the Rock Falls Townsite Company, Payne's last settlement, and had been with Payne when the boomer was taken to Fort Smith by the U.S. army. A former blacksmith who had served with the Texas Confederate army, Eckelberger died at Oklahoma City on March 7, 1897, of the hiccups. *Daily Oklahoma State Capital*, March 9, 1897.
[18] *Purcell Register*, March 2, 1888; *Wichita Eagle*, December 7, 1888.
[19] *Ibid.*, January 4, 1889.
[20] *Ibid.*, January 11, 1889.

21 *Ibid.*
22 *Ibid.*
23 *Ibid.*
24 *Ibid.*
25 *Ibid.*, March 22, 1889.
26 *Ibid.*
27 *Daily Inter-Ocean* (Chicago), April 11, 1889.
28 Henry H. Stafford statement, Harn Collection.
29 Ernest C. Hamil statement, Harn Collection.
30 Report, Lieutenant John M. Carson, Jr., to Post Adjutant, Fort Reno, 1888-1889, RG 393, NA.
31 *Kansas City Gazette*, March 20, 1889.
32 Report, Carson to Adjutant, Fort Reno, April 5, 1889, RG 393, NA. This may well have been Harry Hill's old claim at the Wantland Ranch. In the run, W. A. Arnold settled on the SW ¼, Section 5, T11N, R2W, which is now split diagonally by Interstate 40. W. A. Arnold Affidavit, Harn Papers.
33 *Ibid.*
34 *Kansas City Gazette*, March 21, 1889.
35 *Ibid.*
36 *Ibid.*, March 25, 1889.
37 *Ibid.*
38 *Ibid.*, March 28, 1889.
39 *Wichita Eagle*, March 28, 1889.
40 *New York Herald*, April 13, 1889.
41 *Wichita Eagle*, March 28, 1889.
42 Report, Carson to Post Adjutant, Fort Reno, March 28, 1889, RG 393, NA.
43 *Daily Inter-Ocean*, April 11, 1889.

CHAPTER IV
Bound for Utopia

1 *St. Louis Post Dispatch*, April 21, 1889.
2 *Omaha Bee*, April 7, 1889; *Daily State Capital* (Topeka), April 8, 1889.
3 *Kansas City Gazette*, April 2, 1889.
4 *Wichita Eagle*, April 5, 1889.
5 *Kansas City Gazette*, April 5, 1889; H. C. Peterson, ed., "The Opening of Oklahoma from a European Point of View," *The Chronicles of Oklahoma*, Vol. XVII, No. 1 (March, 1939), p. 24.
6 *Daily Inter-Ocean*, April 8, 1889.
7 *Ibid.*; *Chicago Tribune*, April 8, 1889; *Chicago Herald*, April 13, 1889.
8 April 9, 1889.
9 *Fort Worth Gazette*, January 31, 1889; *Chicago Tribune*, April 14, 19, 1889.
10 *Fort Smith Elevator*, January 31, 1889; *Chicago Tribune*, April 14, 1889.
11 *Daily State Capital*, April 11, 16, 1889.
12 *Daily Inter-Ocean*, April 19, 1889; *Daily State Capital*, April 11, 19, 1889.
13 *Omaha Bee*, April 14, 18, 21, 1889.
14 *Chicago Herald*, April 13, 1889.
15 *Chicago Tribune*, April 19, 1889.
16 *Ibid.*
17 *Ibid.*
18 *New York Sun*, April 17, 1889; *St. Louis Republic*, April 17, 23, 1889.
19 *Kansas City Star*, April 17, 1889.
20 *Ibid.*
21 *Ibid.*, April 18, 1889.

22 *Ibid.*
23 *Ibid.*, April 17, 1889.
24 *New York Sun*, April 17, 1889; *Indianapolis Sentinel*, April 17, 1889.
25 *Daily State Capital*, April 19, 1889.
26 *Chicago Tribune*, April 16, 1889.
27 *Kansas City Star*, April 16, 19, 1889.
28 *Ibid.*
29 *New York Sun*, April 17, 1889.
30 *Kansas City Star*, April 17, 1889; *St. Louis Republic*, April 18, 1889.
31 *St. Louis Republic*, April 22, 1889.
32 *Milwaukee Sentinel*, April 18, 1889.
33 *Kansas City Star*, April 22, 1889.
34 *Ibid.*
35 *Ibid.*
36 *Ibid.*
37 *Chicago Tribune*, April 22, 1889.
38 *St. Louis Republic*, April 20, 1889.
39 April 19, 1889.
40 *Daily State Capital*, April 16, 1889.
41 *Kansas City Star*, April 19, 1889.
42 *Wichita Weekly Beacon*, April 10, 24, 1889.
43 *New York Herald*, April 14, 1889.
44 *Ibid.*, April 20, 1889.
45 *Chicago Tribune*, April 22, 1889.
46 *Guthrie Daily News*, November 30, 1889; B. B. Chapman, "Oklahoma District of 89ers in Court," Notes from Original Sources, Box 9, Reel 6, MM-42, Oklahoma State Library. Upon arriving back in Winfield, Haight said there were twenty soldiers lined up on the platform, and when anyone alighted a soldier would tap him on the shoulder and tell him to be ready to hop back on the train when it rolled out. *Winfield Courier*, April 11, 1889.
47 *New York Sun*, April 17, 1889; *Chicago Herald*, April 22, 1889; *St. Louis Republic*, April 17, 23, 1889.

CHAPTER V
Exodus from Arkansas City

1 *Chicago Tribune*, April 16, 1889.
2 *Ibid.*, April 17, 1889.
3 *Kansas City Star*, April 17, 1889.
4 *Ibid.*
5 *St. Louis Republic*, April 19, 1889.
6 Memoirs of John Barnes, *Sunday Oklahoman*, April 19, 1964.
7 *New York Tribune*, April 20, 1889; *Daily Inter-Ocean*, April 21, 1889.
8 *St. Louis Republic*, April 23, 1889.
9 *New York Tribune*, April 20, 1889.
10 *Ibid.*
11 *Sunday Oklahoman*, April 19, 1964.
12 *New York Tribune*, April 1889.
13 *Arkansas City Republican-Traveler*, April 25, 1889.
14 Prettyman undoubtedly went on to the Oklahoma line, but any photos he may have taken there are not to be found.
15 *Arkansas City Republican-Traveler*, April 25, 1889.
16 *Daily Inter-Ocean*, April 23, 1889.
17 *Ibid.*

[18] *St. Louis Republic*, April 21, 1889.
[19] *Kansas City Star*, April 22, 1889.
[20] *Arkansas City Republican-Traveler*, April 25, 1889; *St. Louis Republic*, April 22, 1889.
[21] *St. Louis Republic*, April 21, 1889.
[22] *New York Herald*, April 21, 1889.
[23] *Ibid.*, April 22, 1889.
[24] *Chicago Herald*, April 22, 1889.

CHAPTER VI
South from Caldwell

[1] *Kansas City Star*, April 19, 1889; *New York Herald*, April 20, 1889.
[2] *Kansas City Gazette*, April 19, 1889.
[3] *St. Louis Republic*, April 18, 1889.
[4] *Kansas City Star*, April 19, 1889.
[5] Eugene Stetler, "Rivers a Problem to Homesteaders," *Kingfisher Free Press, 75th Anniversary Issue*, April 13, 1964, p. 136.
[6] *Caldwell Journal*, February 28, 1889.
[7] *St. Louis Republic*, April 18, 1889.
[8] *New York Herald*, April 13, 1889; *Kansas City Star*, April 20, 1889.
[9] *St. Louis Republic*, April 18, 1889.
[10] *New York Herald*, April 13, 1889.
[11] *St. Louis Republic*, April 15, 17, 1889.
[12] *Ibid.*, April 18, 1889.
[13] *Caldwell Journal*, April 25, 1889.
[14] *Ibid.*
[15] *St. Louis Republic*, April 20, 1889. *Caldwell Journal* editor Swarthout counted 891 wagons before becoming weary of the chore, and they continued to roll through Caldwell the rest of the day, through the night, and during the following morning.
[16] *St. Louis Republic*, April 20, 1889.
[17] *Kansas City Star*, April 19, 1889.
[18] *Caldwell Journal*, April 25, 1889.
[19] Stetler, "Rivers a Problem to Homesteaders," p. 136.
[20] *Caldwell Journal*, May 2, 1889.
[21] Stetler, "Rivers a Problem to Homesteaders," p. 136.
[22] Harry Finley, "Recollections," *The Chronicles of Oklahoma*, Vol. LV, No. 1 (Spring, 1977), pp. 57-58.
[23] B. B. Chapman, "The Legal Sooners of 1889 in Oklahoma," *The Chronicles of Oklahoma*, Vol. XXV, No. 3 (Autumn, 1957), p. 398.
[24] Dr. Charles W. Fisk, "Dr. Fisk's Own Memoirs of Land Opening," *Kingfisher Free Press, 75th Anniversary Issue*, April 13, 1964, pp. 92-94. See also Claude Meacham, "'Oh, Joe, Here's Your Mules' Was Cry of '89ers on First Night in Oklahoma," *ibid.*, p. 139.
[25] *St. Louis Republic*, April 20, 1889; *Chicago Tribune*, April 16, 1889.
[26] *New York World*, May 5, 1889.
[27] *New York Herald*, April 20, 1889. Cole started his own newspaper, *The New World*, to help in his recruiting for the colony. Harry Hill was a director of the organization. *The New World* (first published in Wichita), March 30, 1889.
[28] *Caldwell Journal*, May 2, 1889.

CHAPTER VII
Purcell Passage

[1] *St. Louis Republic*, April 17, 1889.
[2] *Kansas City Star*, April 20, 1889. A correspondent for the *New York Herald* reported by wire from Wichita that this was "wild and exaggerated" and that the facts were that a deputy marshal went over into Oklahoma and arrested a few boomers without any special difficulty. April 22, 1889. But other newspaper accounts verify that the incident did take place.
[3] *Chicago Tribune*, April 22, 1889.
[4] *Ibid.*
[5] *Kansas City Gazette*, April 22, 1889.
[6] *St. Louis Republic*, April 17, 1889.
[7] Harn Collection, Oklahoma Historical Society.
[8] *New York Times*, April 22, 1889.
[9] *Chicago Herald*, April 22, 1889.
[10] *St. Louis Republic*, April 23, 1889; *Kansas City Star*, April 22, 1889.
[11] *Kansas City Star*, April 22, 1889.
[12] *New York Times*, April 23, 1889.
[13] *Ibid.*
[14] *Ibid.*
[15] *Ibid.*
[16] *Ibid.*
[17] *Ibid.*
[18] *Ibid.*

CHAPTER VIII
A Land Surrounded

[1] April 19, 1889.
[2] *St. Louis Republic*, April 22, 1889.
[3] *Wichita Beacon*, April 10, 24, 1889.
[4] *Wichita Eagle*, May 10, 1889.
[5] Julius A. Penn, "Roughing It in the '80s," *Daily Oklahoman Special 89er Edition*, April 22, 1909.
[6] *Chicago Tribune*, April 18, 1889.
[7] Meachem, "Oh, Joe, Here's Your Mule," p. 139.
[8] *Kansas City Gazette*, April 22, 1889.
[9] Mina Patterson Interview, Indian-Pioneer Papers, Vol. 93, OHS, pp. 98-101.
[10] *Chicago Tribune*, April 22, 1889.
[11] *Kansas City Gazette*, April 22, 1889.
[12] Penn, "Roughing It in the '80s."
[13] Montford Johnson, the son of the agent for the Chickasaws who came with them from Mississippi, was born at Tishomingo, I.T., in 1844. He ran the 7BC, 7E, and Figure 8 brands, among others. *Cheyenne Transporter* (Darlington, I.T.), March 27, 1883; August 12, 1886.
[14] Harn Collection.
[15] *Ibid.*
[16] *Ibid.*
[17] *Ibid.*
[18] *Chicago Tribune*, April 18, 1889.
[19] Dan W. Peery, "The First Two Years," *Oklahoma, the Beautiful Land*, pp. 146-151.

CHAPTER IX
The Insiders

[1] March 29, 1889.
[2] Inspector Cornelius MacBride report, Guthrie, May 8, 1889, *Senate Executive Document No. 33*, 51st Cong., 1st Sess., p. 12.
[3] Chapman, "Legal Sooners of 1889 in Oklahoma," p. 389.
[4] *New York Times*, April 16, 1889.
[5] Marshal W. C. Jones to Attorney General, Topeka, Kansas, May 9, 1889, NA, Justice Department, No. 4190, File 3485-1889.
[6] *New York Times*, April 16, 1889.
[7] Marshal T. B. Needles to Attorney General, Guthrie, May 24, 1889, NA, Justice Department, No. 4176, File 3485-1889.
[8] List of Deputies Appointed by T. B. Needles, Marshal, Indian Territory, *Senate Executive Document No. 33*, p. 4.
[9] April 18, 1889.
[10] Chapman, "Legal Sooners of 1889 in Oklahoma," p. 394.
[11] *Chicago Tribune*, April 22, 1889.
[12] April 22, 1889.
[13] Inspector J. A. Pickler to John W. Noble, Guthrie, May 8, 1889, *Senate Executive Document No. 33*, pp. 7-10.
[14] MacBride report, *Senate Executive Document No. 33*, p. 12.
[15] *New York Herald*, April 23, 1889.
[16] S. W. Proudfit, ed., *Decisions of the Department of the Interior and General Land Office*, Vol. XII, *Standley v. Jones*, pp. 253-256.
[17] *Chicago Tribune*, April 19, 1889.
[18] *New York Herald*, April 13, 1889.
[19] "Postmaster G. A. Beidler Was Rushed," Oklahoma City—Early File, OHS; Chase Beidler, "The First Post Office," *Oklahoma, the Beautiful Land*, pp. 55-57.
[20] Beidler, "The First Post Office," pp. 55-57.
[21] *New York Herald*, April 14, 1889.
[22] Victor Murdock, "Dennis T. Flynn," *The Chronicles of Oklahoma*, Vol. XVIII, No. 2 (June, 1940), pp. 107-114; Dennis T. Flynn, "The First Twenty-Four Hours in Oklahoma in 1889," *Oklahoma, the Beautiful Land*, pp. 58-63.
[23] *Wichita Eagle*, April 3, 1889.
[24] Assistant Adjutant General J. C. Kelton to Major General Crook, Washington, D.C., April 16, 1889, *Senate Executive Document No. 72*, p. 7.
[25] *New York Times*, April 20, 1889; *Daily Inter-Ocean*, April 20, 1889.
[26] *Daily Inter-Ocean*, April 20, 1889.
[27] *St. Louis Republic*, April 20, 1889.
[28] *Emporia News*, April 25, 1889; *Oklahoma Daily Capital*, June 26, 1889.
[29] *St. Louis Republic*, April 22, 1889; Fort Sill Post Returns, NA.
[30] *New York Times*, April 20, 1889.
[31] Arthur W. Dunham, "A Pioneer Railroad Agent," *Oklahoma, The Beautiful Land*, pp. 47-55.
[32] John Womack, *Norman—An Early History, 1820-1900* (Norman, Oklahoma: privately published, 1976), pp. 20-21.
[33] Stan Hoig, *The Early Years of Edmond* (Edmond, Oklahoma: Central State University Press, 1976), p. 7.
[34] *U.S. Supreme Court Reports*, Vol. 37, US 147-150, pp. 490-492.
[35] *Oklahoma Weekly Capital* (Guthrie), April 5, 1890.
[36] Proudfit, *Decisions*, Vol. XXI, *Metz v. Seely*, pp. 148-150.
[37] W. H. Matthews Interview, Indian-Pioneer Papers, OHS, Vol. 76, pp. 73-74.
[38] B. B. Chapman, "Oklahoma City, from Public Land to Private Property," *The Chronicles of Oklahoma*, Vol. XXXVII, No. 2 (Summer, 1959), pp. 219-221.
[39] *Ibid.*; J. A. Pickler to John W. Noble, May 8, 1889, Guthrie, *Senate Executive Document No. 33*, pp. 7-10.

⁴⁰ Seminole Town and Improvement Co. Plat of Oklahoma City, NA, Division K, Oklahoma Townsites, Box 140. Though there is no evidence that General Dave Littler was ever in Edmond, his name on the town plat indicates a connection between Littler and the Seminole Town and Improvement Company which drew up the plat.
⁴¹ Original copy of charter in Kansas State Historical Society, *Corporations Copy Books*, Office of Secretary of State, Vol. 36, 172.
⁴² Pickler to Noble, May 8, 1889, *Senate Executive Document No. 33*, pp. 7-10.
⁴³ *Ibid.*
⁴⁴ Luther B. Hill, *History of the State of Oklahoma*, p. 231.
⁴⁵ *Chicago Tribune*, April 23, 1889.
⁴⁶ Chapman, "Legal Sooners of 1889 in Oklahoma," p. 398.
⁴⁷ *Chicago Tribune*, April 23, 1889.

CHAPTER X
To Jordan by Coach

¹ *Kansas City Star*, April 22, 1889.
² *St. Louis Republic*, April 23, 1889.
³ *Wichita Eagle*, April 26, 1889.
⁴ *St. Louis Republic*, April 23, 1889.
⁵ *Arkansas City Republican-Traveler*, April 25, 1889.
⁶ April 25, 1889.
⁷ *St. Louis Republic*, April 23, 1889.
⁸ *Ibid.*
⁹ *Daily Inter-Ocean*, April 23, 1889.
¹⁰ *Kansas City Star*, April 22, 1889.
¹¹ *New York Herald*, April 23, 1889.
¹² Hamilton Wicks, "The Opening of Oklahoma," *Cosmopolitan*, September, 1889, pp. 460-470.
¹³ *Arkansas City Republican-Traveler*, April 25, 1889.
¹⁴ *St. Louis Republic*, April 23, 1889.
¹⁵ *Wichita Eagle*, April 26, 1889.
¹⁶ *Arkansas City Weekly Republican-Traveler*, April 25, 1889.
¹⁷ *Kansas City Star*, April 22, 1889.
¹⁸ *Daily Inter-Ocean*, April 23, 1889; *Arkansas City Republican-Traveler*, April 25, 1889.
¹⁹ *Dallas Morning News*, April 22, 1889.
²⁰ *Daily Inter-Ocean*, April 23, 1889.
²¹ *New York Herald*, April 23, 1889.
²² *Ibid.*
²³ *Milwaukee Sentinel*, April 23, 1889.
²⁴ *Daily Inter-Ocean*, April 23, 1889.
²⁵ *St. Louis Republic*, April 23, 1889.
²⁶ *Chicago Herald*, April 23, 1889.
²⁷ *Kansas State Journal*, April 22, 1889. Newspaper accounts vary on the number of trains. Some say eight, some ten, and several say twenty. The *Wichita Eagle*, citing an interview with a Santa Fe official, indicated there were over 1,000 people on the first train and on each of "the other ten," which would make eleven in all. April 26, 1889.

CHAPTER XI
Harrison's Hoss Race

1. *Wichita Eagle*, April 26, 1889; *Milwaukee Sentinel*, April 23, 1889.
2. *St. Louis Republic*, April 23, 1889.
3. *Ibid.*
4. *Wichita Eagle*, April 26, 1889; *Caldwell Journal*, April 25, 1889.
5. *St. Louis Republic*, April 23, 1889.
6. *Wichita Eagle*, April 26, 1889; *Daily Inter-Ocean*, April 23, 1889.
7. *Wichita Eagle*, April 26, 1889.
8. *Ibid.*
9. *Arkansas City Republican-Traveler*, April 25, 1889.
10. *Ibid.*
11. *Ibid.*
12. *Ibid.*
13. *Ibid.*
14. *Caldwell Journal*, May 2, 1889.
15. *Ibid.*
16. *St. Louis Republic*, April 24, 1889.
17. *Ibid.*
18. *Ibid.*
19. *Kansas City Gazette*, April 23, 1889.
20. *Chicago Tribune*, April 23, 1889; *New York Herald*, April 23, 1889.
21. *Ibid.*
22. Indian-Pioneer Papers, Karl Bornemann Interview, Vol. 16, pp. 16-25; Frank A. Myers Interview, Vol. 81, pp. 169-172; Andrew Dale Robertson Interview, Vol. 98, pp. 16-21.
23. *Edmond Booster*, April 21, 1889.
24. *St. Louis Republic*, April 23, 1889.
25. *Kansas City Times*, April 23, 1889.
26. *New York Times*, April 23, 1889.
27. *Ibid.*
28. *Oklahoma Times-Journal*, December 4, 1891.
29. Harn Papers, W. R. Massey Affidavit.

CHAPTER XII
Guthrie and the Eight O'Clock Crowd

1. *Milwaukee Sentinel*, April 19, 1889.
2. April 13, 1889.
3. *Wichita Eagle*, March 22, 1891.
4. *Kansas City Gazette*, March 28, 1889; *Emporia News*, April 4, 1889.
5. *Oklahoma Capital*, April 6, 1889.
6. *Kansas City Star*, April 16, 1889.
7. *Ibid.*
8. *Oklahoma Capital*, April 13, 1889.
9. *Wichita Eagle*, April 13, 1889.
10. Cornelius MacBride and J. A. Pickler to John W. Noble, Guthrie, May 9, 1889, *Senate Executive Document No. 33*, pp. 16-18.
11. *Wichita Eagle*, April 26, 1889.
12. *Dallas Morning News*.
13. *St. Louis Republic*, April 24, 1889.
14. Cornelius and J. A. Pickler to John W. Noble, Guthrie, April 27, 1889, *Senate Executive Document No. 33*, pp. 1-2.
15. *St. Louis Republic*, April 24, 1889.

[16] Frank J. Best, "Recollections of April 22, 1889," *The Chronicles of Oklahoma*, Vol. XXI, No. 1 (March, 1943), pp. 28-32.
[17] *Winfield Courier*, May 19, 1889.
[18] *Oklahoma Capital*, May 4, June 1, 1889.
[19] *Winfield Courier*, May 19, 1889.
[20] *Wichita Eagle*, November 29, 1889.
[21] *St. Louis Republic*, April 24, 1889.
[22] MacBride and Pickler to Noble, John Dille to Noble, *Senate Executive Document No. 33*, pp. 16-18.
[23] *Ibid.* A number of newspaper accounts say that it was a man named William Johnson who submitted the plat at 12:15. *St. Louis Republic*, April 24, 1889.
[24] *Senate Executive Document No. 33*, pp. 12-13.
[25] MacBride Report, *ibid.*; Pickler to Noble, *ibid.*, pp. 16-18; *Oklahoma Weekly Capital*, November 23, 1889; John Dille and C. M. Barnes to Comm., General Land Office, January 25, 1890, NA, RG 49, Misc. Letters Received.
[26] B. B. Chapman, "Guthrie, from Public Land to Private Property," *The Chronicles of Oklahoma*, Vol. XXIV, No. 1 (Spring, 1956), pp. 78-80.
[27] *Guthrie Daily News*, November 30, 1889.
[28] Frank Hilton Greer, "Early Romance of Oklahoma," *Oklahoma, the Beautiful Land*, pp. 82-88.
[29] *Wichita Eagle*, April 26, 1889.
[30] Chapman, "Guthrie, from Public Land to Private Property," pp. 65-69.
[31] *Daily Inter-Ocean*, April 23, 1889; *St. Louis Globe-Democrat*, May 2, 1889.
[32] *New York Herald*, April 23, 1889.
[33] *Ibid.*, April 24, 1889.
[34] *Ibid.*
[35] *St. Louis Republic*, April 24, 1889.
[36] Greer, "Early Romance," pp. 82-88.
[37] *Ibid.*
[38] *New York Herald*, April 24, 1889.
[39] Omer K. Benedict, "When Oklahoma Territory Swung Wide Her Gates," *Oklahoma Yesterday—Today—Tomorrow*, pp. 414-418.
[40] Wicks, "Opening of Oklahoma," *Cosmopolitan*, September, 1889.

CHAPTER XIII
The Grab at Oklahoma Station

[1] *Harper's Weekly*, April 23, 1892, p. 230.
[2] Dunham, "A Pioneer Railroad Agent," p. 56.
[3] *Harper's Weekly*, April 23, 1889, p. 390. Some witnesses claimed the surveyors were at work well before noon; one man said they were at work as early as 10 a.m. Luther B. Hill, *History of the State of Oklahoma*, p. 231.
[4] Martin C. Lawrence and Thomas J. Moore affidavits, Harn Papers, OHS.
[5] Samuel L. Beidler, brother to the postmaster, was the first claimant on the quarter section directly west (the Sommers's claim, NW ¼, Section 27). It was charged that Samuel Beidler never resided on the land and wholly abandoned it. He relinquished the claim on October 10, 1889. *Oklahoma Times-Journal*, July 28, 1891.
[6] *Senate Executive Document No. 33*, pp. 7-13.
[7] Proudfit, *Decisions*, Vol. XIII, pp. 66-71; Chapman, "Legal Sooners of 1889 in Oklahoma," p. 411.
[8] *Senate Executive Document No. 33*, p. 8; Oklahoma Tract Book, No. 2.
[9] Chapman, "Legal Sooners of 1889 in Oklahoma," p. 396.
[10] Oklahoma Tract Book, No. 2.

[11] Chapman, "Oklahoma City, from Public Land to Private Property," Vol. XXXVII, No. 4 (Winter, 1959-1960), p. 473; Proudfit, *Decisions*, Vol. XIII, pp. 409-411.
[12] Chapman, "Oklahoma City, from Public Land to Private Property," pp. 459-469.
[13] *Ibid.*
[14] *Ibid.*
[15] Proudfit, *Decisions*, Vol. XIII, pp. 66-71.
[16] *Ibid.*, Vol. XVI, pp. 132-135.
[17] Robe Carl White, "Experiences at the Opening of Oklahoma in 1889," *The Chronicles of Oklahoma*, Vol. XXVII, No. 1 (Spring, 1949), p. 56.
[18] Chapman, "Oklahoma City, from Public Land to Private Property," Vol. XXXVII, No. 2 (Summer, 1959), pp. 223-224.
[19] *Oklahoma Weekly Capital*, March 15, 1890; William J. McClure, "The First Legal Settler in Oklahoma City," *Oklahoma, the Beautiful Land*, pp. 72-77.
[20] Gault Affidavit, Harn Papers, OHS.
[21] *Oklahoma Daily Journal*, July 1, 1891.
[22] Richard Harding Davis, "The West from a Car Window," *Harper's Illustrated Weekly*, April 23, 1892, pp. 389-390.
[23] Chapman, "Oklahoma City, from Public Land to Private Property," pp. 225-229.
[24] Mrs. J. B. Charles, "Personal Reminiscences," *Oklahoma, the Beautiful Land*, pp. 223-224.
[25] *St. Louis Globe-Democrat*, April 24, 1889.
[26] Captain D. F. Stiles to Post Adjutant, Camp at Oklahoma City, December 20, 1889, *Senate Executive Document No. 72*, pp. 50-53.
[27] T. M. Richardson, "Fifty Years Ago in Oklahoma City," *Oklahoma, the Beautiful Land*, pp. 224-227.
[28] Calvin S. Harrah, "Experiences of Frank Harrah," *Oklahoma, the Beautiful Land*, pp. 224-227.
[29] J. A. Ryan, "Run from 'South End' Stirring Event," *Oklahoma, the Beautiful Land*, pp. 152-153; Walter E. Larsh, "Early Day Railroading," *Oklahoma, the Beautiful Land*, pp. 165-166; J. A. Burt, "The New Country," *Oklahoma, the Beautiful Land*, pp. 322-323.
[30] Davis, "The West from a Car Window," pp. 389-390.
[31] Richardson, "Fifty Years Ago," 224-227.
[32] Joseph B. Thoburn, *History of Oklahoma*, Vol. II, pp. 634-635, citing *Oklahoma City Daily Times*, November 15, 1890.
[33] *Ibid.*
[34] Stiles to Adjutant, *Senate Executive Document No. 72*, pp. 50-53.
[35] *Daily Oklahoman*, April 22, 1899.
[36] T. M. Richardson, "How the Run Looked from Down South," newspaper clipping, Oklahoma Vertical File, OHS.

CHAPTER XIV
New Empire

[1] Chapman, "Legal Sooners of 1889 in Oklahoma," p. 397.
[2] *Ibid.*, p. 402.
[3] *Kansas City Star*, April 23, 1889.
[4] *Ibid.*
[5] Marion Tuttle Rock, *Illustrated History of Oklahoma*, p. 171; *New York Times*, April 27, 1889; *Kansas City Star*, April 24, 1889.
[6] Rock, *Illustrated History of Oklahoma*, p. 172. There is an indication that the westliners first planned to name their plat "Kingfisher" but changed. *Chicago Tribune*, April 24, 1889.

[7] Jacob Willits Interview, Indian-Pioneer Papers, Vol. 50, pp. 129-140.
[8] "Settlers Came to Land Office to File on Claims," *Kingfisher Free Press, 75th Anniversary Issue*, April 13, 1964, p. 2; Rock, *Illustrated History of Oklahoma*, p. 173.
[9] *Chicago Tribune*, April 24, 1889.
[10] *Ibid.*, April 25, 1889.
[11] *New York Times*, April 27, 1889; *Wichita Eagle*, September 6, 1889.
[12] Proudfit, *Decisions*, Vol. XIV, pp. 13-17.
[13] Hoig, *The Early Years of Edmond*, pp. 7-8.
[14] Stella Fordice, "History of Edmond, Oklahoma" (Unpublished Master of Arts thesis, Norman: University of Oklahoma, 1927), p. 6; *Edmond Sun*, January 22, 1931.
[15] *U.S. Supreme Court Reports*.
[16] Testimony of A. F. Jackson, Harn Papers, OHS. See also affidavits of Charles Smith, Fred W. Sugden, Captain Joseph Anderson, Miss Ann C. Anderson, and O. N. Jaynes.
[17] J. A. Pickler to John W. Noble, Guthrie, May 14, 1889, *Senate Executive Document No. 33*, pp. 19-20.
[18] *Ibid.*; Jackson Testimony, Harn Papers.
[19] Fordice, "History of Edmond," p. 13.
[20] *Ibid.*
[21] *U.S. vs. Eddie B. Townsend, Peter Anglea*, Harn Papers, OHS.
[22] *Dallas Morning News*, April 25, 1889.
[23] Affidavit, Thomas G. Miller, July 22, 1892, General Land Office Records, Oklahoma Townsite File, NA.
[24] Rock, *Illustrated History of Oklahoma*, pp. 176-177.
[25] Edmond Townsite Application, General Land Office Records, Oklahoma Townsite File, Docket 4. The application carries the notice that it was received by the Guthrie Land Office by mail on April 25 and that it conflicted with filings made on April 22 by William Johnson and on April 24 by C. A. Compton.
[26] *Edmond Sun, Illustrated Supplement*, March 1, 1917.
[27] Pickler to Noble, *Senate Executive Document No. 33*, pp. 19-20.
[28] *U.S. Supreme Court Reports*, Vol. 148 US, pp. 533-537.
[29] Womack, *Norman—An Early History*, pp. 11-19.
[30] *Ibid.*, p. 20.
[31] *Ibid.*, pp. 24-28.
[32] *Oklahoma Times-Journal*, August 21, 1891.
[33] Rock, *Illustrated History of Oklahoma*, pp. 174-175.
[34] *Ibid.*, pp. 179-180.
[35] Proudfit, *Decisions*, Vol. XIV, pp. 146-154.
[36] B. B. Chapman, "Founding of El Reno," *The Chronicles of Oklahoma*, Vol. XXXIV, No. 1 (Spring, 1956), pp. 79-108.
[37] Proudfit, *Decisions*, Vol. XIV, pp. 153-154; *Congressional Record*, January 23, 1890, p. 740. Historian B. B. Chapman felt that Noble had done Foreman an injustice with his ruling. Chapman, "Founding of El Reno," p. 108.
[38] Chapman, "Founding of El Reno," p. 108, citing *Oklahoma Democrat* (El Reno), February 13, 1892.
[39] *Ibid.*, p. 92, fn 35; *Daily Oklahoman Special 89er Edition*, April 22, 1909; Julius A. Penn, "Roughing It in the '80s."
[40] John Womack, unpublished paper, "Noble."
[41] Mrs. Prater, "We Came, We Stayed," *Oklahoma, the Beautiful Land*, pp. 220-222; Mrs. Catalina Prater Interview, Indian-Pioneer Papers, Vol. 76, pp. 360-372.
[42] John Womack, "Noble."
[43] B. B. Chapman, *The Founding of Stillwater* (Oklahoma City: Times-Journal Publishing Company, 1948), pp. 36-77.

44 *Oklahoma Daily Capital*, May 31, June 16, 1889.
45 W. H. Matthews Interview, Indian-Pioneer Papers, Vol. 78, pp. 73-78.
46 Rock, *Illustrated History of Oklahoma*, p. 181.
47 *Ibid.*, p. 183; B. B. Chapman, "Perkins Townsite: An Archival Case Study," *The Chronicles of Oklahoma*, Vol. XXV, No. 2 (Summer, 1947), pp. 82-91.
48 *Wichita Eagle*, August 30, 1889.
49 *Oklahoma Daily State Capital*, June 28, 1889.
50 *St. Louis Republic*, April 22, 1889.
51 *Wichita Eagle*, July 5, 14, 1889.
52 Original claimants to Section 34 were Emerson B. Thorne, NE; Nathaniel P. Moran, NW; James J. Thorne, SE; and Thaddeus D. McCall, SW.
53 *Wichita Eagle*, June 28, September 27, 1889.

CHAPTER XV
The "Bubble Towns"

1 *New World* (Kingfisher), May 25, 1889.
2 *Oklahoma Daily Capital*, May 12, 1889.
3 *Ibid.*
4 *Ibid.*
5 Chapman, "The Founding of El Reno," p. 87; John L. Rice Interview, Indian-Pioneer Papers, Vol. 52, pp. 305-306.
6 *Wichita Eagle*, May 10, 1889.
7 Rice Interview, Indian-Pioneer Papers, pp. 305-306.
8 *Wichita Eagle*, June 21, 1889; Rice Interview, Indian-Pioneer Papers, p. 305-306; *Pacific Reporter, Potter vs. Hall*, Vol. 65, p. 841.
9 *New World*, June 8, 1889; Rice Interview, Indian-Pioneer Papers, p. 305.
10 *Wichita Eagle*, July 12, 1889.
11 *Oklahoma Daily Capital*, June 23, 1889.
12 Charles Hazelrigg, "The Christian Church of Sheridan, Oklahoma," *The Chronicles of Oklahoma*, Vol. XX, No. 4 (December, 1942), pp. 398-399.
13 John W. Morris, *Ghost Towns of Oklahoma* (Norman: University of Oklahoma Press, 1977), pp. 70-71; Rock, *Illustrated History of Oklahoma*, p. 183; *Oklahoma Weekly Capital*, May 24, 1890.
14 *Wichita Eagle*, August 16, November 29, 1889. It must be noted that, contrary to the prevailing notion, there were only a few black people who participated in the run of April 22, 1889. An exhaustive study by John Womack, entitled "Blacks, the First Year in Oklahoma," revealed less that fifty blacks who are believed to have participated in the run. Womack compared the Federal Land Tract records listing first claimants, but not by race, against the 1890 Territorial Census, which lists race, and found only 42 blacks. These were most heavily concentrated in the area north of Kingfisher. Another grouping of black homesteaders was located south of the Military Timber Reservation on the North Canadian. It is believed that most of the 3,000 blacks listed as citizens of the original run area in June 1890 came in following the April 22 event. This undoubtedly was caused in great part by the social prejudices of the day.
15 *Wichita Eagle*, November 15, 1889.
16 *New World*, May 18, June 15, 1889; Rock, *History of Oklahoma*, pp. 182-183.
17 *Wichita Eagle*, July 26, 1889.
18 *Ibid.*, August 16, 1889.
19 *New World*, August 10, 1899.
20 *Chicago Tribune*, April 24, 1889; *Daily Inter-Ocean*, April 24, 1889.
21 *Senate Executive Document No. 33*, p. 20.
22 Map of Oklahoma and Indian Territories, dated 1895, Oklahoma State Library.

This map and others of the period locate Columbia northeast of Wanamaker. However, one early account in the May 31, 1889, *Wichita Eagle* described the plan of an Omaha man to establish a new town by that name on the dividing ridge of the North and South Canadian rivers halfway between Fort Reno and Oklahoma City. Information on many of these former Oklahoma towns can be found in Townsite Records, General Land Office, NA. In Box 129, for instance, the transscript of *John B. Watt vs. Townsite of Columbia City* (SE ¼, Section 13, and NE ¼, Section 24, T11N, R6W) indicates that this location once had two storehouses, a blacksmith shop, livery stable, and three residences. W. S. Rice had a small stock of goods and was also postmaster at Columbia City.

CHAPTER XVI
The Sooner Cases

[1] The early settlers found ironic amusement in the story of a "fast" oxen or mule which miraculously beat all others. Several poems were written about this facet of the run. One is "Captain Caha's Mules," by Ezra Banks in Dan W. Peery, "The First Two Years," *The Chronicles of Oklahoma*, Vol. VII, No. 3 (September, 1929), pp. 268-288.
[2] Hill, *History of the State of Oklahoma*, p. 257.
[3] James L. Brown, "Early and Important Litigations," *Sturm's Oklahoma Magazine*, Vol. VIII, No. 2 (April, 1929), pp. 26-30.
[4] *Ibid.*
[5] "Roy and Estelle Hoffman—89ers," *Oklahoma, the Beautiful Land*, pp. 197-208.
[6] Hill, *History of the State of Oklahoma*, p. 257.
[7] Harn to Commissioner General Land Office, undated, Harn Papers, OHS.
[8] Hill, *History of the State of Oklahoma*, pp. 259-260.
[9] *Ibid.*
[10] *Ibid.*, p. 261.
[11] By-laws of Crutcho Organization, May 11, 1889, Harn Papers, OHS.
[12] *Ibid.*
[13] *Oklahoma Times-Journal*, December 25, 1891.
[14] *Ibid.*, January 9, 1891.
[15] George W. Gibson Affidavit, Harn Papers, OHS.
[16] Chapman, "Oklahoma District 89ers in Court," Notes, Oklahoma State Library.
[17] Numerous affidavits, including W. E. Banks, S. T. Williams, F. H. Hunter, J. D. Troop, W. M. Thornton, plus others in brief in *U.S. vs. Anton Caha*, Harn Papers, OHS.
[18] *U.S. Supreme Court Reports*, pp. 152-211.
[19] *Oklahoma Daily Capital*, June 9, 1889.
[20] *U.S. Supreme Court Reports*, pp. 152-211.
[21] Hill, *History of the State of Oklahoma*, p. 260.
[22] *Ibid.*, pp. 258-259; Proudfit, *Decisions*, Vol. XIV, pp. 13-17.
[23] *Oklahoma Times-Journal*, February 26, 1892.

CHAPTER XVII
The Land Fights at Oklahoma City

[1] *U.S. vs. J. C. Adams*, Harn Papers.
[2] *Oklahoma City Daily Times*, October 21, 1889.
[3] Chapman, "Oklahoma City, from Public Lands to Private Property," pp. 46-63.
[4] Affidavit, William McClure, Frank Gault Case, Harn Papers, OHS.

[5] Affidavit, William McClure, Frank Johnson Case, Harn Papers, OHS.
[6] *Oklahoma Reports*, Vol. V, p. 174, *John A. Meyers vs. U.S.*
[7] Oklahoma Tract Books, Vols. 3-4.
[8] Gault Affidavit, Harn Papers, OHS.
[9] Affidavits, Harn Papers, OHS. Edmond Fillson claimed that Gault, Brusha, and the others could not have made the ride in less than one and three-quarters hours because of the country's being full of black jack and running oak with projecting roots and branches for six miles. Judge J. L. Brown wondered why Gault and several others were not in the penitentiary. *Oklahoma Daily Times*, September 11, 1892.
[10] Chapman, "Oklahoma City, from Public Land to Private Property," p. 236, fn. 42.
[11] G. Turner Affidavit, Harn Papers, OHS.
[12] Oklahoma Tract Books, Vols. 3-4.
[13] *Odell vs. Bourne, Oklahoma Reports*, Vol. 5, p. 570; *Oklahoma City Daily Times*, November 8, 1889.
[14] *Oklahoma Weekly Capital*, March 15, 1890.
[15] Proudfit, *Decisions*, Vol. XIII, pp. 66-71.
[16] *Ibid.*, Vol. XVIII, pp. 31-35.
[17] *Ibid.*; *Oklahoma Daily Journal*, June 19, 1891.
[18] *Oklahoma Times-Journal*, July 28, 1891.
[19] Oklahoma Tract Books, Vols. 3-4. Sommers, as a U.S. Commissioner, administered the oaths of office to the provisional officials of Oklahoma City, including William L. Couch as mayor. Chapman, "Legal Sooners of 1889 in Oklahoma," p. 386, fn. 9.
[20] Proudfit, *Decisions*, Vol. XV, pp. 267-270; *Oklahoma City Times-Journal*, January 1, 1892.
[21] Chapman, "Oklahoma City, from Public Land to Private Property," pp. 473-476.
[22] *Ibid.*, pp. 453-459; *Oklahoma Daily Journal*, June 14, 1891.
[23] Proudfit, *Decisions*, Vol. XVI, pp. 132-135.
[24] *U.S. vs. Meshack Q. Couch*, Harn Papers, OHS; Kuhlman, Lee, Couch Affidavits, Harn Papers; Oklahoma Tract Books, Vols. 3-4.
[25] *Oklahoma Gazette*, August 19, 25, 1889.
[26] Oklahoma Tract Books, Vols. 3-4.
[27] *Oklahoma Reports*, Vol. 5, p. 127; *Oklahoma Times-Journal*, October 16, 1892; Oklahoma Tract Books, Vols. 3-4.
[28] Jackson Affidavit, Harn Papers, OHS; Proudfit, *Decisions*, Vol. XXI, pp. 16-61; *Oklahoma Times-Journal*, October 16, 1892; Oklahoma Tract Books, Vols. 3-4.
[29] *Oklahoma Times-Journal*, February 26, 1892; *Oklahoma Daily Capital*, December 3, 1890.
[30] *Oklahoma Daily Journal*, July 1, 1891; Newspaper clipping, "The Curt Blackburn Case," Harn Papers, OHS.
[31] *Oklahoma Times-Journal*, June 2, 1894; Oklahoma Tract Books, Vols. 3-4.
[32] *Oklahoma Reports*, Vol. 1, p. 336, *Grant Stanley vs. U.S.* In running for public office in 1902, Grant Stanley defended himself in an Edmond speech. Among other things, he said that he had been the attorney for every claim but two within a mile and a half of the Oklahoma City townsite, and that all of his clients had admitted to being sooners except Katie Woodruff. *Edmond Enterprise*, October 16, 1902.
[33] *Oklahoma Daily Times-Journal*, July 28, 1892; *Supreme Court Of Oklahoma*, Vol. 41, p. 357.

CHAPTER XVIII
Other Sooner Cases

[1] Proudfit, *Decisions*, Vol. XIV, pp. 593-595.
[2] Chapman, "Legal Sooners of 1889 in Oklahoma," p. 413.
[3] Proudfit, *Decisions*, Vol. XXI, pp. 284-287.
[4] *Ibid.*, Vol. XVII, pp. 414-417.
[5] *Ibid.*, pp. 47-54.
[6] *Ibid.*, Vol. XV, pp. 584-585; Chapman, "Oklahoma District 89ers," Notes.
[7] *Oklahoma Times-Journal*, November 18, 1893.
[8] Proudfit, *Decisions*, Vol. XVII, pp. 162-168.
[9] *Ibid.*, Vol. XII, pp. 654-661; pp. 562-568; Chapman, "Guthrie, from Public Land to Private Property," pp. 70-78.
[10] Proudfit, *Decisions*, Vol. XII, pp. 654-668; Chapman, "Guthrie, from Public Land to Private Property," pp. 65-69.
[11] Proudfit, *Decisions*, Vol. VII, pp. 402-404.
[12] Chapman, "Guthrie, from Public Land to Private Property," pp. 78-86.
[13] Proudfit, *Decisions*, Vol. XVI, pp. 375-378.
[14] *Ibid.*, Vol. XVIII, pp. 112-115.
[15] Chapman, *The Founding of Stillwater*, pp. 37-77.
[16] *Oklahoma Times-Journal*, December 4, 1891.

CHAPTER XIX
The Eighty-Niners—I

[1] Eugene D. Stetler, "Kingfisher North Line," *Kingfisher Free Press 75th Anniversary Issue*, April 13, 1964, p. 136.
[2] Robert Galbreath Interview, Indian-Pioneer Papers, Vol. 25, pp. 319-322; Vol. 74, pp. 171-173.
[3] Interview of Endsley Jones, *Ibid.*, Vol. 5, pp. 515-518.
[4] William Kenworthy, "The Opening of Oklahoma, OHS Vertical Files.
[5] Grant Shoop Interview, Indian-Pioneer Papers, Vol. 73, pp. 22-29.
[6] Winifred L. Morton (Salesbury), "No. Seven Colony," *Oklahoma, the Beautiful Land*, pp. 242-248.
[7] Ada Baskins Jorgenson, "Stakes Her Claim with the American Flag," *Oklahoma, the Beautiful Land*, pp. 269-270; Ada Baskins Jorgenson Interview, Indian-Pioneer Papers, Vol. 62, pp. 451-453.
[8] Edna Helm Ahrens Interview, Indian-Pioneer Papers, Vol. 66, pp. 33-37.
[9] Andrew David Robertson Interview, *ibid.*, Vol. 98, pp. 16-21.
[10] Mina Patterson Interview, *ibid.*, Vol. 93, pp. 98-107.
[11] Karl Reichert Interview, *ibid.*, Vol. 58, pp. 3-11; Anna Reichert Interview, *ibid.*, Vol. 70, pp. 464-471.
[12] De'Leslaine R. Davis Interview, *ibid.*, Vol. 53, pp. 89-93.
[13] Karl Bornemann Interview, *ibid.*, Vol. 16, pp. 16-25.

CHAPTER XX
The Eighty-Niners—II

[1] Mrs. Welling Haynes Interview, Indian-Pioneer Papers, Vol. 28, pp. 345-352; Mrs. C. E. Haynes, "Experiences of a Pioneer Woman," *Oklahoma, the Beautiful Land*, pp. 212-213.
[2] Charles C. Alling Interview, Indian-Pioneer Papers, Vol. 12, pp. 292-302.
[3] James K. Hastings, "The Opening of Oklahoma," *The Chronicles of Oklahoma*, Vol. XXVII, No. 1 (Spring, 1949), pp. 70-75.

[4] M. T. Hoover Interview, Indian-Pioneer Papers, Vol. 29, pp. 421-427.
[5] Matilda Pontius Interview, *ibid.*, Vol. 40, pp. 208-215.
[6] Alfretta Jennings, "The Jennings Family Goes Adventuring," *Oklahoma, the Beautiful Land*, pp. 272-276.
[7] Laura (Mrs. C. A.) Barnum, "Six Stakes on Same Land, But Woman Claimant Won Out," *Kingfisher Free Press, 75th Anniversary Issue*, April 13, 1964, p. 22.
[8] Byron Dick Webb Interview, Indian-Pioneer Papers, Vol. 75, pp. 156-164.
[9] William T. Rogers Interview, *ibid.*, Vol. 42, pp. 254-258.
[10] James McKee Owen, "Reminiscences," *The Chronicles of Oklahoma*, Vol. XXIV, No. 2 (Summer, 1956), pp. 217-221.
[11] A. M. Debolt, "Battle with 'Jumpers,'" *Oklahoma, the Beautiful Land*, p. 95.
[12] L. F. Carroll, "The Diary of an Eighty-Niner," *The Chronicles of Oklahoma*, Vol. XVI, No. 1 (March, 1938), pp. 66-69.
[13] Joseph W. Bouse Interview, Indian-Pioneer Papers, Vol. 1, pp. 261-273; Oklahoma Tract Books, Vols. 3-4.
[14] Thoburn and Wright, *Oklahoma, a History*, Vol. II, pp. 893-894.
[15] April 21, 1889.

Bibliography

Archival

Barde Collection, Oklahoma Historical Society.

Chapman, Berlin B. "Oklahoma District of 89ers in Court," Notes from Original Sources, Box 9, Reel 6, MM-42, Oklahoma State Library.

Clipping Book, OHS.

Couch, Eugene. "A Pioneer Family," manuscript, OHS.

Dangerfield, Royden J., ed., "The Autobiography of Samuel Crocker," manuscript, OHS.

Harn Papers, OHS.

Indian-Pioneer Papers, OHS.

Original Charter, Seminole Town and Improvement Company, Kansas State Historical Society.

Vertical Files, OHS: 89er Collection.

Womack, John. Unpublished paper on founding of Noble, personal files. Unpublished paper "Blacks, the First Year in Oklahoma."

Articles

Barnum, Mrs. E. A. (Laura). "Six Stakes on Same Farm, But Woman Claimant Won Out," *Kingfisher Free Press 75th Anniversary Issue*, April 13, 1964.

Beidler, Chase. "The First Post Office," *Oklahoma, the Beautiful Land* (Oklahoma City: Times-Journal Publishing Co., 1943).

Benedict, Omer K. "When Oklahoma Territory Swung Wide Her Gates," *Oklahoma Yesterday—Today—Tomorrow* (Guthrie: Co-operative Publishing Co., 1930).

Best, Frank J. "Recollections of April 22, 1889," *The Chronicles of Oklahoma*, Vol. XXI, No. 1 (March, 1943).

Brown, James L. "Early and Important Litigation," *Sturm's Oklahoma Magazine*, Vol. VIII, No. 2 (April, 1909).

Brownlee, George. "Northliners Late for First Lots in Kingfisher," *Kingfisher Free Press 75th Anniversary Issue*, April 13, 1964.

Buck, Solon J., "The Settlement of Oklahoma," *Wisconsin Academy of Science, Arts and Letters*, September, 1907.

Cade, Cash M. "The Day of Days," *Oklahoma, the Beautiful Land* (Oklahoma City: Times-Journal Publishing Co., 1943).

Carroll, L. F. "The Diary of an Eighty-Niner," *The Chronicles of Oklahoma*, Vol. XVI, No. 2 (March, 1938).

Casey, Naomi Taylor, "Cowboy King Won Race of '89," *Orbit Magazine*, April 17, 1977.

Chapman, Berlin B. "Founding of El Reno," *The Chronicles of Oklahoma*, Vol. XXIV, No. 1 (Spring, 1956).

_____ . "Freedmen and the Oklahoma Lands," *Southwestern Social Science Quarterly*, Vol. 29 (September, 1948).

_____ . "Guthrie, from Public Lands to Private Property," *The Chronicles of Oklahoma*, Vol. XXXIII, No. 1 (Spring, 1955).

_____. "The Legal Sooners of 1889 in Oklahoma," *The Chronicles of Oklahoma*, Vol. XXXV, No. 3 (Autumn, 1957).

_____. "Oklahoma City, from Public Lands to Private Property," *The Chronicles of Oklahoma*, Vol. XXXVIII, No. 2 (Summer, 1959); Vol. XXXVIII, No. 3 (Autumn, 1959); Vol. XXXVIII, No. 4 (Winter, 1959-1960).

_____. "Perkins Townsite: An Archival Case Study," *The Chronicles of Oklahoma*, Vol. XXIV, No. 2 (Summer, 1947).

Charles, Mrs. J. B. "Personal Recollections," *Oklahoma, the Beautiful Land* (Oklahoma City: Times-Journal Publishing Co., 1943).

Chrisney, Joseph C. "The Promised Land," *Oklahoma, the Beautiful Land* (Oklahoma City: Times-Journal Publishing Co., 1943).

Clark, Laura G. (Mrs. Ivan), "Six Children of Pioneer Weimer Family Still Living," *Kingfisher Free Press 75th Anniversary Issue*, April 13, 1964.

Davis, Richard Harding. "The West from a Car Window," *Harper's Illustrated Weekly*, April 23, 1892.

Dunham, A. W. "A Pioneer Railroad Agent," *The Chronicles of Oklahoma*, Vol. II, No. 1 (March, 1924).

_____. "Oklahoma City Before the Run," *The Chronicles of Oklahoma*, Vol. XXXVI, No. 1 (Spring, 1958).

Dunjee, Roscoe, "Negroes Pioneered in Many Fields in the Early Days," *Daily Oklahoman Special 89er Edition*, April 23, 1939.

Finley, Harry. "Recollections," *The Chronicles of Oklahoma*, Vol. LV, No. 1 (Spring, 1977).

Fisk, Dr. Charles W. "Dr. Fisk's Own Memoirs of Land Opening," *Kingfisher Free Press 75th Anniversary Issue*, April 13, 1964.

Flynn, Dennis T. "The First Twenty-Four Hours in Oklahoma in 1889," *Oklahoma, the Beautiful Land* (Oklahoma City: Times-Journal Publishing Co., 1943).

Foster, George D., and Foster Children, "Pioneer Woman Forded Cimarron Daily," *Kingfisher Free Press 75th Anniversary Issue,* April 13, 1964.

Greer, Frank Hilton. "Early Romance of Oklahoma," *Oklahoma, the Beautiful Land* (Oklahoma City: Times-Journal Publishing Co., 1943).

Gustin, Alvin M. "An 89er Speaks," *Oklahoma, the Beautiful Land* (Oklahoma City: Times-Journal Publishing Co., 1943).

Harrah, Calvin S. "Experiences of Frank Harrah," *Oklahoma, the Beautiful Land* (Oklahoma City: Times-Journal Publishing Co., 1943).

Hastings, James K. "The Opening of Oklahoma," *The Chronicles of Oklahoma*, Vol. XXVII, No. 1 (Spring, 1949).

Haynes, Mrs. C. E. "Experiences of an Oklahoma Pioneer Woman," *Oklahoma, the Beautiful Land* (Oklahoma City: Times-Journal Publishing Co., 1943).

Hazelrigg, Charles. "The Christian Church of Sheridan, Oklahoma," *The Chronicles of Oklahoma*, Vol. XX, No. 4 (December, 1942).

Hill, Herbert C. "Hill Family Came from Texas in Ox-Drawn Wagons," *Kingfisher Free Press 75th Anniversary Issue,* April 13, 1964.

Hoffman, Roy. "Roy and Estelle Hoffman—89ers," *Oklahoma, the Beautiful Land* (Oklahoma City: Times-Journal Publishing Co., 1943).

Holznapfel, John. "The Kansas Oklahoma Colony," *Oklahoma, the Beautiful Land* (Oklahoma City: Times-Journal Publishing Co., 1943).

Howard, William Willard, "The Oklahoma Movement," *Harper's Illustrated Weekly*, May 4, 1889.

Jennings, Alfretta. "The Jennings Family Goes Adventuring," *Oklahoma, the Beautiful Land* (Oklahoma City: Times-Journal Publishing Co., 1943).

Jorgenson, Ada Baskins. "Stakes Her Claim with the American Flag," *Oklahoma, the Beautiful Land* (Oklahoma City: Times-Journal Publishing Co., 1943).

Kane, Mrs. Matthew J. "Kingfisher Elects a Provisional City Government," *Oklahoma, the Beautiful Land* (Oklahoma City: Times-Journal Publishing Co., 1943).

Kelley, E. H. "When Oklahoma City Was Seymour and Verbeck," *The Chronicles of Oklahoma*, Vol. XXVII, No. 4 (Winter, 1949-1950).

Kenworthy, William. "The Opening of Oklahoma," OHS Vertical Files, from *Kansas City Times*.

Knight, Charlie. "The Top of the World—1889," *Oklahoma, the Beautiful Land* (Oklahoma City: Times-Journal Publishing Co., 1943).

Larsh, Walter E. "Early Day Railroading," *Oklahoma, the Beautiful Land* (Oklahoma City: Times-Journal Publishing Co., 1943).

Marble, A. D. "Oklahoma Boomers, Trials and Troubles," *Sturm's Oklahoma Magazine*, Vol. 6, No. 5 (July, 1908).

McClure, William J. "The First Legal Settler in Oklahoma City," *Oklahoma, the Beautiful Land* (Oklahoma City: Times-Journal Publishing Co., 1943).

Meachem, Claude. "'Oh, Joe, Here's Your Mules' Was Cry of '89ers on First Night in Oklahoma," *Kingfisher Free Press 75th Anniversary Issue*, April 13, 1964.

Messenbaugh, Mrs. L. F. "Reminiscences of Pioneer Days," *Oklahoma, the Beautiful Land* (Oklahoma City: Times-Journal Publishing Co., 1943).

Morton, Winifred L. (Salesbury). "No. Seven Colony," *Oklahoma, the Beautiful Land* (Oklahoma City: Times-Journal Publishing Co., 1943).

Murdock, Victor. "Approach to Notable Date, April 22," *Oklahoma, the Beautiful Land* (Oklahoma City: Times-Journal Publishing Co., 1943).

Owen, J. M. "Reminiscences of an '89er of Oklahoma City," *The Chronicles of Oklahoma*, Vol. XXXIV, No. 2 (Summer, 1956).

Parfry, Mrs. Jennie M. "In My Dreaming, I Call It Holy Land," *Kingfisher Free Press 75th Anniversary Issue*, April 13, 1964.

Peery, Dan W. "The First Two Years," *Oklahoma, the Beautiful Land* (Oklahoma City: Times-Journal Publishing Co., 1943).

_____ . "Colonel Crocker and the Boomer Movement," *The Chronicles of Oklahoma*, Vol. XIII, No. 3 (September, 1935).

Penn, Julius A. "Roughing It in the '80s," *Daily Oklahoman*, April 22, 1909.

Perry, Mrs. S. J. (Faye S.). "A. E. Stalnaker Was Early-Day Surveyor Here," *Kingfisher Free Press 75th Anniversary Issue*, April 13, 1964.

Peterson, H. C., translator and editor. "The Opening of Oklahoma from the European Point of View," *The Chronicles of Oklahoma*, Vol. XVII, No. 1 (March, 1939).

Prater, Mrs. "We Came, We Stayed," *Oklahoma, the Beautiful Land* (Oklahoma City: Times-Journal Publishing Co., 1943).

Richardson, T. M. Jr. "Fifty Years Ago in Oklahoma City," *Oklahoma, the Beautiful Land* (Oklahoma City: Times-Journal Publishing Co., 1943).

_____ . "How the Run Looked from Down South," Oklahoma City Vertical File, OHS.

Rucker, Alvin. "Postmaster and Population Before the Run," *Daily Oklahoman*, April 16, 1933.

Russell, Edith B. "Why We Came," *Oklahoma, the Beautiful Land* (Oklahoma City: Times-Journal Publishing Co., 1943).

Ryan, J. A. "Run from 'South End' Stirring Event," *Oklahoma, the Beautiful Land* (Oklahoma City: Times-Journal Publishing Co., 1943).

Schreffler, Doyle H. "A Journey," *Oklahoma, the Beautiful Land* (Oklahoma City: Times-Journal Publishing Co., 1943).

"Settlers Came to Land Office to File Claims," *Kingfisher Free Press 75th Anniversary Issue*, April 13, 1964.

Scott, Angelo C. "The First Week in Oklahoma City," *Oklahoma, the Beautiful Land* (Oklahoma City: Times-Journal Publishing Co., 1943).

Stetler, Mrs. Archie (Stella). "Homesteaders Wanted Water on Their Land," *Kingfisher Free Press 75th Anniversary Issue*, April 13, 1964.

Stetler, Eugene. "Rivers a Problem to Homesteaders," *Kingfisher Free Press 75th Anniversary Issue*, April 13, 1964.

Thurman, Dr. J. H. "The Doctor Takes a Bride," *Oklahoma, the Beautiful Land* (Oklahoma City: Times-Journal Publishing Co., 1943).

Terrill, I. N. "The Sooners," *Sturm's Oklahoma Magazine*, Vol. 8, No. 2 (April, 1909).

_____ . "The Boomers' Last Raid," *Sturm's Oklahoma Magazine*, Vol. 8, No. 2 (April, 1909).

Walker, Dr. Delos. "Out of the Raw Material," *Oklahoma, the Beautiful Land* (Oklahoma City: Times-Journal Publishing Co., 1943).

Way, Mrs. Ross R. "From California to Oklahoma," *Oklahoma, the Beautiful Land* (Oklahoma City: Times-Journal Publishing Co., 1943).

Wetzel, John J. "Cooked for Carpenters," *Oklahoma, the Beautiful Land* (Oklahoma City: Times-Journal Publishing Co., 1943).

White, Robe Carl. "Experiences at the Opening of Oklahoma," *The Chronicles of Oklahoma*, Vol. XXVII, No. 1 (Spring, 1949).

Wicks, Hamilton. "The Opening of Oklahoma," *Cosmopolitan*, September, 1889.

Williams, Loren. "The Original Oklahoma Boomer," *The Oklahoma News*, December 20, 1936.

Willmott, Irene Etta Cruce. "Recollections of an '89er," *Oklahoma, the Beautiful Land* (Oklahoma City: Times-Journal Publishing Co., 1943).

Womack, John. "Countdown to the Run," *Cleveland County Reporter*, April 17, 1980.

Books

Aldrich, Gene. *Black Heritage of Oklahoma* (Edmond, Oklahoma: Thompson Book & Supply Co., 1973).

Burright, Orrin Ulysses. *The Sun Rides High* (Wichita Falls, Texas: Nortex Publishing Inc., 1973).

Chapman, Berlin Basil. *The Founding of Stillwater* (Oklahoma City: Times-Journal Publishing Co., 1948).

Eighty-niners, The. *Oklahoma, The Beautiful Land* (Oklahoma City: Times-Journal Publishing Co., 1943).

Ernest, Lynn. *Pawnee Bill and the Oklahoma Boomers* (Chicago: The White House Publishers, 1927).

Hill, Luther B. *The History of the State of Oklahoma.* 2 vols. (Chicago: Lewis Publishing Co., 1908).

Hoig, Stan. *The Early Years of Edmond* (Edmond, Oklahoma: Central State University Press, 1976).

Matthews, William B. *The Settlers Map & Guide Book* (Washington, D.C.: Wm. H. Lepley Electric Power Printer, 1889).

Morris, John W. *Ghost Towns of Oklahoma* (Norman: University of Oklahoma Press, 1977).

Morris, Lerona Rosamond. *Oklahoma Yesterday—Today—Tomorrow* (Guthrie, Oklahoma: Co-operative Publishing Co., 1930).

Oklahoma—A Guide to the Sooner State (Norman: University of Oklahoma Press, 1941).

Rock, Marion Tuttle. *Illustrated History of Oklahoma* (Topeka, Kansas: C. B. Hamilton & Son, 1890).

Shirley, Glenn. *Pawnee Bill* (Albuquerque: University of New Mexico Press, 1958).

Thiel, Sidney, comp. *The Oklahoma Land Rush* (Washington, D.C.: Works Projects Administration, NA).

Thoburn, Joseph B., and Wright, Muriel H. *Oklahoma—A History of the State and Its People*, 4 vols. (New York: Lewis Historical Publishing Co., Inc., 1929).

Womack, John. *Norman—An Early History, 1820-1900* (Norman: published by the author, 1976).

Wood, S. N. *The Boomers or the True Story of Oklahoma* (Topeka, Kansas: Bond and Neill, 1885).

Government Documents Published

Congressional Record

Federal Reporter

Oklahoma Criminal Reports

Oklahoma Decisions Reported in Pacific Reporter

Oklahoma Reports

Oklahoma Statutes Annotated

Pacific Reporter

Pacific Reporter, 2nd Series

Proudfit, S. W., ed. *Decisions of the Department of the Interior and the General Land Office.*

Report of the Secretary of War, 1889.

Senate Executive Document No. 33, 51st Cong., 1st sess.

Senate Executive Document No. 72, 51st Cong., 1st sess.

U.S. Reports

U.S. Supreme Court Reports

Government Documents
Unpublished

Adjutant General, Office of, Letters Received, 1881-1889.

Fort Reno, Letters Received, Record Group 393, National Archives.

General Land Office, Letters Received, Record Group 60, File 3485, Nos. 4716, 4190.

U.S. War Department, Office of Adjutant General, Papers Relating to the Intrusion by Unauthorized Persons into Indian Territory, Including Invasions into Oklahoma Territory, the Cherokee Strip, and Greer County, Texas. Boxes 425-442, 18 reels.

Newspapers

Arkansas City Republican-Traveler
Caldwell Journal
Cheyenne Transporter (Darlington, I.T.)
Chicago Herald
Chicago Tribune
Cleveland County Reporter (Norman)
Daily Inter-Ocean (Chicago)
Daily Oklahoman (Oklahoma City)
Daily State Capital (Topeka)
Dallas Morning News

Edmond Enterprise
Edmond Sun
Emporia News
Fort Smith Elevator
Fort Worth Gazette
Harper's Illustrated Weekly
Guthrie Daily Capital
Guthrie Daily News
Guthrie Getup
Indian Chieftain (Vinita, I.T.)
Indian Citizen (Atoka, I.T.)
Indian Journal (Muskogee, I.T.)
Indianapolis Sentinel
Kansas City Gazette
Kansas City Globe
Kansas City Star
Kingfisher Daily World
Kingfisher Free Press
Milwaukee Sentinel
Muskogee Phoenix
New World (Kingfisher)
New York Herald
New York Sun
New York Times
Oklahoma Chief
Oklahoma City Daily Times
Oklahoma Daily Capital (Guthrie)
Oklahoma Democrat (El Reno)
Oklahoma Gazette (Oklahoma City)
Oklahoma Standard (Stillwater)
Oklahoma Times-Journal
Omaha Bee
Purcell Register
St. Louis Globe-Democrat
St. Louis Post-Dispatch
St. Louis Republic
Wichita Beacon
Wichita Eagle
Winfield Courier

Index

— A —

Abilene, Kansas, 230
Abilene Cattle Trail, 96, 182
Acres, Nelson F., Internal Revenue Collector, 103
Adair, Lt. Samuel W., 31, 86, 89, 104, 133
Adams, J. C., 192, 196, 197, 208
Admire, Jacob V. "Cap," 106, 165; named Receiver of Moneys at Kingfisher, 106
Ahrens, Martin, 230
Alfred station, 25, 102, 111, 112, 177, 178, 240
Alling, Charles C., 237, 238, 239
Allman, John, 171
American Freedmen's Fund, supporting black boomers, 184
Anderson, Capt. Joseph, 168
Anglea, Hardy C., 169
Ansley, W. W., deputy marshal, 103
Anthony, Kansas, 181
Arapaho Indians, 36, 167, 211
Arbuckle Cattle Trail, 30, 37, 172
Arkansas, 5
Arkansas City, Kansas, 4, 5, 6, 14, 19, 20, 23, 31, 32, 40, 41, 45, 48, 55, 56, 58, 59, 61, 62, 66, 73, 74, 76, 79, 83, 88, 90, 102, 103, 104, 105, 106, 107, 111, 113, 116, 117, 118, 122, 123, 124, 125, 131, 136, 147, 157, 168, 170, 176, 177, 179, 205, 207, 219, 226, 228, 229, 230, 237, 238, 239, 240, 241, 243; Summit Street, 62; boomers, 146; *Dispatch*, 120; *Republican-Traveler*, 120; *Traveler*, 4; *Weekly Republican*, 116
Arkansas City-Fort Reno cutoff, 78
Arkansas River, 60, 62, 118
Arnold, W. A., 39, 40, 41, 43, 190
Ashinger, Charles F., 161
Atlantic & Pacific Railroad, 137

— B —

Baker, Capt. H. D., 141, 142
Ball, 186
Barlow, Lucian H., 204
Barnard, Kansas, 241
Barnes, Cassius M., 103, 106, 143, 194, 205, 219; named Receiver of Moneys, 103
Barnes, Rep. George T., of Georgia, 7
Barnes, John H., 220
Barnum, Mrs. E. A. (Laura Brown), 242
Barrett survey of 1873, of Oklahoma, 171

Barrow's crossing, 96, 98, 191, 213
Barrow's farmhouse, 97; boomer camp at, 97
Baskins, Ada, 229, 230
Beaver Creek, 178
Beidler, Chase, 106, 107
Beidler, George A., Oklahoma station postmaster, 106, 107, 153, 154, 204, 205
Beidler, R. Linn, 106, 107
Belcher, W. H., 204
Bell, John C., deputy marshal, 103
Bergs Colony, 47
Berry, 186
Best, Frank, 140
Beulah, 186
Bickford, C. B., 32, 213
Big Turkey Creek, 79
Birge City (Edmond), 171
Bixler, M. J., 201
Black Bear River, 66, 67, 120, 128
Black Bear Trail, 67, 68, 127
Blackburn, Curt, 209
Blacks, origins of boomers in Oklahoma, 46; as cavalrymen, 77; as cowboys, 172; settling in Oklahoma, 184; as boomers, 185; participating in Oklahoma land run, 234
Blair, Marion, 184, 185
Blakeslee, Charles W., 177
Blanchard, Carley, 156, 201
Bluff City, Kansas, 229
Bluff Creek, 74, 75
Bockfinger, Henry H., 219
Bohemian settlers, 97, 98, 192, 193
Boomer crossing, 96
Boomer train, 88, 121, 133, 134, 170, 177, 213, 226
Boomers (settlers, rushees, land seekers), 5, 6, 9, 9, 18, 20, 27, 28, 35, 37, 38, 44, 55, 60, 61, 62, 65, 66, 67, 68, 69, 71, 73, 85, 87, 91, 94, 97, 106, 112, 116, 125, 128, 129, 132, 133, 153, 195; black, 40; camps of, 22; leaders of, 10; reasons for coming to Oklahoma, 92
Booth, John W., 199
Bornemann, Karl, 234, 235
Bothel, D. C., 182
Boudinot, Col. Elias C., 3, 16
Bourn, E. W., 201
Bouse, Joseph W., 244, 245
Bowman, 186
Bracht, Emil, 245
Bross, J. H., 179

Brown, Andrew J., 203
Brown, J. L., 201
Brown, Nellie, 242, 37
Brusha, J. W., 198, 199, 200
Bryant, Jim, 177
Bryant, Mrs. Jim, 177
Bubble towns, 180; list of, 186
Buckhead, 186
Buffalo Springs, 68, 72, 77, 78, 79, 92, 114, 124, 129, 130, 166, 223; boomers starting at, 167
Bullfoot Ranch, 34, 235
Burford, John H., Register of Deeds, Oklahoma City land office, 205, 208
Burks, Garnett, 177, 221
Burt, Father J. A., 160
Burton, John, 203

— C —

Caddo Indian reservation, 178
Caha, Capt. Anton, 97, 192, 193
Caldwell, Kansas, 5, 19, 22, 41, 48, 49, 55, 71, 72, 73, 74, 75, 76, 78, 79, 90, 91, 92, 173, 181, 194, 223, 224, 225; Board of Trade, 22; boomers camped at, 72; fairgrounds, 78; *Journal*, 74
Caldwell, Belle, 207
Calhoun, Calvin A., 205, 206
Call, James W., 215
Camp Couch, 155
Camp Price, 19
Canadian, 186
Cannon, Rep. Joseph, of Illinois, 10
Cannon Ball Stage Line, 72
Cantonment Trail, 93
Carpenter, Col. C. C., 4, 12, 16
Carroll, L. F., 244
Carson, Lt. John M. Jr., 38, 39, 40, 41, 43, 190
Cartwright, John P., 213
Case, 186
Cashion, 132
Cattle syndicates, control Oklahoma lands, 11; oppose opening of Oklahoma, 12
Cedar, 186
Chaddick, 186
Chamberlain, Charles, 113, 114, 152
Chandler, George, Ass't Sec'y of the Interior, 212
Chapin, John G., 211, 212
Cherokee Coal and Iron Railroad, 153
Cherokee Indians, 8
Cherokee Nation, 8, 218

277

Cherokee Outlet (also Strip), 25, 52, 56, 61, 63, 66, 68, 71, 73, 74, 78, 91, 118, 120, 121, 123, 125, 180, 236; cattlemen, 74
Cherokee Strip Live Stock Association, 12, 33; opposes opening of Oklahoma, 12
Cheyenne Indian scouts, 31, 35
Cheyenne Indians, 24, 36, 167, 211
Cheyenne-Arapaho Indian reservation, 173 (see also Darlington Indian agency)
Chicago, Illinois, 41, 45, 53; *Daily Inter-Ocean*, 43, 120; *Herald*, 120; *Tribune*, 91, 114
Chicago Oklahoma Colony, 45, 47, 48, 53, 167, 171
Chickasaw Indians, 8, 26
Chickasaw Nation, 8, 18, 19, 40, 83, 95, 111, 133, 172, 175, 178, 190
Chikaskia River, 19, 237, 239
Childer, Edd, 132
Chilocco Creek, 19
Chilocco Indian School, 23, 62
Chisholm Cattle Trail, 130, 182, 224, 235
Chisholm Creek, 22
Choctaw Coal & Railway Company, 138, 153, 181, 182, 200
Choctaw Indians, 8
Choctaw Nation, 138
Chrisney, Joseph C., 34
Chrisney, Indiana, 34
Cimarron, 178, 184
Cimarron City, 178, 182, 183
Cimarron River, 25, 50, 58, 72, 75, 100, 123, 127, 128, 137, 146, 178, 182, 184, 185, 210, 220, 238, 243; bridge over, 228
Cincinnati (Ohio) *Commercial Gazette*, 120
Clark, Frank E., 172
Clark, George R., deputy marshal, 103
Clarke, Sidney, 5, 7, 12, 13, 113, 154, 157
Clarkson, 186
Clayton, 186
Clayton, Gen. W. H. H., 103, 141, 143; files townsite plat of Guthrie, 143
Cleveland (Ohio) *Leader*, 119
Cleveland, Pres. Grover, 7, 15
Clifton Hotel, Purcell, 26, 27, 28
Coffeyville, Kansas, 244
Cohn, Mark S., 142, 143, 219

Cole, Charles, 219, 220; sued by T. M. Golden, 219
Cole, E. C., 22, 23, 56, 79, 167
Cole, T. F., 169
Cole Colony, 79
Coletown, 167
Collins, Charles, deputy marshal, 102
Collins, Ed, deputy marshal, 103
Colony, Kansas, 57
Colony Crowd, 57, 158
Colorado, 5, 55, 92
Columbia, 186
Combs, Leslie, 216
Conception, 186
Congressional Record, 174
Conway, Arkansas, 46
Cook, Frank, 197, 200, 201
Cook, Vestal, 197, 201
Cooper, George, 226
Cooper, Capt. George H., 118
Cooper, George W., 48
Cooper's colony, 226
Copper, Robert, 220, 221
Cottonwood Creek, 25, 56, 137, 143, 144, 147, 149, 182, 219, 228, 229
Couch, Charles B., 155
Couch, John M., 155
Couch, Joseph, 112
Couch, M. Q. "Quint," 112
Couch, Meshack H., 112, 155, 206
Couch, Thomas H., 112, 208
Couch, William L., 4, 5, 6, 7, 11, 12, 13, 16, 18, 21, 23, 28, 30, 40, 41, 58, 112, 113, 138, 157, 159, 176, 192, 195, 197, 208; elected mayor of Oklahoma City, 197
Couch boomers, 190, 194, 195
Couch family, 112, 155
Council Grove, 32, 186
Cow Creek, 96, 177
Cowboys, 27, 47, 74, 77, 85, 86, 90, 91, 93, 121, 128, 129; used as press couriers, 120
Cowley, Kansas, 144
Cowley County, Kansas, 57, 156, 237; townsite colony, 144
Cox, R. L., deputy marshal, 102
Crandall, L. H., 113
Crawford Opera House, Wichita, Kansas, 11
Creek Indians, 3, 8, 14, 16, 42
Creek Nation, 12, 102
Crescent, 179, 238
Crescent Townsite Company, 179
Crocker, Samuel, 5, 6, 7, 11, 12, 13, 15,

28, 112, 155, 158, 198, 199, 201
Crutcho Creek, 23, 37, 39, 98, 135, 158, 190, 191, 193
Crutcho Flat, 200
Crutcho Organization, protects sooners, 190, 191

— D —

Daisey, Nanitta A. H., 88, 120, 139, 170
Dallas (Texas) *Morning News*, 88, 120, 170
Darlington Indian agency, 31, 32, 36, 71, 91, 83, 102, 138, 174, 180, 181, 235
Darlington, William T., 174
Darlington-Fort Reno area, 92, 124, 132, 235
Davis, Anson A., 174
Davis, De'Leslaine R., 234
Dawson, John M., 197
Dead Man's Crossing, 32
DeBolt, A. M., 243, 244
Decker, William, 31
Decker building, at Oklahoma station, 32, 33
Deep Fork River, 32, 37, 99, 100, 208, 243, 244; trestle bridge over, 208
Deer Creek, 56, 182, 229
Delaney, Carroll, receiver of moneys, Oklahoma City land office, 205, 208
Denison, Texas, 138
Denver, 186
Denver, Colorado, 94
DeTar, Edward, 155, 205
Dick, Louis O., 157, 198
Dille, Jehu E., 142, 143
Dille, John I., Register of Deeds, Guthrie land office, 103, 106, 143, 194, 205, 219
Dodge City, Kansas, 242
Dodsworth, 186
Donald, I. N., 229, 230
Dover, 184, 211
Downing's ford, 96, 191
Downing's Grove, boomer camp at, 97
Downs, 184
Downs Townsite Company, 184
Dreeson, B. J., 173
Drum, W. E., 171
DuBois, Col. J., 181
Duncan, Sandford, 176, 221
Dunham, A. W., 33, 110, 152
Durland, Otto C., 209
Dyer, Col. D. B., 118, 138, 142, 167; agent to Cheyenne-Arapaho Indians, 118

— E —

Eades, J. D. ("Kiowa"), 43
Earlie, Chief John [Ottawa], 6, 8
East Guthrie vs. Veeder B. Paine, 216, 217
Eckelberger, T. W., 34, 38, 39, 155, 205, 206
Eda, 186
Edmond, 112, 113, 169, 170, 171, 185, 194, 228, 230; townsite plat of, 171; station, 25, 56, 88, 100, 103, 111, 113, 145, 167, 168, 208, 229, 243
Eggleston, T. C., 35, 36, 43
Eighty-Niners, 223
El Reno, 173, 174, 175, 193, 215, 231, 232, 234; Townsite Company, 173
Elliott, Temp, deputy marshal, 103
Emporia, Kansas, 34, 48, 226
Emporia colony, 226
Ephraim Creek, 68
Evans, J. S., 31, 32
Ewing, 37

— F —

Fairbanks, George, 238, 239
Fall Creek, 72
Feagins, James W., 144, 218, 219
5th United States Cavalry, 18, 62, 86, 91, 104, 108, 110, 122, 153; Troop C, 121; Troop D, 122, 125; Troop K, 73
Fisher, George W., 191
Fitzgerald, Thomas, 214
Fitzgerald, Xenophon, 217, 218
Flinn, Peter Oliver, 234
Flynn, Dennis T., 107, 108, 119, 142; appointed postmaster at Guthrie, 107
Forbush, Capt. W. C., 153
Foreman, John A., 174, 175
Fort Elliott, Texas, 110
Fort Gibson, 46, 242
Fort Leavenworth, Kansas, 49, 73, 108, 109
Fort Lyon, Colorado, 110
Fort Reno, 18, 31, 32, 34, 37, 38, 43, 52, 56, 71, 73, 90, 91, 92, 93, 94, 95, 102, 110, 131, 173, 175, 178, 181, 182, 192, 213, 214, 230-231, 233, 234, 235
Fort Reno Road, 156
Fort Reno-Caldwell stage route, 34, 56, 71, 72, 78, 90, 179, 211
Fort Scott, Kansas, 6
Fort Sill, 32, 34, 110
Fort Smith, Arkansas, 46; black boomers from, 46

279

Fort Supply, 110
Fort Wayne, Indiana, 49
Fort Worth, Texas, 88, 168, 216; *Gazette*, 120
Fossett, William D., 165, 166, 167; sued by townsite of Kingfisher, 193
Foster, Judge C. G., 109, 110, 142
Foster, Lt. Fred W., 66, 67, 68, 123, 127
Foster's crossing, 96
Fowler, John, 208, 209
Franklin, 186
Frisco, 181, 182; convention, 181, 185; township, 215
Frost, J. E., 113, 142, 154
Fry, William, 236
Fuller, Eugene, 198, 199
Fuller, Perry, 191
Fuller, Randall, 198, 199
Fuller-Russell Town Site Company of Arkansas City, Guthrie, and Oklahoma City, 47
Furbush, W. R., 46
Furlong, John, 6, 28

— G —

Gage, 233
Gainesville, Texas, 4
Galbreath, Robert, 224, 225
Gallimore's crossing, 96, 98
Galloway, Judge John M., United States Commissioner, 6, 109, 141, 144
Gamblers, at Oklahoma station, 30; at Arkansas City, 59; at Purcell, 87; at Guthrie station, 147
Garrett, D. B., 185
Gault, Frank M., 158, 189, 198, 199, 200
George Miller Ranch, 78
Gibson, George W., 32, 33, 34, 192, 196
Gibson, Mrs. George, 192
Giffin, Abiel W., 215, 216
Gilbert, Pleasant M., 32, 199
Gillett, Sen. F. E., 179
Godfrey, J. T., 181
Golden, T. M., vs. Charles Cole, 219
Golden, T. M., 219, 220
Goring, John, 185
Grand Army of the Republic (G.A.R.), 56, 75
Green, Col. D. R. "Cannonball," 72, 130
Greencastle (Indiana) *Star Press*, 120
Greer, Frank, 138, 144, 145, 226
Greff, Lewis A., 201

Greiffenstein, William, 98
Gueda Springs, Kansas, 6, 20
Guthrie, Judge John, 109, 118, 141, 142
Guthrie Settlers' Association, 146
Guthrie station, 19, 25, 41, 42, 43, 45, 49, 50, 57, 58, 87, 90, 91, 100, 103, 104, 107, 108, 109, 110, 111, 113, 116, 123, 127, 136, 137, 138, 139, 142, 144, 146, 147, 149, 150, 155, 159, 161, 164, 166, 167, 169, 170, 176, 179, 182, 183, 193, 203, 205, 207, 211, 216, 217, 218, 219, 221, 226, 228, 229, 236, 240, 241, 242; land office established at, 42; Eastern District Land Office at, 43; land office at, 102, 103, 105, 106, 108, 143, 146, 157, 170, 171, 172, 187, 195, 201, 204, 205, 212, 221; Guthrie House Hotel at, 139, post office, 142; townsite group, 145

— H —

Hagin, Eugene, assistant United States Attorney, 142
Haight, N. A., 57
Haines, Rachel Anna, 112, 155, 206, 207
Hall, 186
Hall, Capt. W. C., 91, 131
Hamill, Kid, 38, 107
Hardesty, John W., 171
Harkins, Col. G. W., 8, 9
Harn, W. F., 169, 189, 190, 193
Harper, Kansas, 181
Harper's Illustrated Weekly, 120
Harrah, Frank, 160
Harrison, Pres. Benjamin, 16, 22, 29, 41, 42, 44, 71, 101, 102, 106, 108, 137, 141
Harrison, 182, 185
Hartsell, 186
Hastings, James K., 238, 239, 240
Hay, Daniel, deputy marshal, 103
Hayes, Capt. Jack, 62, 63, 64, 65, 68, 128
Haynes, Mrs. Welling, 236
Hefley, J. L., 110-111, 172, 173
Helm, Edna, 230
Hennessey, 179, 183, 184
Hennessey Massacre, 179, 224
Herron, 186
Hico, 186
Higgins, Dr. Robert W., 196
Hill, "Oklahoma Harry," 12, 19, 20,

21, 22, 24, 25, 26, 28 29, 30, 36, 37, 38, 40, 72, 130, 138, 183
Hill, Arthur, 216
Hills, O. O., 135, 221, 222
Hoover, M. T., 240
Howe, Henry, 203
Hubbard, George E., 78, 164, 167
Huckleberry, James H., deputy marshal, 103, 143, 217
Hudson, J. A., 113
Hunnewell, Kansas, 19, 21, 58, 78
Hurt, William S., 215
Husband, David, 176

— I —

Illinois, 49, 54, 102, 167
Indian Appropriation Bill of 1889, 14, 22
Indian Meridian, 99, 245
Indian police, 38, 239
Indian scouts, 37, 39, 93
Indian Territory, 4, 5, 6, 7, 8, 9, 11, 12, 13, 16, 17, 18, 19, 22, 23, 24, 45, 46, 55, 58, 62, 75, 78, 88, 92, 101, 102, 110, 120, 137, 138, 163, 216, 217, 225, 232
Indiana, 53; settlers from ("Hoosiers"), 45
Indianapolis (Indiana) *Sentinel*, 119
Indians, 8, 12, 16, 18, 27, 119
Ingalls, 186
Ingalls, Sen. John J., of Kansas, 14
Ingram, George, 46
International Order of Odd Fellows, 94, 166
IOA cattle ranch, 99, 168
Iowa, 11, 51
Iowa Indian reservation, 99, 168, 216, 219, 220, 243, 244
Iowa State *Leader*, 120; *Register*, 119-120
Ismet, Peter, 200
Italy, 178

— J —

Jackson, A. F., 168
Jackson, Ambrose F., 207
Jaynes, O. N., 168
Jenkins's crossing, 96
Jennings, Alfretta, 241
Jennings, J. P., deputy marshal, 102
Jennings, J. S., 6
Jensen, Thomas, 175

Jerome, James, 216, 217
Johnson, Charles F., 199
Johnson, Montford [Chickasaw], 96, 172
Jones, Asa, deputy marshal, 102, 143, 155, 200
Jones, Endsley, 225, 226
Jones, Marshal William C., 101, 102, 104, 113, 139, 153, 154, 157, 159
Jordan, Dr. Francis M., 212-213
Jorgenson, Henry, 230

— K —

Kansas, 4, 5, 6, 11, 18, 19, 22, 23, 25, 33, 35, 37, 47, 49, 55, 57, 58, 61, 63, 68, 72, 75, 92, 102, 103, 111, 146, 147, 149, 157, 223, 235, 236, 244; blacks, 184; boomers, 13; border, 71, 73, 78, 81, 223
Kansas City, Missouri, 5, 6, 48, 52, 53, 62, 67-68, 115, 226; Board of Trade, 6; Interstate-Oklahoma Legislative Memorial, 7; Union Depot, 48, 49, 50, 51, 52; *Gazette*, 22, 29, 137; *Graphic*, 119; *Star*, 76, 119, 120; *Times*, 4, 5, 16, 104, 119, 142, 226
Kansas State Penitentiary, 102
Kenworthy, William, 226
Kesler, Willis, 200
Keyes, M. J., deputy marshal, 102
Kickapoo Flats, 135
Kickapoo Indian reservation, 46, 99, 243
Kickapoo Indians, village of, 243, 244
Kickapoo station, 48, 99
Kicking Bird, 6, 179
Kingfisher, 42, 43, 72, 75, 78, 90, 91, 94, 103, 114, 124, 129, 130, 131, 138, 166, 173, 179, 182, 184, 185, 216, 224, 225, 226, 229, 230, 242; stagecoach relay station at, 42, 71; land office established at, 42; Western District Land Office at, 43, 102, 105, 114, 187, 212, 215; station, 56, 73, 90, 91, 164, 165, 215; townsite, 167
Kingfisher Creek, 91, 92
Kingkade, Andrew, 110, 172, 173
Kingman, Kansas, 72, 179
Kingsbury, C. H., 197
Kiowa, Kansas, 107, 181; *Herald*, 107
Klinglesmith, J. W., 175
Koonce, J. B., deputy marshal, 102, 154, 198
Kuhlman, H. George, 206

281

— L —

Lafayette County, Missouri, 50
Lake Erie, Ohio, 238
Lakeview, 186
Lamb, W. F., 200
Land seekers, *see* Boomers
Langston, 220
Lannon, C. P., 178
Larned (Kansas) *Chroniscope*, 119
Larsh, D. L., 172, 173
Larsh, Walter E., 160
Las Vegas (Nevada) *Optic*, 120
Laughlin, M. M., 220
Laurie station, 228
Lawrie, 186
Lee, Robert J., 206
Lewis, A. P., 28
Lexington, 100
Liberty, 186
Lightning Creek, 158, 191, 192, 193
Lightning Creek Combination, protects sooners, 191
Lillie, Maj. Gordon W. ("Pawnee Bill"), 19, 20, 21, 22, 55, 78, 79
Lima, 186
Lincoln, 184, 185
Linden, Kansas, 229
Lisbon, 131, 166
Little Rock, Arkansas, black boomers from, 46
Littler, Gen. David T., 46, 104, 113
Livingston, Harry, 118
Lockwood, M. L., 200
Logan County, 230
Long-O crossing, 96, 97, 192
Long-O Ranch, 96
Loo, Sam, 43
Love, Robert [Chickasaw], 26
Lowry, Robert, 176, 220

— M —

MacArthur, Capt. Arthur, 109, 139, 140; father of Douglas, 109
MacBride, Cornelius, Interior Department inspector, 104
Madden, Ed, deputy marshal, 102
Mansur, Rep. Charles H., of Missouri, 11, 12, 28
Maples, Ezra, 219
Marshall, 183
Martin, Rev. H. H., 185
Martin, James, 171
Martin, Samuel D., 220

Maryland, 47, 49, 56
Masonic Order, 94
Massachusetts, 49
Massey, George W., 198
Mathewson, 182
Mathewson, William M. ("Buffalo Bill"), 182
Mathewson City, 182
Matthews, Sam, 177, 178
May, Kate E., 206
McAlester, 138
McClure, William J., 98, 99, 158, 197, 198
McComb, Lt. A. C., 17, 35, 36
McCormack, James, 205, 206
McDonaugh, George L., deputy marshal, 103
McGinty, Pat, 236
McGranahan, James, 34, 106, 107; postmaster at Oklahoma station, 34; replaced as postmaster, 107
McGranahan, Sarah, 34
McLane, C. R., 118
McNalley, Joe, 81, 82
McPeek, George S., 218
McPherson (Kansas) *Freeman*, 120
Mendota station, 24, 25
Mennonites, operate Indian school, 93
Merritt, Brig. Gen. Wesley, 73, 108, 109, 110, 151, 153
Meyers, John A., 198
Michigan, 49, 167
Miles, John D., agent to Cheyennes & Arapahos, 167
Miller, 186
Miller, Ben, 33
Miller, Nathan N., 206
Miller, Thomas G., 170
Miller, W. H. H., United States Att'y Gen., 102, 108
Milwaukee, Wisconsin, 51; *Sentinel*, 120
Minick, Dr. J. M., 56, 91, 92, 181, 185, 186
Minneapolis, Kansas, 223
Minor, C. E., 177
Missouri, 4, 5, 44
Missouri Pacific Railroad, 46
Mitts, T. J., deputy marshal, 103
Mohler, O. E., deputy marshal, 103
Monroe, William, 212
Moonlighters, 100
Moore, 244; station, 30, 113 (*see also* Verbeck station)

282

Morena, 186
Mormons, 45
Morton, Winifred, 228, 229
Moss, Thomas, 199
Mowrey, Al, 56
Mulhall, Zack, 111, 112, 177; assistant livestock agent for Santa Fe, 177
Mulhall, 178, 218
Munford, Dr. Morrison, 5, 7, 104, 142
Murdock, Marsh, 11, 19, 20
Murphy, John M., 191
Murphy, Samuel, 201
Murray, Rev. James, 57, 158, 159
Muskogee, 102
Mustang Creek, 39, 192, 193, 212
Myrtle, 186

— N —

Nebraska, 75
Needles, Marshal Thomas B., 102, 103, 104
Negroes, *see* Blacks
New Mexico, 5
New York, New York, 46, 50, 118; *Herald*, 119; *Press*, 120; *Times*, 50, 89, 103
New York, 49
Newspapers, list of correspondents reporting on opening of Oklahoma, 119-120
Nine-Mile Flats, 99
No-Man's Land, 92, 225, 233
Noble, John A., Sec'y of the Interior, 105, 108, 174, 175, 177, 193, 194, 205, 206, 217, 218, 219
Noble, 176; townsite plat of, 176
Norman, Abner, 171
Norman station, 26, 30, 103, 110, 113, 159, 160, 171, 172, 173, 175; townsite plat of, 172
Norman Townsite Company, 172
Norman's Camp, 172
North Canadian River, 4, 30, 35, 37, 39, 43, 48, 56, 93, 94, 98, 99, 124, 135, 152, 155, 178, 180, 181, 182, 185, 191, 192, 197, 198, 205, 207, 212, 213, 214; east of Fort Reno, 90, 92, 95, 233, 234, 243, 244
North Carolina, black boomers from, 46
Northliners, boomers starting at north edge of Oklahoma, 167

— O —

O'Rourke, Richard ("Stage Line Dick"), 49
O. K. Cattle Company, 235
Odell, Daniel J., 155, 200, 201
Ohio, 47, 56, 69
Oklahoma (Oklahoma country, Oklahoma lands, Oklahoma district—not state), 3, 4, 5, 6, 10, 12, 13, 14, 15, 17, 19, 20, 21, 23, 25, 26, 27, 28, 29, 35, 36, 38, 41, 44, 45, 47, 49, 50, 51, 52, 53, 55, 56, 58, 59, 60, 63, 64, 67, 68, 69, 71, 72, 73, 74, 81, 83, 87, 89, 90, 92, 95, 97, 98, 99, 101, 102, 103, 104, 107, 108, 109, 110, 112, 113, 119, 124, 125, 127, 132, 133, 135, 136, 137, 140, 144, 149, 150, 164, 169, 173, 175, 176, 178, 181, 187, 188, 190, 191, 192, 193, 197, 200, 203, 204, 206, 207, 209, 210, 211, 212, 213, 214, 217, 218, 219, 223, 224, 226, 228, 230, 233, 234, 236, 238, 240, 242, 243, 244, 245; and squatters' rights, 28; border, 61, 74, 79, 93, 94, 122, 125, 241
Oklahoma bill, to open Oklahoma to settlement, 5, 7, 11, 12, 13, 14, 15, 22
Oklahoma boomer crusade, 207
Oklahoma boomers, 4, 14; convention held at Arkansas City, 14
Oklahoma Capital, 138, 144
Oklahoma Capital City Town Site and Improvement Company, 46
Oklahoma City (Oklahoma station), 27, 31, 32, 112, 113, 154, 164, 166, 182, 189, 191, 193, 194, 200, 204, 207, 209, 211, 215; station, 18, 22, 23, 24, 25, 30, 31, 32, 33, 34, 35, 37, 38, 39, 40, 41, 43, 57, 58, 83, 87, 88, 90, 98, 102, 103, 104, 106, 107, 108, 109, 110, 112, 113, 116, 135, 138, 145, 152, 153, 154, 155, 156, 157, 158, 160, 161, 162, 168, 170, 188, 191, 192, 194, 195, 196, 197, 198, 202, 205, 206, 207, 208, 209, 213, 221, 243, 244; post office building at, 36; land office, 187, 197, 203, 205, 206, 208, 209, 222; established, 187; townsite, 198
Oklahoma Co-Operative Townsite and Homestead Company, 35, 84
Oklahoma colonies, 46, 55, 78
Oklahoma Colony of the Real Estate Homestead and Emigration Association for the State of Kansas, 47

283

Oklahoma country, *see* Oklahoma
Oklahoma district, *see* Oklahoma
Oklahoma fever, 46, 52, 235
Oklahoma Homestead and Town Company, 174
Oklahoma lands, *see* Oklahoma
Oklahoma legion, 84
Oklahoma Mercantile Co., 157
Oklahoma movement, 11, 19, 21, 184
Oklahoma Panhandle, 92
Oklahoma question, 7, 11
Oklahoma settlement, 11, 22, 142
Oklahoma State Capital, 226
Oklahoma station, *see* Oklahoma City
Oklahoma Territorial Legislature, 200
Oklahoma Territory, 108, 245
Oklahoma Territory Supreme Court, 187, 201, 207, 209
Oklahoma Times, 43
Oklahoma Town Company of Meade Center, 47, 57, 158, 159
Oklahoma War Chief, 5, 15
Old Santa Fe crossing, 96
Old soldier colonies, 56, 68, 77, 91, 92, 228
Omaha, Nebraska, 47, 52, 192; *Bee*, 120
Omer, 186
Orlando, 178, 236, 238, 240, 241
Orme, Edward, 206
Otoe Springs, 219
Ottawa Indians, 7
Owen, James McKee, 243
Oxford, Kansas, 240
Oxford colony, 241

— P —

Paine, Veeder B., 145, 217; sued by East Guthrie townsite, 216
Paradise, 186
Parker, Capt. D. L., 46
Parker, Colonel, 208
Patterson, John, deputy marshal, 102, 144
Patterson, Lee, 232, 233
Patterson, Mina Wade, 232, 233
Pauls Valley, 175
Pauls Valley Townsite Company, 175
Pawnee Bill Colonization Company, 20, 79
Pawnee Bill Wild West Show, 19
Pawnee Indian Reservation, 19
Pawnee Indians, 24
Payne, Capt. David L., 4, 11, 12, 16, 17, 18, 19, 20, 28, 30, 32, 34, 37, 47, 58, 68, 112, 206, 207
Payne, Ransom, deputy marshal, 102, 144, 145, 217, 218
Payne's Oklahoma Colony, 48, 119, 176, 204, 221
Payne-Couch boomers, 60, 83
Pearce, H. L., 12
Peel, Rep. Samuel W., of Arkansas, 10, 14
Peery, W. T., 96
Peery crossing, 96
Penn, Julius A., 175
Pennsylvania, 49
Peoria, Illinois, 54
Perkins, 167, 178
Perkins, Cong. Bishop W., of Kansas, 7, 9, 14, 22, 174
Perry, William, United States Attorney, 142
Peters, Clay, 202, 203
Peters, Rep. Samuel B., of Kansas, 10, 107
Phelps, Frank S., 206
Pickett, C. C., 99
Pickler, John A., Public Land Office inspector, 105, 171, 185, 186
Pierce, H. A., 141
Pikey's crossing, 96
Pittsburgh (Pennsylvania) *Commercial Gazette*, 119
Plumb, Sen. Preston B., of Kansas, 14, 38, 107
Poisal, Snake Woman [Arapaho], 214
Ponca agency, 24, 64, 144, 219
Ponca Indian reservation, 24
Ponca Indians, 119
Ponca station, 24, 64, 65, 119, 120
Ponca Trail, 63, 67, 68, 241
Pond Creek, 56, 71, 72, 76, 79, 130, 180
Pontious, Matilda, 240
Pontoon bridge, across Salt Fork, 64
Pott line, 100, 112
Pottawatomi Indian reservation, 82, 98, 99, 100
Preston, H. L., 120
Prettyman, W. S., 66
Proctor, Redfield, Sec'y of War, 108
Public domain, 11, 14, 16
Purcell, 18, 23, 26, 27, 35, 36, 40, 41, 55, 57, 81, 82, 83, 84, 86, 87, 88, 97, 98, 108, 110, 111, 124, 133, 135, 139, 147, 152, 159, 160, 161, 168, 170, 172, 175, 176, 203, 207, 213, 235, 244; *Register*, 34; station, 87

— Q —

Quincy, 186

— R —

Radcliff, Virgil, 208, 209
Radebaugh, Mary, 208
Radebaugh, Samuel H., 32, 33, 34, 37, 38, 39, 40, 43, 153; operates Oklahoma station hotel, 36
Rainey, George, 183
Ralston, 186
Rarrick, Capt. O. S., deputy marshal, 102, 103, 144
Ratts, Oliver N., 213, 214
Red Fork, 184, 225; renamed Dover, 184; station, 31, 225
Red Fork Ranch, 211, 225
Red Fork Trail, 244
Red Hill, at Purcell, 26, 89, 133, 176; St. Augustine Catholic mission on, 26
Red Rock Creek, 239
Red Rock, 238; station, 24, 64, 68, 120
Red Wing, 184, 185
Reece, Jasper, deputy marshal, 103
Reichert, Karl, 233, 234
Rennie, Albert, 172, 175, 176
Rennie, James, 175
Reno City, 180, 181, 182, 234
Reynolds, Milton W. ("Kicking Bird"), 6, 13, 20, 119, 179
Reynolds, T. C., 200
Richardson, T. M., 160
Riddle, Solomon S., 212
Robb, Almira C. Wilkerson, 202, 203
Roberts, Jacob C., Register of Deeds, Kingfisher land office, 106
Robertson, Andrew Dave, 230, 231, 232
Robinson, F. R., 45, 48
Rock Creek, 236
Rock Island, 182
Rock Island Hotel, 72, 77, 131
Rock Island Railroad, 48, 49, 53, 56, 71, 72, 79, 178, 179, 180, 181
Rock Island stage line, 130
Rogers, William, 242
Rushees, see Boomers
Ryan, J. A., 160
Ryan, Rep. Thomas, of Kansas, 14

— S —

Sac and Fox Indian agency, 32, 244
Sac and Fox Indian reservation, 99, 145, 216, 244
Sacred Heart Mission, operated by Catholics, 99
Salt Fork of Arkansas River, 24, 63, 64, 66, 72, 76, 77, 78, 120, 144, 223, 237, 239, 241, 243; bridge over, 64, 65, 128
San Francisco (California) *Call and Bulletin*, 119
Santa Fe House, Guthrie, 139; Purcell, 17
Santa Fe Railroad, 4, 5, 18, 23, 27, 30, 31, 45, 48, 53, 58, 65, 71, 81, 90, 103, 108, 109, 111, 112, 113, 115, 116, 123, 124, 125, 136, 138, 140, 144, 147, 157, 160, 161, 167, 171, 172, 176, 177, 178, 180, 182, 185, 188, 194, 198, 200, 205, 206, 208, 212, 218, 235, 239, 244, 245; attorney for, 15; bridge at Purcell, 86
Sapulpa, 137, 184
Schofield, Maj. Gen. J. W., 108
Scott, Capt. S. H., 46
Secret leagues, in Oklahoma, 44, 189, 190
Seeley, Albert, 111, 177
Seminole Indians, 3, 8, 14, 16, 42
Seminole Townsite and Improvement Company, 88, 112, 113, 138, 142, 154, 157, 158, 167, 168, 171, 172, 195; surveyors for, 168, 172, 173; townsite plat of Oklahoma City, 159
7-C Flats, 99
7-C ranch, 98, 100, 124, 135, 158, 197, 198, 201, 203, 209, 221, 244
7th United States Cavalry, troops H & K, 110
Seward station, 226, 228, 229
Shawnee Town, 98, 99
Shawneetown Road, 98, 99, 158, 197, 209
Sheridan, 183
Sherman, Texas, 46
Shoop, Lincoln Grant, 226, 228
Sikes, Dan, 63
Silver, 186
Silver City, in Chickasaw Nation, 33, 95; crossing, 96

285

Skeleton Creek, 68, 77, 124
Sluss, Judge H. C., 19
Smith, Alexander B., 111, 167, 168, 169, 171, 194; *vs. Eddy B. Townsend*, 194
Smith, E. G., 173
Smith, Hoke, Sec'y of the Interior, 203, 207
Smith, Capt. Jesse G., 47, 52
Smith, John R., 167, 168, 171
Snyder, 29, 186
Snyder, Lt. Col. Simon, 110, 153
Soldier Creek, 98, 135, 158, 191, 199, 200
Sommers, C. F., 31, 32, 33, 106, 107, 110, 153, 154, 202, 203, 204; United States Commissioner, 204
Sommers, Eva, 31
Sooners, 100, 101, 188, 192, 193, 194, 195, 198, 206, 211, 212, 213, 221, 222, 245; at Guthrie station nicknamed Eight O'Clock Crowd, 140; "legal," 194; commit perjury to protect claims, 195, 198, 206
Sorenson, Conradina, 202, 203
South Canadian River, 17, 18, 26, 27, 28, 30, 34, 40, 51, 57, 82, 83, 86, 95, 96, 98, 99, 100, 132, 133, 151, 152, 158, 160, 173, 175, 178, 191, 192, 193, 196, 213, 214, 235; crossings of, 96
South Oklahoma City, 159, 205 ,206, 243
Southwestern Kansas Immigration Society, 47
Speer, Billy, 226
Spencer, 222
Spice, W. M., 182
Springer, Rep. William M., of Illinois, 5, 8, 9, 10, 11, 13, 14, 15, 46
Springer Oklahoma Bill, 6, 11, 13, 21
Springfield, Illinois, 46, 104, 139
Springfield, Missouri, 167, 238; colony, 170-171
Springvale, 186
St. Augustine Catholic Mission, at Purcell, 85
St. Joseph, Missouri, 205
St. Louis, Missouri, 53, 111; *Post-Dispatch*, 245; *Republic*, 104, 119, 139
St. Louis & San Francisco Railroad, 71, 181, 184, 185
Standard, 186
Stanley, Grant, 209
Star Mail and Stage Company, 213

Stearrett, George, United States District Court Clerk, 142
Steen, John, 111, 168
Stetler, Eugene, 223
Stetler, M. O., 223, 224
Stevens, J. O., deputy marshal, 102
Stiles, Capt. D. F., 151, 152, 159
Stillwater, 176, 219; townsite plat of, 176
Stillwater Creek, 67, 124, 128, 176, 220
Stillwater Town Company, 176, 221
Stilwell, Jack, deputy marshal, 102, 181
Stone, W. M., assistant commissioner, General Land Office, 204
Stone, William W., Commissioner, General Land Office, 218
Sumner, E. V., United States Commissioner, 193
Swarthout, R. B., 74, 77
Syke, J. M., 178

— T —

Taft, Frank A., 212
Tahlequah, 242
Taylor, John B., 212
Taylor, John D., 212
Taylor, Thomas, deputy marshal, 103, 219
10th United States Infantry, 151, 153
Terrill, I. N., 219
Texas, 4, 5, 18, 19, 82, 102; Panhandle, 51, 92
Thompson, James, 175
Thornton, George, 33, 155, 205
Thurston, 52, 186
Tobee, 186
Tonkawa, 237
Topeka, Kansas, 46, 72, 109, 113, 141, 184, 185; United States district court at, 109; *Commonwealth*, 31; *Journal*, 20
Touse, Frank, 46, 47
Townsend, Eddy B., 99, 168, 169, 171; sued by Alexander Smith, 194
Townshend, Rep. Richard W., of Illinois, 7
Townsite companies, 55; list of, 47
Townsite of Kingfisher vs. John H. Wood and William Fossett, 193, 205
Tulsa, 137, 244
Turkey Creek, 73, 224
Turkey Track ranch, 145, 216
Turner, B. J., deputy marshal, 103

286

Turner, Edgar, 213
Turner, Fenton, 143
Turner, J. Wheeler, 169

— U —

United States Army, 4, 18, 20, 43, 58, 65, 68, 74, 75, 86, 91, 92, 95, 98, 106, 125, 130, 139, 149, 199, 220, 239, 242; Quartermaster Department, 31; Division of the Missouri, 108
United States Bureau of Indian Affairs, 4, 33
United States Congress, 4, 5, 7, 9, 11, 13, 14, 21, 141, 204; Senate-House joint committee, 15
United States Department of the Interior, 61
United States deputy marshals, 85, 88, 101, 104, 139, 143, 151, 153, 154, 229; list of, 102-103
United States deputy tax collectors, 101
United States General Land Office, 69, 106, 166, 174, 189, 194, 198, 201, 203, 205, 205, 206, 208, 212, 214, 217, 218, 219
United States House of Representatives, 5, 7, 9, 13, 14, 22; Committee on Territories, 8, 9, 13; Indian Affairs Committee, 14
United States marshals, 109, 159
United States Post Office Department, 107
United States Senate, 14; Committee on Territories, 13; Public Lands Committee, 13
United States Supreme Court, 171, 187, 193, 218
UF cattle ranch, in Pottawatomi reservation, 98
Union City, 178
Utah, 55

— V —

Van Voorhees, S. K., 169
Van Wyck, Sen. Charles H., of Nebraska, 7
Varnum, John, deputy marshal, 103
Verbeck station, 26, 30, 159; renamed Moore station, 26
Vermont, 51
Veteran City, 181
Virginia, 186

— W —

Wabash Railroad, 48
Wade, Col. J. C., 108, 135, 221
Waggoner, T. R., mayor of Norman, 173
Waite, Lt. Henry, 68, 122, 125
Walden, W. B., 48
Walden Colony, of Kansas City, 48
Walker, Dr. Delos, 57
Walker, 186; station, 176
Wall, Anson, 206
Wallace, Willie A., 209, 210
Walnut Creek, at Arkansas City, 45, 60, 69; settlements on, 60, 69
Walters, John, deputy marshal, 102
Wanamaker, 184
Wandel, 186
Wantland Crutch-O Ranch, 37
Ward, Tom, 30
Washington, D.C., 5, 7, 13, 14, 15, 21, 22, 28, 73, 105, 106, 108, 128, 147, 189
Wass, Napoleon B., 175
Waterloo, 186
Weaver, Gen. James B., Sen. of Iowa, 5, 7, 11, 12, 13, 15, 40, 41, 97, 157, 193
Weaver, Capt. W. J., deputy marshal, 102
Webb, Byron Dick, 242
Wellington, Kansas, 56, 173, 181
Wellington Consolidated Land and Town Company of Oklahoma, 47
Wells, C. T., 99
Wells-Fargo Express Company, 138
Wellston, 99, 244
West Guthrie, 219
West Guthrie townsite group, 144
West Oklahoma City, 197
West Virginia, 47, 56
Wharton station, 120, 121, 146
Wheeler, Jacob, deputy marshal, 103
Whisler, 186
White, Ewers, deputy marshal, 102, 154, 155, 156, 201
White Bead Hill, 175
Wichita, Kansas, 11, 12, 13, 19, 20, 21, 23, 35, 43, 55, 56, 72, 79, 92, 98, 101, 120, 173, 181, 193, 207, 241; Board of Trade, 19, 21, 22; colony, 79, 148; *Beacon*, 56; *Eagle*, 6, 11, 19, 23, 26, 27, 55, 101, 120, 145, 153; *Journal*, 120; *Republic*, 6; United States District Court at, 193; Horse and Mule Market, 19; Interstate Oklahoma Convention, 11, 12

287

Wicks, Hamilton, 118, 149
Wild Horse Trail, 67, 128
Wiley, Mary, 236
Wilkins, W. J., deputy marshal, 103
Wilkinson, Huger, 200
Williamson, George, 226
Williamson, Sidney, 226
Willow Springs station, 23, 63, 119, 219
Wilson, J. W., 113
Wilson, Joseph, United States Commissioner, 142
Winans, J. F., 204, 205
Winfield, Kansas, 55, 57, 58, 138, 176, 221, 226, 241; colony, 63, 64, 100, 144, 176
Winfield Crowd, 144
Winter and Townsley Colony, 47
Winters, Smith, deputy marshal, 103
Wood, John W., 114, 165, 166, 167; sued by townsite of Kingfisher, 193, 205
Woodruff, Frank H., 202-203
Woodruff, Katie, 158, 161, 203, 209
Woodruff, Luman C., 203, 209, 210
Woodson, Capt. A. L., 18, 19, 22, 23, 56, 68, 73, 74, 76, 77, 79, 91, 92, 114, 129
Woodward station, 110, 233
Wright, Thomas, deputy marshal, 103, 156, 206
Wyatt, Capt. D. F., deputy marshal, 102

— Y —

Yates, 186
Yellow Bull Crossing, 237
Yukon, 32, 193, 212, 245

— Z —

Z. V. Cattle Ranch, 239
Zion, 186